DISCOVERING AFRICAN-AMERICAN ST. LOUIS:

A GUIDE TO HISTORIC SITES

By John A. Wright

Edited by Jean E. Meeh Gosebrink, St. Louis Public Library

Candace O'Connor, Missouri Historical Society

PRESS MISSOURI HISTORICAL SOCIETY

Missouri Historical Society Press • St. Louis

The Missouri Historical Society Press
P.O. Box 11940, St. Louis, Missouri 63112-0040

Printed in the United States of America
by Fiedler Printing Company
St. Louis, Missouri
Designed by Lee Harris

ISBN 1–883982–00–6

First Edition
Library of Congress Catalog Card Number: 93-079983

Cover Illustration: Kenneth Calvert

Cover art includes: (left to right, bottom row) Lucy Delaney,
Julia Davis Branch Library, Archer Alexander;
(top row) Homer G. Phillips, Jefferson Bank demonstrators,
Dr. Martin Luther King, Jr., statue, Olive Chapel AME Church.

To my wife Sylvia and our three sons,
John, Jr., David, and Curtis, and my daughter-in-law
Carmel and grandson John III, with the hope that one day
they will see our city live out the true
meaning of brotherhood

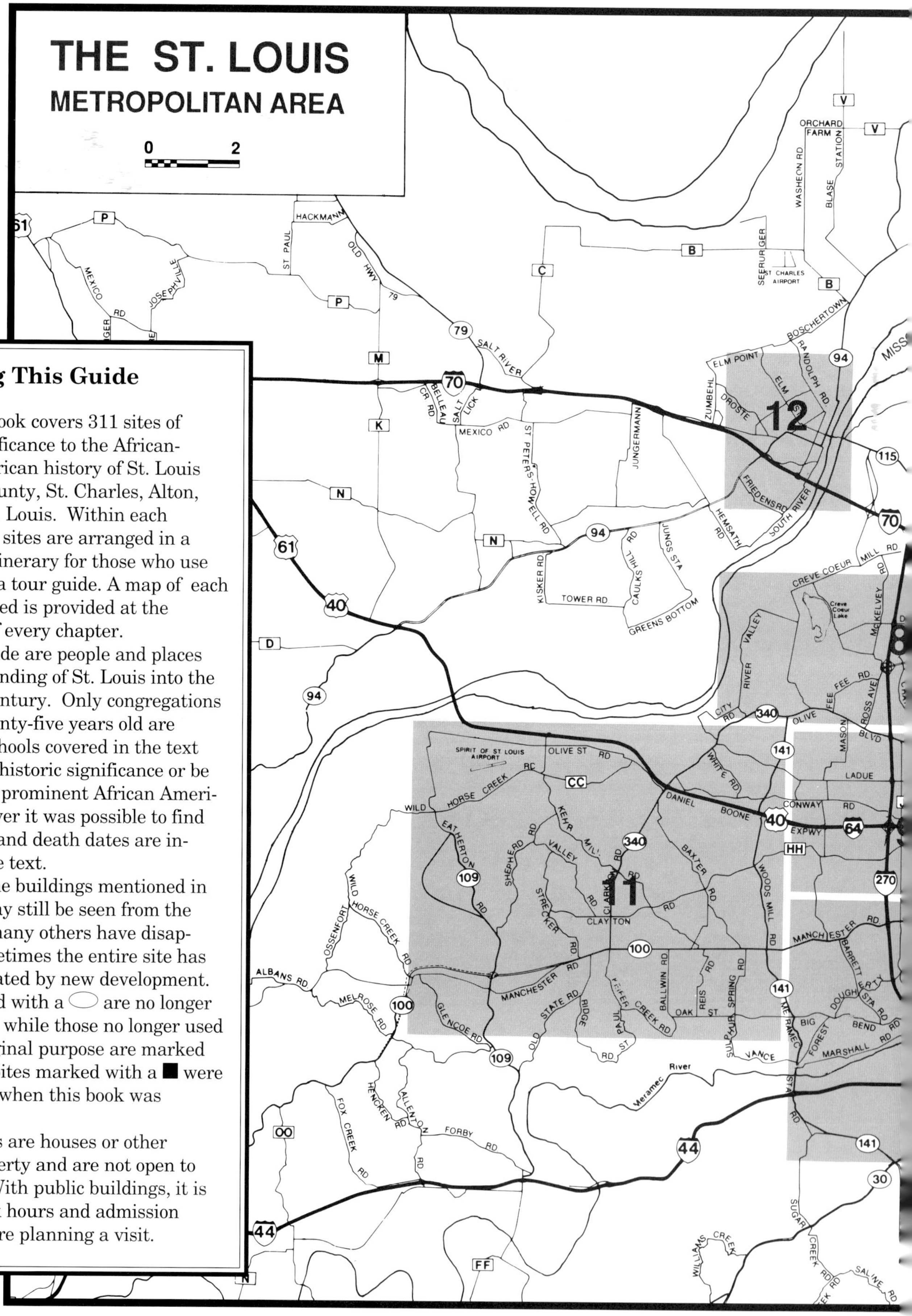

On Using This Guide

This book covers 311 sites of significance to the African-American history of St. Louis City and County, St. Charles, Alton, and East St. Louis. Within each chapter, the sites are arranged in a suggested itinerary for those who use the book as a tour guide. A map of each area discussed is provided at the beginning of every chapter.

In this guide are people and places from the founding of St. Louis into the twentieth century. Only congregations at least seventy-five years old are included. Schools covered in the text had to have historic significance or be named for a prominent African American. Whenever it was possible to find them, birth and death dates are included in the text.

Some of the buildings mentioned in this book may still be seen from the street, but many others have disappeared; sometimes the entire site has been obliterated by new development. Sites marked with a ⬭ are no longer in existence, while those no longer used for their original purpose are marked with a ⬬. Sites marked with a ■ were in existence when this book was printed.

Many sites are houses or other private property and are not open to the public. With public buildings, it is best to check hours and admission charges before planning a visit.

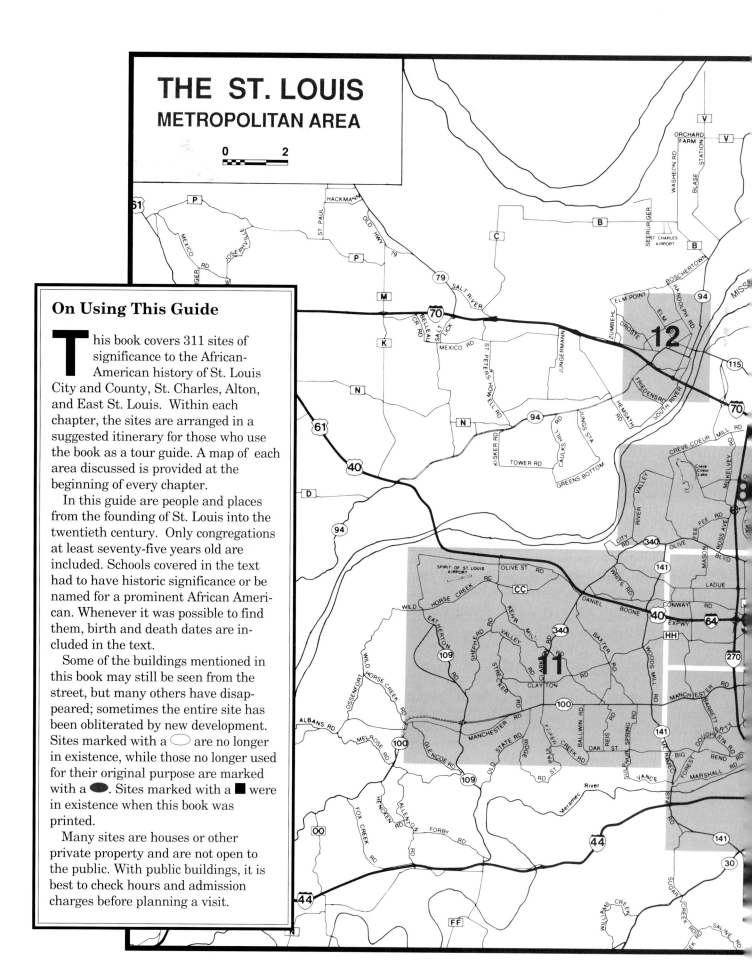

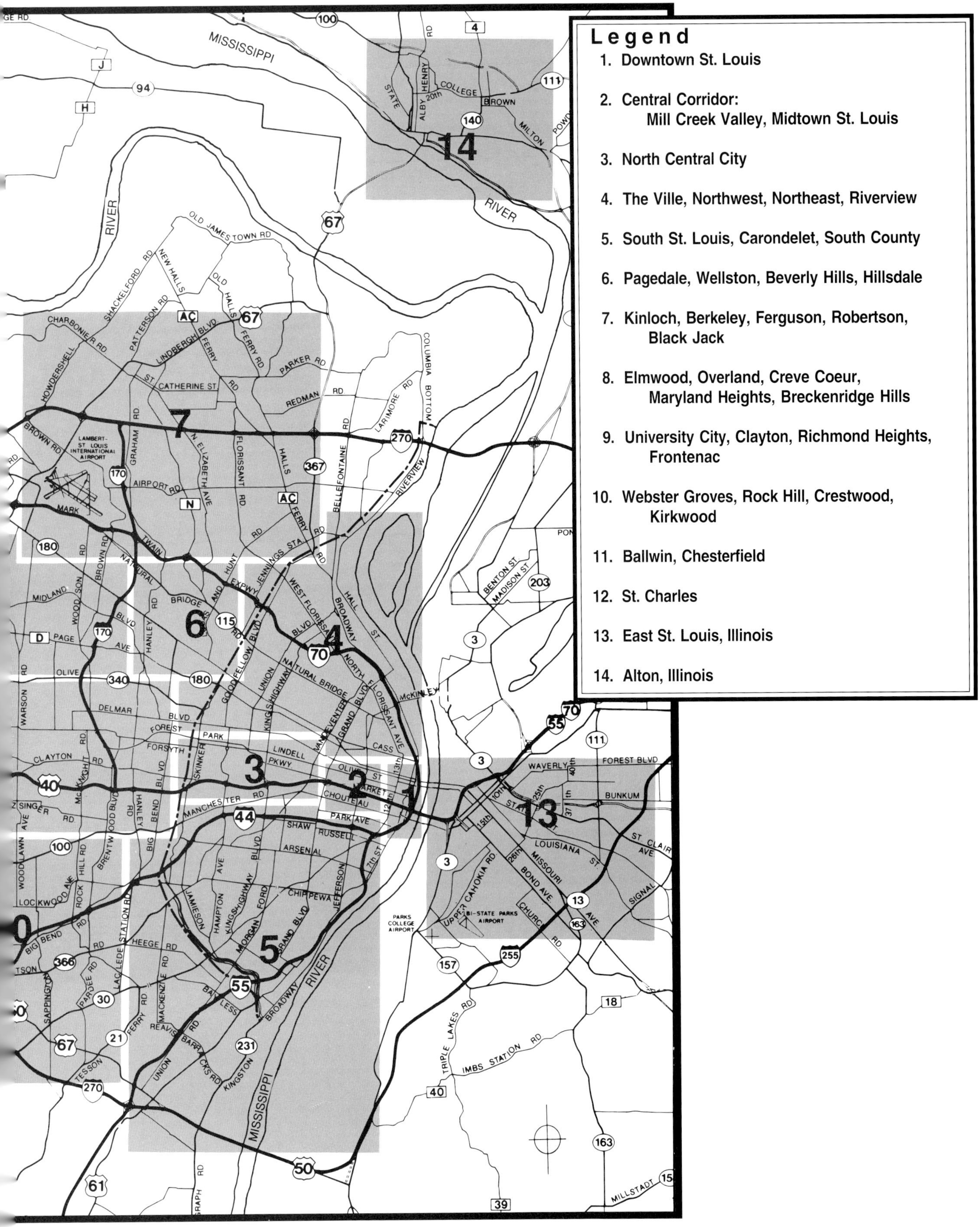
Legend
1. Downtown St. Louis
2. Central Corridor: Mill Creek Valley, Midtown St. Louis
3. North Central City
4. The Ville, Northwest, Northeast, Riverview
5. South St. Louis, Carondelet, South County
6. Pagedale, Wellston, Beverly Hills, Hillsdale
7. Kinloch, Berkeley, Ferguson, Robertson, Black Jack
8. Elmwood, Overland, Creve Coeur, Maryland Heights, Breckenridge Hills
9. University City, Clayton, Richmond Heights, Frontenac
10. Webster Groves, Rock Hill, Crestwood, Kirkwood
11. Ballwin, Chesterfield
12. St. Charles
13. East St. Louis, Illinois
14. Alton, Illinois
MISSISSIPPI
RIVER
MISSISSIPPI RIVER
LAMBERT-ST LOUIS INTERNATIONAL AIRPORT
PARKS COLLEGE AIRPORT
BI-STATE PARKS AIRPORT
OLD JAMESTOWN RD
CHARBONIER RD
LINDBERGH BLVD
ST CATHERINE ST
PARKER RD
REDMAN RD
COLUMBIA BOTTOM
AIRPORT RD
FLORISSANT RD
BELLEFONTAINE RD
RIVERVIEW
NATURAL BRIDGE
DELMAR BLVD
FOREST PARK
LINDELL PKWY
OLIVE ST
CHOUTEAU
PARK AVE
MANCHESTER RD
SHAW
RUSSELL
ARSENAL
CHIPPEWA
LOUISIANA
MISSOURI
BOND AVE
ST CLAIR AVE
FOREST BLVD
BUNKUM
WAVERLY
IMBS STATION RD
TRIPLE LAKES RD
MILLSTADT

Author's Acknowledgments

I would like to express a special thanks to the following individuals who made this project possible: the late Julia Davis, who encouraged me throughout the project and provided me with valuable sources of information; Willie Loving, a former resident of Baden; Doris Frazier of Westland Acres; Mildred Cobbs of Robertson; Cheryl Clayton, Katie Wright, Charles Tigue, and Jean Faulkner of East St. Louis; Josephine Beckwith of Alton; Esley Hamilton of the St. Louis County Parks Department; the St. Louis Art Museum Education Department; and Charles Brown, St. Louis Mercantile Library.

I would be remiss if I did not also extend special thanks to Robert Fritz, superintendent for the Ferguson-Florissant School District, who gave the initial approval for this project, and to Brendolyn Baily Burch, director of the Technical Assistance Unit for the Missouri Department of Elementary and Secondary Education, for her interest in the project and her help in securing funding for production of the original material. Special thanks also go to Donna Corno, Sheri Beirne, Patricia Jost, Cheryl Lanos, Pat Whitener, Doris Marshall, Linda Smith, Clint Vance, Diane Scollay, Shirley Wittner, Carol Shoults, Betty Windsor, Carmen Elfgen, Cathy Hoffmann, Edna Jackson, Rina Krasney, Carol Mullen, Robert Manges, and Marina Medrano in the Ferguson-Florissant School District; to Billye Crumpton; Charles Burgess, St. Louis Public Schools; Marie Boykin, St. Louis City Hall; Patricia Adams, Missouri Historical Society; and Robert Tabscott, Elijah P. Lovejoy Society.

John A. Wright
Assistant Superintendent for Personnel,
Ferguson-Florissant School District

Editors' Acknowledgments

We would like to add our thanks to the staff members at the St. Louis Public Library and at the Missouri Historical Society, along with people from the community, who helped make this project possible.

Among Missouri Historical Society staff, we appreciate the help of: Robert Archibald, Karen Goering, and Joseph Porter with project review and support; Sharon Conner and Brandon Sterling with research; Dina Young with historical data; Katharine Corbett, Patricia Adams, and Mary Seematter with site review; Duane Sneddeker and Kirsten Hammerstrom with photo selection; David Schultz with photography; Bettye Dew with copy editing; David Miles with proofreading and captions; and Jacqueline Dace with manuscript preparation.

Among St. Louis Public Library staff members, we are grateful to: Glen Holt; Mary Mulroy; Cynthia Ruggeri, for help with research and preparation of the bibliography and index; Tom Pearson, Noel Holobeck, Cynthia Millar, Suzy Frechette, and Tim Willman for research; Barbara Stewart Murphy, Jeanette Smith, and Nicolette Ehernberger for site suggestions.

Members of the community have also assisted us with information and historic photos. They include: Annette Bridges, Scott Joplin House State Historic Site; Charles Brown and John Neal Hoover, St. Louis Mercantile Library; the Carondelet Historical Society; Robert Fishbone, On the Wall Productions; Paula Homan, St. Louis Cardinals' Hall of Fame; Deanna Kohlburn, Madison County Historical Society; Grace Monroe, Alton Black Pioneers; Ann Morris, Western Historical Manuscript Collection, University of Missouri–St. Louis; John Porter, Clayton Historical Society; Zadie Ratliff, St. Louis Public Schools photo archives; Robert St. Peters, Alton Landmarks Association; Irene Smith, Ferguson Historical Society; and Martin Towey, archives of the Archdiocese of St. Louis.

Our special thanks to Henrietta Ambrose and Alice Windom for site review; Robert Archibald and Glen Holt for writing the foreword; Henry Givens, Jr. and Congressman William L. Clay for writing the introduction; and Lee Harris for his design, photography, and mapmaking work.

Candace O'Connor
Editor,
Missouri Historical Society Press

Jean E. Meeh Gosebrink
Head, Special Collections
St. Louis Public Library

Contents

Foreword

Since the founding of St. Louis in 1764, African Americans have played an integral role in the community's history and culture. They served as *voyageurs* in the early fur-trade days; they owned businesses and worked aboard the boats when the steamboat dominated St. Louis trade. While some were held as slaves in St. Louis, others were free blacks who formed what one of them called "a colored aristocracy." As their numbers increased late in the nineteenth century, their significance also grew in the economic, cultural, and social life of the community.

Early in 1992, St. Louis Public Library issued a thirty-page pamphlet, *The African-American Heritage of St. Louis: A Guide*, which identified forty-six selected heritage sites with religious, educational, artistic, or cultural significance. In a matter of weeks, the Library distributed more than five thousand copies. The pamphlet received national press coverage and was sent to addresses in nearly thirty states.

Just as the Library was publishing the guide and considering a reprint, the Missouri Historical Society was also planning a new edition of a book, *St. Louis Black Heritage Trail*, written in 1989 by John A. Wright, assistant superintendent in the Ferguson-Florissant School District. His book included 214 sites of historic or cultural importance to the African-American community. The original twenty-five hundred copies of Dr. Wright's book, produced by his district, had quickly been distributed.

Staff members from the two institutions met and decided that, since the goals of their two projects were so similar, it would make sense to collaborate. Over the past year, they have worked closely with Dr. Wright to produce an expanded guide to places of importance to the African-American experience in the St. Louis metropolitan area, including Alton and East St. Louis, Illinois. The result is this new book, *Discovering African-American St. Louis: A Guide to Historic Sites*.

The guide, which describes more than three hundred sites, reflects the many contributions made by African Americans to the history of the St. Louis region. Historic churches, news-papers, theaters, social and cultural centers, hospitals, businesses, parks, and homes; sites connected with political leaders, military heroes, musical stars, and sports figures; and schools, post offices, playgrounds, and streets named for prominent African Americans are included. Users of the guide can make connections with this important aspect of local history by walking or driving past these sites, by visiting the places that are open to the public, or by reading about their significance.

Some of the sites, such as the Shelley house in the 4600 block of Labadie, exist amid a streetscape that is little changed from the 1940s. Standing in front of this national landmark, one can admire the courage of the J. D. Shelley family and their attorney George L. Vaughn when they took their fight against the enforcement of racially restrictive housing covenants to the United States Supreme Court. Other sites no longer look the way they did when the important events described in the guide took place there. And a great many of the historically significant buildings mentioned in this book have disappeared, victims of road construction, urban renewal, suspicious fires, and community neglect. The reader will need to imagine, for example, the bustling African-American community of more than eighteen thousand people who lived in the Mill Creek Valley area and the central city around 1900. The historic images in the book will help readers conjure up lost buildings and neighborhoods.

This publication is not definitive. We encourage those who use it to suggest new material for a future edition. In the meantime, we hope that this publication will help St. Louis residents and visitors become more aware of the area's rich African-American heritage.

Robert R. Archibald
President,
Missouri Historical Society

Glen E. Holt
Executive Director,
St. Louis Public Library

Introduction

The role played by black Americans in the history of our country has been ignored, distorted, and downplayed by those who write for periodicals and newspapers, by those who write the textbooks, and, most importantly, by the so-called master historians.

It is vitally important, therefore, that we as black people chronicle the people, events, and monuments that are relevant to our own history. We do this not because we want to be segregated from our larger communities, but because we would be omitted otherwise.

That we have to develop our own addenda to history books and other publications even today is a sad indictment of the goals of equality that Americans so frequently mouth. Little effort has been made to right the wrongs so unjustly placed on our people by centuries of inaccurate depictions of the role of black people in the development of our country.

We will have reached a milestone when blacks, whites, and other racial and ethnic groups learn to collaborate in putting together history books of the future. Only then will we be able to tell the true story of every group in our society. Not only will this be of value to those who had been ignored previously, but it will provide a strong base of understanding for those who have been led to believe that only their history is important.

Discovering African-American St. Louis: A Guide to Historic Sites is a fine example of what can be accomplished by those who have the foresight, dedication, and fortitude to pick up the mantle and fill a void when it is apparent that our story has not been told. Here in the St. Louis area there have been many, many contributions by blacks that previously had never been amassed in a single publication. Many of the early landmarks have been destroyed; many others still exist, but it is important to know about them all. They form a link to the past.

This publication will serve as a rich resource for people of all backgrounds and will kindle pride in the hearts of many who are familiar with the people and places described.

The Hon. William L. Clay
Congressman,
First District, Missouri

It has been aptly noted that to be ignorant of history is to be doomed to a repetition of its mistakes. This same very wise observation could well be applied to the cultural heritage of a people. Not to know and cherish one's cultural heritage—particularly the story of one's forebears and their accomplishments—is to run the terrible risk of living with low self-esteem and with all the dire psychological consequences that flow therefrom.

Discovering African-American St. Louis: A Guide to Historic Sites, a highly valuable volume resulting from the careful research of Dr. John A. Wright, was written to provide African Americans—particularly those who live or have lived in the St. Louis metropolitan area—with vital bits of information about the lives and contributions of their black forebears who lived, toiled, and contributed to the development of this region. This historical information is presented as if the reader were on a tour, discovering for himself or herself landmarks, structures, monuments, and other commemorations of the lives and contributions of African Americans in this region.

The book consists of photographs, quotations from documents, and fragments from history and provides a valuable reference for all Americans—though particularly for African Americans who wish to enrich their lives and strengthen their sense of personal worth through a knowledge of their cultural heritage. It is, therefore, with great pleasure that I commend Dr. Wright both for the diligent research that went into the writing of this book and for his recognition of the need for such a document for African Americans of all ages. His is a truly valuable book. I strongly recommend that all who teach the young and aspire to know more of the true past become thoroughly acquainted with this work and use it to help American youth of all ethnic backgrounds to know and appreciate the contributions of African Americans to the development of our Greater St. Louis area. Toward this noble end, I am reminded of the words of Joseph Anderson, who quite rightly noted:

> There is nothing that solidifies and strengthens a nation [or a people] like reading the nation's [people's] history, whether that history is recorded in books or embodied in customs, institutions, and monuments.

If only all of us would remember well and continue in our everyday lives to practice this sound advice!

Henry Givens, Jr.
President,
Harris-Stowe State College

Downtown St. Louis

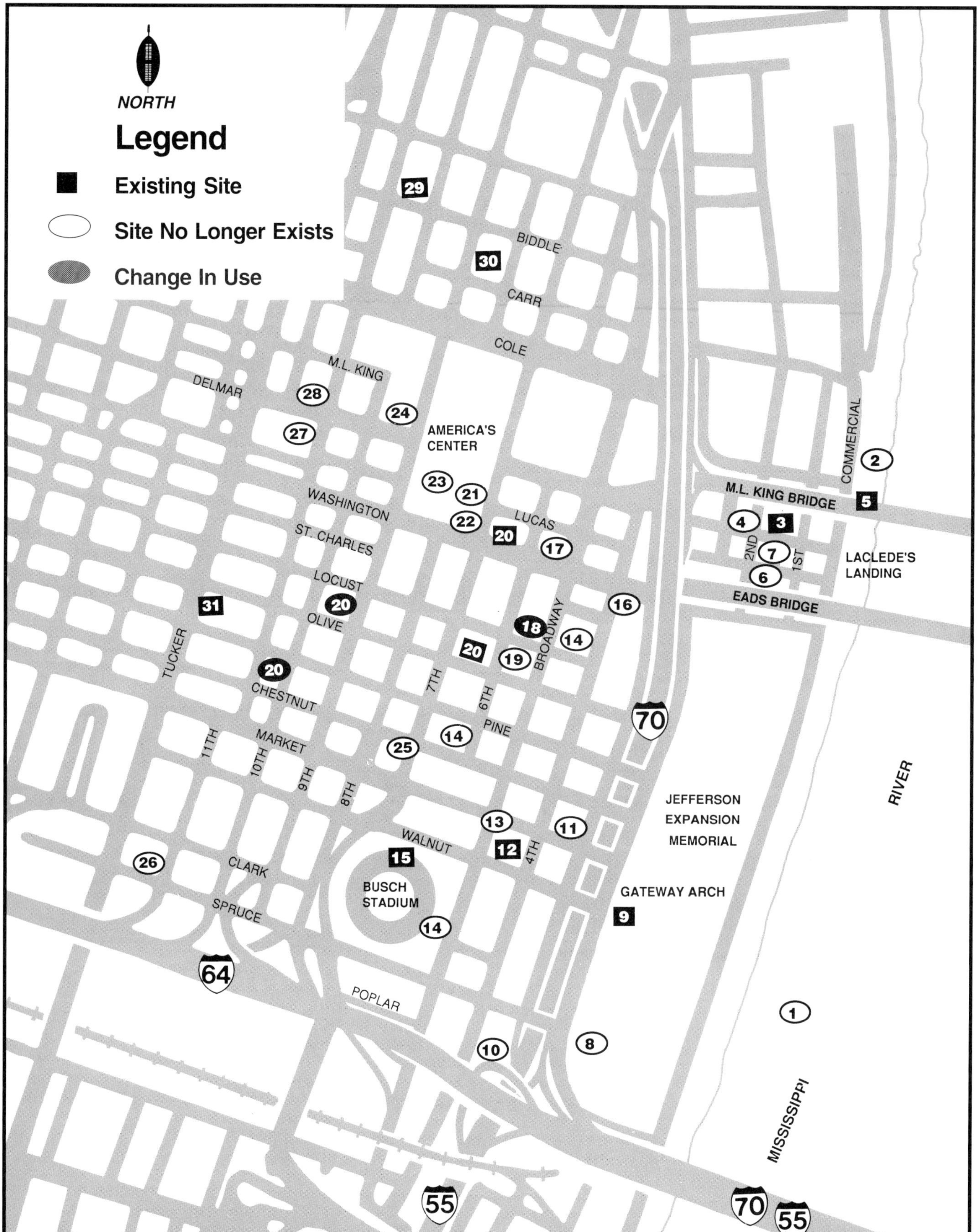

Downtown St. Louis

Chapter 1

From its founding, St. Louis has served as the Gateway to the West for African Americans. Free blacks and slaves were among the early settlers of the Creole village. According to the 1799 census, the St. Louis population included 56 free blacks, 268 slaves, and 601 whites. One free black was a woman known as Esther, who in 1793 petitioned Spain and was given a grant of taxable land in what is now Laclede's Landing.

The village grew into an important center for trade and commerce after the 1803 Louisiana Purchase. On September 23, 1804, an expedition led by Meriwether Lewis (1774-1809) and William Clark (1770-1838) left to explore the Louisiana Territory, then came back to St. Louis after traveling more than eight thousand miles in two years. The only black among the party was York (ca. 1775-ca. 1815), Clark's slave, who once saved Clark's life and gained the confidence of Native Americans along the route. After his return, Clark became the first governor of the Missouri territory. He later freed York and many of his other slaves.

Some African Americans were prominent property owners and tradesmen in the pre-Civil War city, which still hugged the banks of the Mississippi River. At the same time, areas such as "Happy Hollow," bounded by Gratiot, Sixth, Papin, and Seventh streets, were filled with shacks and tenements housing both poor blacks and whites.

In 1879, the St. Louis riverfront served as the portal for thousands of black "Exodusters" fleeing the oppressive conditions of the South for a better life in Kansas and other parts of the West. The emigrants lived on wharf boats and in camps along the river. Relief societies organized by black St. Louisans and their local churches provided funds and emergency services for the travelers.

During the twentieth century, the riverfront has continued to provide inspiration for authors and songwriters. Black poet Langston Hughes (1902-67) said that the St. Louis riverfront inspired him to write his poem, "The Negro Speaks of Rivers." And musician W. C. Handy (1873-1958) recalled the sounds of the levee in his world-famous song, "St. Louis Blues."

Freedom School ⬭ 1

Mississippi River

By the late 1840s, several schools and many classes for blacks were being conducted in church basements, among them the Chambers Street Baptist Church, the First African Baptist Church, St. Paul African Methodist Episcopal Church, and the Central Baptist Church. The Sisters of St. Joseph also ran a school for the instruction of black Catholic girls.

In 1847, arguments over the extension of slavery into territories acquired after the Mexican War, along with the fear felt by Missouri slaveowners that a class of literate free blacks would be rebellious, impelled the Missouri General Assembly to act. It passed a law that stated: "No person shall keep or teach any school for the instruction of negroes or mulattoes in reading or writing in this STATE." In the same year the Assembly also forbade blacks to hold meetings.

According to community tradition, the Reverend John Berry Meachum (1789-1854), a former slave and pastor of First African Baptist Church in St. Louis, defied the law by building a steamboat and anchoring it in the Mississippi River. The boat served as a "floating school" on which hundreds of black children were educated in the 1840s and 1850s with the help of teachers from the East. Because the river was under federal jurisdiction, Meachum's school was allowed to continue operating.

See also: First African Baptist Church
Bellefontaine Cemetery

Sen. Blanche Kelso Bruce site ⬭ 2

Steamboat Columbia
Keokuk Packet Company
34 North Commercial Street

Blanche Kelso Bruce (1841-98), who later became a senator from Mississippi, was born a slave in Virginia. He moved to outstate Missouri in the early 1850s with the family of his master, William Perkinson. By the mid-1850s, he had come to St. Louis, where he worked along the levee. He later attended Oberlin College, then returned to St. Louis after the Civil War as an employee on the steamboat *Columbia*, which sailed between St. Louis and Council Bluffs, Iowa.

In 1868, he bought a plantation in Bolivar, Mississippi, and amassed a fortune. Entering politics in 1870, he became sergeant-at-arms for the Mississippi State Senate; in 1874, he was elected United States senator and served until 1881. At the end of his term, he served as register of the treasury until 1889, recorder of deeds in the District of Columbia until 1895, and finally register of the treasury again until his death. One newspaper recalled that Bruce "scorned the use of the phrase 'colored men' "; he often declared, "I am a Negro and proud of it."

Clamorgan Alley ■ 3

North-south alley running from Washington Avenue to Morgan Street, parallel to First and Second streets on Laclede's Landing

Clamorgan Alley, originally called "Commercial Alley," is named for Jacques Clamorgan (?-1814), a West Indian native who arrived in St. Louis in the 1780s. Clamorgan, possibly of Welsh, Portuguese, Spanish, and African heritage, was a fur trader, merchant, financier, and land speculator who owned land in what is now Laclede's Landing. His home was on the site of what is now the Peper Tobacco Company, 701–17 North First Street. Before the acquisition of the Louisiana Territory by the United States in 1803, Clamorgan was one of the founders of the Missouri Company, which promoted trade and sent expeditions up the Missouri River to find an all-water route to the Pacific. He explored Texas and traded along what became the Santa Fe Trail, linking St. Louis to Spanish territory through what is now New Mexico. In 1804, he was appointed judge of the Court of Common Pleas and Quarter Sessions by Governor W. H. Harrison. He rented his house to the government to be used as a jail.

Clamorgan is known to have fathered four children by mulatto women. At his death, he left those children an estate of nearly one thousand dollars. The French community accepted the declared off-spring of such unions and protected their rights of inheritance. Members of the prominent Clamorgan family were part of the nineteenth-century "colored aristocracy" of St. Louis.

See also: Madame Rutgers estate

Site of land grant to Esther ⬭ 4

723 North Second Street, Laclede's Landing

This location, now occupied by one of the historic Schoelhorn-Albrecht Machine Company buildings, was the site of a 1793 Spanish land grant to Esther, a free mulatto woman. In its collections, the Missouri Historical Society has a copy of the original document containing Esther's land grant request:

> To Mr. Don Zenon Trudeau, Lt. [Gov.]
>
> Humbly imploring, the named Esther, the free mulatto woman, formerly belonging to Mr. Clamorgan and residing in this place, has the honor of laying before you her desire to obtain in this city of St. Louis, at the bottom of the hill, a plot of land measuring 240 feet of frontage by 300 feet of depth, located behind the home of Mr. Clamorgan which stands on the second street ordinarily called Church Street. . . . [The purpose of Esther's request] is to enable her to make a garden and to erect a barn for the shelter of her animals. The supplicant will never cease praying for your prosperity and giving thanks for your goodnesses.
>
> [Given in] St. Louis on this 18th day of July, in the year 1793.
> [Esther's mark is made by an X.]

See also: St. Louis Association of Colored Women's Clubs

Clamorgan Alley

Photo. Courtesy of Dr. John Wright.

Martin Luther King, Jr., Memorial Bridge

Photo by Irv Schankman. Courtesy of the Irv Schankman–Allied Photocolor Collection, the Missouri Historical Society Photograph and Print Collection.

Martin Luther King, Jr., Memorial Bridge ■ 5

Dr. Martin Luther King, Jr., Drive

The Martin Luther King, Jr., Memorial Bridge spans the Mississippi River between St. Louis and East St. Louis. Constructed in 1951 as the Veterans Bridge, it was renamed in 1972 for the Baptist clergyman and civil rights activist who was slain in 1968. The bridge connects with Dr. Martin Luther King, Jr., Drive, both in St. Louis and in East St. Louis. In 1972, Easton Avenue and part of Franklin Avenue were renamed to honor King.

Elijah P. Lovejoy

Engraving. Courtesy of Robert Tabscott.

St. Louis Observer office 6

85 First (formerly Main) Street

In June 1833, the Reverend Elijah Parish Lovejoy (1802-37), newly graduated from Princeton Theological Seminary, returned to St. Louis, where he had previously edited the *St. Louis Times*. This time, he became editor of a Presbyterian newspaper, the *St. Louis Observer*. Soon he turned his editorial attention to "the incubus" of slavery, which "is paralyzing our energies, and like a cloud of evil portent, darkening all our prospects." By October 1835, his anti-slavery editorials had aroused public complaint and threats of mob action against the *Observer* office. After the lynching of Francis McIntosh in 1836, Lovejoy published a detailed account of the tragedy, entitled "Awful Murder and Savage Barbarity." The judge presiding over the grand jury investigation of the affair denounced Lovejoy's brand of abolitionist sentiment. Taking their cue from the judge's remarks, Lovejoy's enemies broke into the *Observer* office three times during the following weeks. After the last attack, which took place on July 21, 1837, Lovejoy decided to move his press to Alton.

See also: Lovejoy assassination site
Lovejoy monument and grave site
Lovejoy press
Site of the Burning of Francis McIntosh

St. Louis Observer

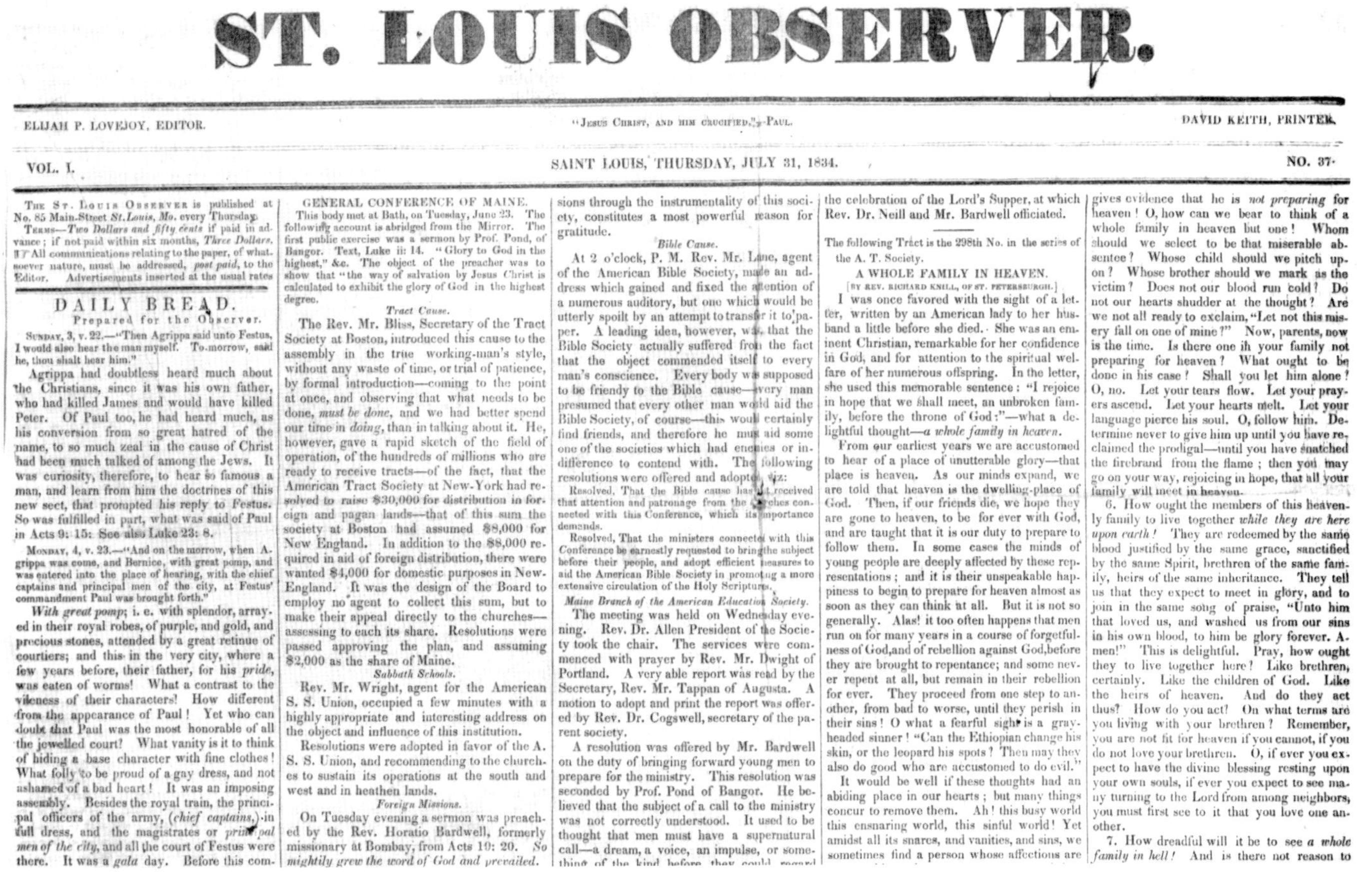

ST. LOUIS OBSERVER.

ELIJAH P. LOVEJOY, EDITOR. "JESUS CHRIST, AND HIM CRUCIFIED."—PAUL. DAVID KEITH, PRINTER.

VOL. I. SAINT LOUIS, THURSDAY, JULY 31, 1834. NO. 37.

THE ST. LOUIS OBSERVER is published at No. 85 Main-Street *St. Louis, Mo.* every Thursday.

TERMS—*Two Dollars and fifty cents* if paid in advance; if not paid within six months, *Three Dollars.* ☞ All communications relating to the paper, of whatsoever nature, must be addressed, *post paid,* to the Editor. Advertisements inserted at the usual rates

DAILY BREAD.

Prepared for the Observer.

SUNDAY, 3, v. 22.—"Then Agrippa said unto Festus, I would also hear the man myself. To-morrow, said he, thou shalt hear him."

Agrippa had doubtless heard much about the Christians, since it was his own father, who had killed James and would have killed Peter. Of Paul too, he had heard much, as his conversion from so great hatred of the name, to so much zeal in the cause of Christ had been much talked of among the Jews. It was curiosity, therefore, to hear so famous a man, and learn from him the doctrines of this new sect, that prompted his reply to Festus. So was fulfilled in part, what was said of Paul in Acts 9: 15: See also Luke 23: 8.

MONDAY, 4, v. 23.—"And on the morrow, when Agrippa was come, and Bernice, with great pomp, and was entered into the place of hearing, with the chief captains and principal men of the city, at Festus' commandment Paul was brought forth."

With great pomp; i. e. with splendor, arrayed in their royal robes, of purple, and gold, and precious stones, attended by a great retinue of courtiers; and this in the very city, where a few years before, their father, for his *pride*, was eaten of worms! What a contrast to the vileness of their characters! How different from the appearance of Paul! Yet who can doubt that Paul was the most honorable of all the jewelled court? What vanity is it to think of hiding a base character with fine clothes! What folly to be proud of a gay dress, and not ashamed of a bad heart! It was an imposing assembly. Besides the royal train, the principal officers of the army, (*chief captains,*) in full dress, and the magistrates or *principal men of the city*, and all the court of Festus were there. It was a *gala* day. Before this com-

GENERAL CONFERENCE OF MAINE.

This body met at Bath, on Tuesday, June 23. The following account is abridged from the Mirror. The first public exercise was a sermon by Prof. Pond, of Bangor. Text, Luke ii: 14. "Glory to God in the highest," &c. The object of the preacher was to show that "the way of salvation by Jesus Christ is calculated to exhibit the glory of God in the highest degree.

Tract Cause.

The Rev. Mr. Bliss, Secretary of the Tract Society at Boston, introduced this cause to the assembly in the true working-man's style, without any waste of time, or trial of patience, by formal introduction—coming to the point at once, and observing that what needs to be done, *must be done*, and we had better spend our time in *doing*, than in talking about it. He, however, gave a rapid sketch of the field of operation, of the hundreds of millions who are ready to receive tracts—of the fact, that the American Tract Society at New-York had resolved to raise $30,000 for distribution in foreign and pagan lands—that of this sum the society at Boston had assumed $8,000 for New England. In addition to the $8,000 required in aid of foreign distribution, there were wanted $4,000 for domestic purposes in New-England. It was the design of the Board to employ no agent to collect this sum, but to make their appeal directly to the churches—assessing to each its share. Resolutions were passed approving the plan, and assuming $2,000 as the share of Maine.

Sabbath Schools.

Rev. Mr. Wright, agent for the American S. S. Union, occupied a few minutes with a highly appropriate and interesting address on the object and influence of this institution.

Resolutions were adopted in favor of the A. S. S. Union, and recommending to the churches to sustain its operations at the south and west and in heathen lands.

Foreign Missions.

On Tuesday evening a sermon was preached by the Rev. Horatio Bardwell, formerly missionary at Bombay, from Acts 19: 20. *So mightily grew the word of God and prevailed.* ... sions through the instrumentality of this society, constitutes a most powerful reason for gratitude.

Bible Cause.

At 2 o'clock, P. M. Rev. Mr. Lane, agent of the American Bible Society, made an address which gained and fixed the attention of a numerous auditory, but one which would be utterly spoilt by an attempt to transfer it to paper. A leading idea, however, was, that the Bible Society actually suffered from the fact that the object commended itself to every man's conscience. Every body was supposed to be friendy to the Bible cause—every man presumed that every other man would aid the Bible Society, of course—this would certainly find friends, and therefore he must aid some one of the societies which had enemies or indifference to contend with. The following resolutions were offered and adopted, viz:

Resolved, That the Bible cause has not received that attention and patronage from the churches connected with this Conference, which its importance demands.

Resolved, That the ministers connected with this Conference be earnestly requested to bring the subject before their people, and adopt efficient measures to aid the American Bible Society in promoting a more extensive circulation of the Holy Scriptures.

Maine Branch of the American Education Society.

The meeting was held on Wednesday evening. Rev. Dr. Allen President of the Society took the chair. The services were commenced with prayer by Rev. Mr. Dwight of Portland. A very able report was read by the Secretary, Rev. Mr. Tappan of Augusta. A motion to adopt and print the report was offered by Rev. Dr. Cogswell, secretary of the parent society.

A resolution was offered by Mr. Bardwell on the duty of bringing forward young men to prepare for the ministry. This resolution was seconded by Prof. Pond of Bangor. He believed that the subject of a call to the ministry was not correctly understood. It used to be thought that men must have a supernatural call—a dream, a voice, an impulse, or something of the kind before they could regard ... the celebration of the Lord's Supper, at which Rev. Dr. Neill and Mr. Bardwell officiated.

The following Tract is the 298th No. in the series of the A. T. Society.

A WHOLE FAMILY IN HEAVEN.

[BY REV. RICHARD KNILL, OF ST. PETERSBURGH.]

I was once favored with the sight of a letter, written by an American lady to her husband a little before she died. She was an eminent Christian, remarkable for her confidence in God, and for attention to the spiritual welfare of her numerous offspring. In the letter, she used this memorable sentence: "I rejoice in hope that we shall meet, an unbroken family, before the throne of God:"—what a delightful thought—*a whole family in heaven.*

From our earliest years we are accustomed to hear of a place of unutterable glory—that place is heaven. As our minds expand, we are told that heaven is the dwelling-place of God. Then, if our friends die, we hope they are gone to heaven, to be for ever with God, and are taught that it is our duty to prepare to follow them. In some cases the minds of young people are deeply affected by these representations; and it is their unspeakable happiness to begin to prepare for heaven almost as soon as they can think at all. But it is not so generally. Alas! it too often happens that men run on for many years in a course of forgetfulness of God, and of rebellion against God, before they are brought to repentance; and some never repent at all, but remain in their rebellion for ever. They proceed from one step to another, from bad to worse, until they perish in their sins! O what a fearful sight is a gray-headed sinner! "Can the Ethiopian change his skin, or the leopard his spots? Then may they also do good who are accustomed to do evil."

It would be well if these thoughts had an abiding place in our hearts; but many things concur to remove them. Ah! this busy world this ensnaring world, this sinful world! Yet amidst all its snares, and vanities, and sins, we sometimes find a person whose affections are ... gives evidence that he is *not preparing* for heaven! O, how can we bear to think of a whole family in heaven but one! Whom should we select to be that miserable absentee? Whose child should we pitch upon? Whose brother should we mark as the victim? Does not our blood run cold? Do not our hearts shudder at the thought? Are we not all ready to exclaim, "Let not this misery fall on one of mine?" Now, parents, now is the time. Is there one in your family not preparing for heaven? What ought to be done in his case? Shall you let him alone? O, no. Let your tears flow. Let your prayers ascend. Let your hearts melt. Let your language pierce his soul. O, follow him. Determine never to give him up until you have reclaimed the prodigal—until you have snatched the firebrand from the flame; then you may go on your way, rejoicing in hope, that all your family will meet in heaven.

6. How ought the members of this heavenly family to live together *while they are here upon earth!* They are redeemed by the same blood justified by the same grace, sanctified by the same Spirit, brethren of the same family, heirs of the same inheritance. They tell us that they expect to meet in glory, and to join in the same song of praise, "Unto him that loved us, and washed us from our sins in his own blood, to him be glory forever. Amen!" This is delightful. Pray, how ought they to live together here? Like brethren, certainly. Like the children of God. Like the heirs of heaven. And do they act thus? How do you act? On what terms are you living with your brethren? Remember, you are not fit for heaven if you cannot, if you do not love your brethren. O, if ever you expect to have the divine blessing resting upon your own souls, if ever you expect to see many turning to the Lord from among neighbors, you must first see to it that you love one another.

7. How dreadful will it be to see *a whole family in hell!* And is there not reason to

St. Louis Times office 7

North side of Lucas, just west of First Street

William Wells Brown (1814-84), born a slave in Kentucky, moved to St. Charles County with his master's family in 1816. Eleven years later, the family moved again, this time to a farm near St. Louis. Brown was hired out in turn as a steamboat steward, a hotel keeper's servant, and a press operator in the printing office of Elijah Parish Lovejoy, who was editor and part-owner of a political newspaper, the *St. Louis Times,* from 1830 to 1832. In 1834 Brown escaped to Canada and freedom. Later, he became a prominent anti-slavery spokesman, an author in the United States and England, and America's first black novel writer. His best-known work is his autobiography, the *Narrative of William W. Brown, A Fugitive Slave* (Boston, 1847).

William Wells Brown

Engraving by R. Andrews, 1847. Courtesy of the Missouri Historical Society Library.

Sutton Blacksmith Shop ◯ 8

94 South Second (formerly Church) Street

Renowned mountain man James Pearson Beckwourth (1798-1866) was born in Virginia, the son of a white Revolutionary War officer and a slave from his household. The family moved to St. Louis County around 1806. In 1812, Beckwourth began an apprenticeship in the blacksmith shop of John Sutton and George Casner, but it ended in 1817 when he quarrelled with Casner. After clerking in his father's trading post, he worked the lead mines near Galena, Illinois, and hired out as a hunter. In 1823, he responded to the call by General William H. Ashley (1778-1838) for men to join a fur-trapping expedition up the Missouri River and into the Rocky Mountains. While Beckwourth earned a reputation for his expert use of such weapons as the bowie knife and the tomahawk, he also became known for his quick temper and his willingness to fight.

Beckwourth went on to become a noted explorer, guide, and scout. His 1856 autobiography, *The Life and Adventures of James Beckwourth*, describes his exploits. He spoke Indian dialects, along with French and Spanish; he also developed good relations with Native Americans, especially the Crow, who named him a chief. With these contacts, he was able to help the United States government in opening new trails into Oregon. In 1850, he discovered an important passage through the Sierra Nevada Mountains, a few miles northwest of what is today Reno, Nevada. He personally guided the first seventeen wagons of settlers through the pass; later, wagon trains on their way to California gold used the pass, first stopping at Beckwourth's nearby ranch. The pass and valley still bear his name.

Another famous early guide and interpreter associated with trading parties that originated in St. Louis was Edward Rose (1790s?-1834?), the son of a white trader and a half-Cherokee, half-black mother. He traveled with Wilson Price Hunt (1783?-1842) on part of his 1811 northwestern expedition and with Manuel Lisa (1772-1820) on his expeditions to the upper Missouri River in 1807 and to the Yellowstone River in 1812. In 1823 he was an interpreter with the Arikara tribe for General Ashley of the Rocky Mountain Fur Company.

Old Cathedral

St. Louis Cathedral. *Lithograph by L. Pomarede, 1835. Courtesy of the Missouri Historical Society Photograph and Print Collection.*

Old Cathedral ■ 9

(Basilica of St. Louis, King of France)

209 Walnut Street

The Basilica, the oldest Catholic cathedral west of the Mississippi River, had been under construction for more than three years when it was completed in 1834. According to a news article published in the 1870s, none of the men working on the cathedral wanted to place the last stone in the belfry until black stonemason William Johnson, an Alton resident, volunteered for the dangerous job. Climbing the steep tower, Johnson put the stone in place; afterwards he received the blessing and thanks of the

Right Reverend Joseph Rosati (1789-1843), bishop of St. Louis. He was also awarded a five-dollar gold piece.

School for African-American girls 10

Third and Poplar streets

In 1845, a Catholic priest, the Reverend Augustin Paris, organized a school for black Catholic girls, most of them daughters of free blacks. The school was located in a brick building at Third and Poplar streets, close to the Cathedral. Three Sisters of St. Joseph taught elementary subjects, French, needlework, and catechism. Children of Catholic slaves received instruction in religion at the school after regular school hours and on the second Sunday of each month. The school was closed in 1846, under pressure of civil authorities.

First African Baptist Church 11

Third and Market (formerly Almond) streets

First African Baptist Church was the first Protestant congregation established for African Americans in St. Louis. All of the city's black Baptist churches developed from it. The church grew out of Sunday school and religious services organized in 1818 by two Baptist missionaries: the Reverend John Mason Peck (1789-1858) and the Reverend James E. Welch (1789-1876).

John Berry Meachum (1789-1854), a former slave who bought freedom for himself and his family, assisted Peck with the school and religious services. In 1822, African-American worshipers formed a separate branch of the church under the direction of Meachum, then a layman. In 1825, after he was ordained a minister, Meachum founded the First African Baptist Church and became its first pastor. A brick church building was erected at the same address in 1827. Membership then numbered about 220, of whom 200 were slaves.

Shortly after the church was built, Meachum and Peck opened a day school at the church under the guise of a Sunday school. This clandestine operation, called "Candle Tallow School," charged a monthly tuition of one dollar for those who could afford to pay. No one, including slaves, was ever turned away.

Meachum also owned a barrel factory and steamboats, one of which was equipped with a library. Between 1826 and 1836, Meachum purchased approximately twenty slaves; he employed them in his factory until they learned a trade and saved enough money to buy their freedom. He remained pastor of First African Baptist Church until his death in 1854. He is buried in Bellefontaine Cemetery.

First African Baptist Church, now First Baptist Church, moved to Fourteenth and Clark streets in 1848, and in 1917 to its present address on Bell Avenue.

See also: First Baptist Church
Bellefontaine Cemetery

Last Sale of the Slaves

Oil painting by Thomas Satterwhite Noble. Courtesy of the Missouri Historical Society Art Collection.

Old Courthouse ■ 12

11 North Fourth Street at Market Street

The Old Courthouse served as the site for the civil courts of St. Louis until 1930. Numerous public gatherings were held in its rotunda, and for a time city hall was located in its north wing. Today, as part of the Jefferson National Expansion Memorial of the National Park Service, the Old Courthouse provides exhibits on early St. Louis history and the city's role in westward expansion.

Along with other property, slaves were once sold as part of public judicial auctions on the east steps of the courthouse, generally in legal estate settlements after their owners had died or declared bankruptcy. In 1861, anti-slavery demonstrators disrupted with catcalls and jeers what is believed to have been the last public auction of slaves in St. Louis.

The most famous event associated with the Old Courthouse was the case of Dred Scott (1799?-1858). A slave who lived in St. Louis, Scott was taken by his owner to live in the free territories of Illinois and Wisconsin. Upon his return to St. Louis, Scott sued to obtain freedom for himself and his wife, Harriet. The first two trials in their case were held in the Old Courthouse in 1847 and 1850. Although the Scotts were awarded their freedom in the second trial, the decision was overturned by the Missouri Supreme Court. A fourth trial in the case took place in May 1854; it was held in Federal District Court in a rented room on the second floor of the Papin Building, then at 38 North Main Street, near what is now the Gateway Arch.

When the Scotts lost the case and their motion for a new trial was overruled, they appealed to the United States Supreme Court on a writ of error. The case was argued before the Supreme Court in Washington, D.C., in February 1856, then again the following December. In 1857, the court declared that a slave was not a citizen and that the Scotts therefore had no legal right to sue in the courts. The court also stated that Congress could not pass laws restricting slavery, since such laws deprived slaveholders of the right to take their property where they wished.

Fort San Carlos

Ink on paper rendering by Clarence Hoblitzelle, 1897. Courtesy of the Missouri Historical Society Art Collection.

This decision was a major contributing factor to the outbreak of the Civil War in 1861. After the Supreme Court decision, ownership of the Scotts was transferred to St. Louisan Taylor Blow (1820-69), who freed them on May 26, 1857. Scott died one year later, in 1858.

In the Old Courthouse, Dred Scott is commemorated in a display on the first floor and in a second-floor courtroom, which is restored to its 1850s appearance.

See also: Calvary Cemetery

Fort San Carlos 13

In the general area of Broadway, Market, Fourth, and Walnut streets

In 1780, during the American Revolution, England planned a large-scale assault on the Mississippi Valley. That April, St. Louis got word that a force of British and Indians was heading toward the town. Don Fernando de Leyba, lieutenant governor of Upper Louisiana, quickly ordered the construction of Fort San Carlos, a rough fortification named in honor of Charles III of Spain. The attack came on May 25, 1780, while many villagers were in the fields outside the fortifications. An estimated six hundred Sioux, Sac, Fox, Potawatomi, Winnebago, and Chippewa, led by Captain Emmanuel Hesse, fired upon the villagers.

Caught by surprise, sixty of the villagers were killed or captured by the Indians. Seven slaves were among the casualties, and thirteen others were taken prisoner. In an 1846 account of the episode, Pascal Cerré (ca. 1771-1849) recalled that one slave who escaped was Louis, owned by the Cerré family. When chased by an Indian he could not outdistance, Louis threw himself flat on the ground, tripped the man, and "before the Indian could recover himself, Louis shot him and brought in the gun as a trophy of victory." Another black, severely wounded, hid in a sinkhole and died there.

Musket and cannon fire from Fort San Carlos quickly repelled the attack. Unable to breach the town's defenses, the Indians withdrew and the British western campaign ended in failure.

Rules of Lynch's Slave Market

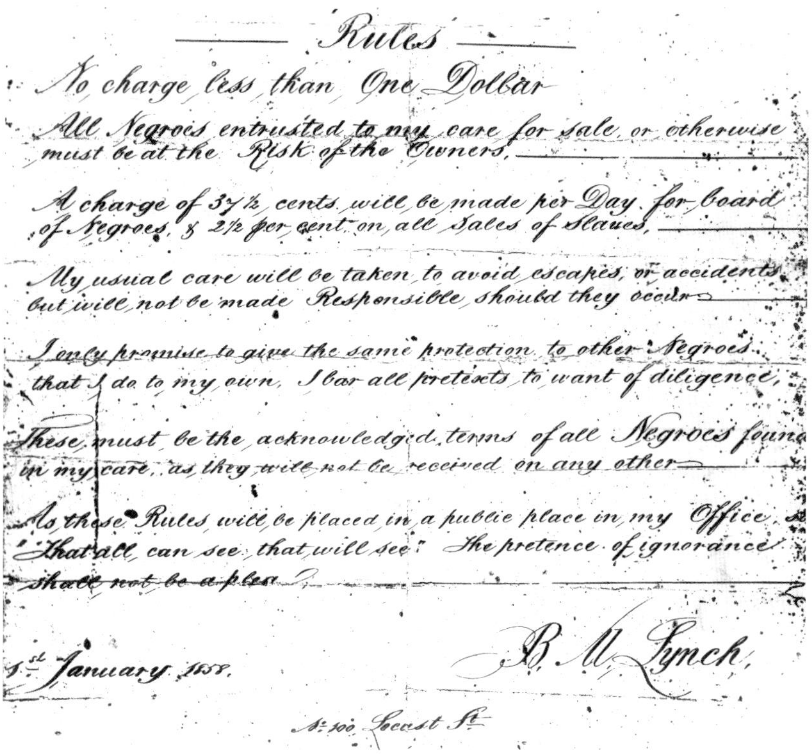

Rules

No charge less than One Dollar

All Negroes entrusted to my care for sale or otherwise must be at the Risk of the Owners.

A charge of 37½ cents will be made per Day for board of Negroes, & 2½ per cent on all Sales of Slaves.

My usual care will be taken to avoid escapes, or accidents but will not be made Responsible should they occur.

I only promise to give the same protection to other Negroes that I do to my own. I bar all pretexts to want of diligence.

These must be the acknowledged terms of all Negroes found in my care, as they will not be received on any other.

As these Rules will be placed in a public place in my Office that all can see that will see. The pretence of ignorance shall not be a plea.

1st January 1858.

B. M. Lynch

No. 100 Locust St.

Broadside, 1858. Courtesy of the Missouri Historical Society Archives.

Slave markets 14

Corbin Thompson's slave market
3 South Sixth Street

Lynch's slave market
100 Locust Street

Lynch's slave pen
Broadway and Clark Street
(formerly Fifth and Myrtle streets)

The 1858 St. Louis directory listed two slave dealers, Corbin Thompson and Bernard M. Lynch. In his advertising, Thompson claimed that his slave pen had "a high and healthy location with ample room." Lynch, a well-known character in his day, was engaged in the slave trade in St. Louis for many years. First he ran a slave market on Locust Street, midway between Fourth and Fifth streets. When his business outgrew those quarters, he purchased the Fifth-and-Myrtle site in 1859, installing barred windows, bolts, and locks to convert it to a secure prison. The Reverend Galusha Anderson (1832-1918), a distinguished Baptist

Lynch's Slave Market

Daguerreotype by Thomas Easterly, 1855. Courtesy of the Missouri Historical Society Photograph and Print Collection.

minister who was pastor of Second Baptist Church in St. Louis from 1858 to 1866, described the desolate quarters:

> The room was in the shape of a parallelogram. It was plastered and had one small window high up near the ceiling. There was no floor but the bare earth. Three backless wooden benches stood next to the walls. There were seven slaves there, both men and women, herded together, without any arrangement for privacy.

Soon after the start of the Civil War, the federal authorities took possession of the building and used it as a military prison. Long concealed in the substructure of the Meyer Brothers Drugstore, the actual slave pens were not dismantled until 1963, when construction of Busch Stadium began.

St. Louis Cardinals Hall of Fame Museum ■ 15

100 Stadium Plaza, on the Walnut Street side of Busch Stadium

The St. Louis Cardinals Hall of Fame Museum, located in the home of the St. Louis Cardinals baseball team, honors professional, semi-professional, and amateur baseball players. The museum displays pictures and memorabilia from the history of baseball in St. Louis. Among the African-American players covered in the exhibits are Bob Gibson

St. Louis Negro League team photo

STANDING LEFT TO RIGHT
MGR. TAYLOR, - PALMS, C. - TRENT, P. - SUTTLES, 1ST. - J. WILLIAMS, P.
HENSLEY, P. - WELLS, S.S. - H. WILLIAMS, C. - CREACY, 3RD.
SITTING
BAT BOY, - J. RUSSELL, 2nd. - BELL, C.F. - B. RUSSELL, RF.
CANNON, P. - DAVIS, P. - REDUS, L.F. - McDONALD, P. -
ST. LOUIS STARS
WORLD'S CHAMPIONS
NATIONAL NEGRO LEAGUE
WORLD'S SERIES (9 GAMES)
ST. L. STARS WON 5 - AMER. GIANTS WON 4

Photo, 1928. Courtesy of the National Baseball Library, Cooperstown, New York.

(1935-) and Lou Brock (1939-), who had outstanding careers with the Cardinals, and Leroy Robert "Satchel" Paige (1906-82), who played for the St. Louis Browns. Another exhibit highlights the history of the Negro Baseball League and its St. Louis team, the Giants, later known as the Stars. The Negro National League career of James "Cool Papa" Bell (1903-91) is also featured.

See also: James "Cool Papa" Bell Avenue
Finley Park

Freedmen's Fair 16

Philharmonic Hall
Fourth Street and Washington Avenue

The Freedmen's Fair, held in Philharmonic Hall during the week of June 22, 1868, was sponsored by the African-American people of Carondelet and Kirkwood to raise funds for building schools and churches in their communities. Moses Dickson (1824-1901) was in charge of the fair, which attracted huge crowds to its many lectures, concerts, and exhibits. Booths set up around the hall sold handiwork, infant clothing, cakes, candies, and fruit; also on sale were pictures of such heroic figures as John Brown (1800-59), Hiram Revels (1827-1900), and Frederick Douglass (1817?-95), as well as depictions of "Emancipation in Missouri." A band played patriotic songs, and the Woodson Family Singers—the nine children of former slave E. S. Woodson, who had bought his freedom in 1848—also provided entertainment.

Elizabeth Keckley

Frontispiece of Elizabeth Keckley, Behind the Scenes *(New York, 1868).*

Elizabeth Keckley home 17

5 Broadway (formerly North Fifth Street), between Washington and Lucas avenues (formerly Green Street)

Elizabeth Hobbs Keckley (1818-1907), born a slave in Virginia, grew up to become a dressmaker to the first lady, Mary Todd Lincoln (1818-82). In her 1868 autobiography, *Behind the Scenes: Thirty Years a Slave and Four in the White House*, she described her life and career. As a young woman, she moved with the Garland family to St. Louis, where she was hired out as a seamstress. In 1855, with the help of some female patrons, she purchased freedom for herself and her son, George, for twelve hundred dollars. In the spring of 1860, she left St. Louis, traveled to Baltimore, and taught dressmaking skills to young black women. Next she moved to Washington, D.C., and began sewing for wealthy women, particularly the wives of politicians. In 1860 she became a "modiste" to the wife of then-Senator Jefferson Davis (1808-89).

Just days before the 1861 inauguration of President Abraham Lincoln (1809-65), Mary Todd Lincoln spilled coffee on the gown she had planned to wear for the celebration. Frantically, she looked for a dressmaker who could quickly make a replacement, and a friend recommended Elizabeth Keckley. Working nonstop, Keckley managed to finish an elegant, rose-colored gown which Lincoln himself called "charming." After the inauguration, Keckley became the modiste and trusted confidante of Mrs. Lincoln.

But when Elizabeth Keckley's book appeared, with its intimate portrait of White House life, Mrs. Lincoln refused to see her again. Though she briefly taught domestic science at Wilberforce University, Elizabeth Keckley spent much of the remainder of her life living quietly in Washington.

Missouri State Convention 18

Mercantile Library Hall
Broadway (formerly Fifth) and Locust streets

This convention met in the Mercantile Library Hall on January 6, 1865, to consider amendments to the Missouri constitution that would emancipate all slaves in the state. On January 11, the sixty-nine delegates, with four dissenters, passed an ordinance abolishing slavery and involuntary servitude "except in punishment of crime." In Jefferson City, Governor Thomas C. Fletcher (1827-99) proclaimed "that henceforth and forever no person within the jurisdiction of this State shall be subject to any abridgement of liberty, except such as the law may prescribe for the common good, or know any master but God."

As reports of the meeting spread throughout St. Louis during the day, all business was suspended, and church bells pealed. African Americans met in their churches, singing hymns and praying late into the night. An official observance was held on January 14. Large crowds—both

Missouri Emancipation Proclamation

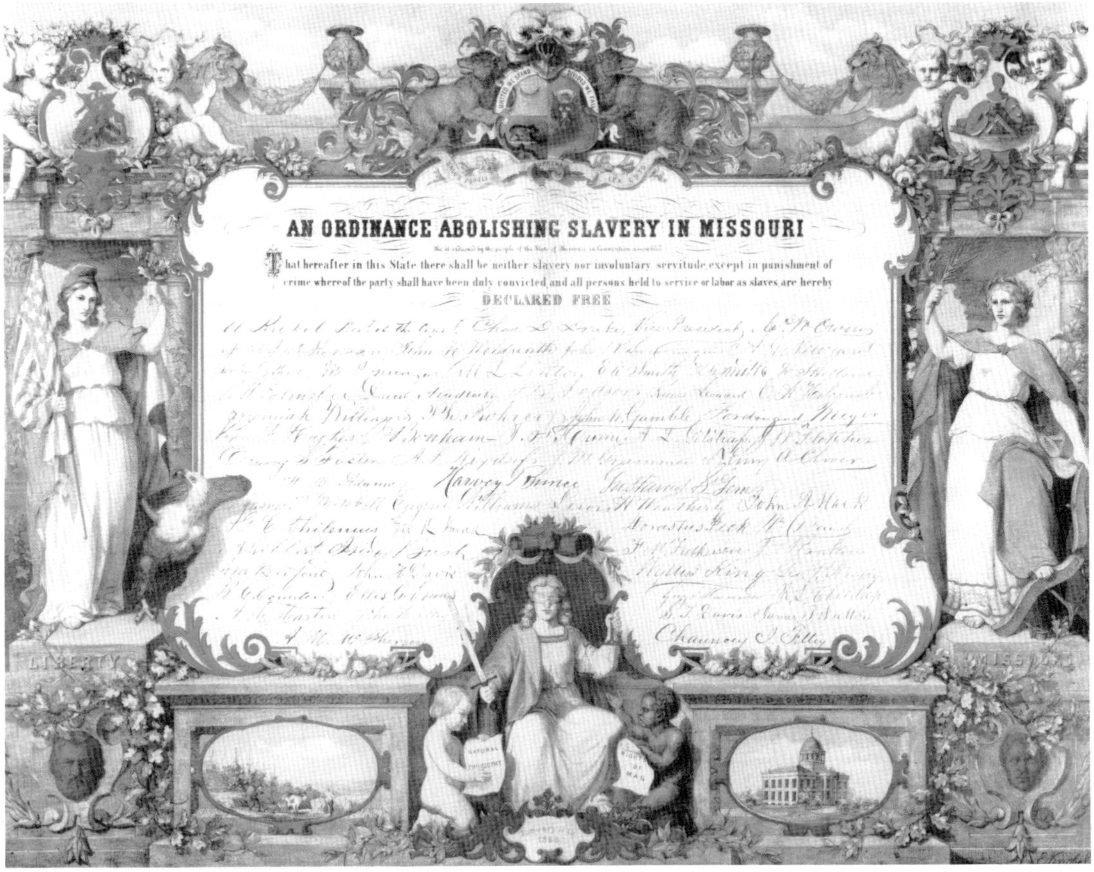

Courtesy of the Missouri Historical Society Photograph and Print Collection.

black and white—paraded through the streets, past buildings decked with flags. In the afternoon, at the request of Mayor James S. Thomas (1802-74), General Grenville M. Dodge (1831-1916) ordered the firing of a sixty-gun salute. As the governor's proclamation was read aloud, the crowd roared its approval. That evening, St. Louis was said to be "aglow with lights in every window and fireworks in the skies."

The ratification of the Thirteenth Amendment to the United States Constitution on December 18, 1865, ended slavery nationally.

Freedmen's National Savings Bank 19

700 Broadway (formerly North Fifth Street)

The St. Louis branch of the national Freedmen's Savings and Trust Company was opened in 1868 by the Reverend W. P. Brooks. The bank had been organized in 1865 by the United States government to help freed slaves achieve a stronger economic position. Brooks, born a slave in Virginia in 1826, moved to Missouri in 1842, purchased his freedom, and became actively involved in the Underground Railroad and in education for African Americans. From 1855 to 1865, he had a wood and coal business in St. Louis. Blacks had little money to save, however. The national bank failed due to insolvency during the financial crisis of 1873 and closed its doors on June 28, 1874. The St. Louis branch had $58,397 on deposit as of January 24, 1874. Creditors ultimately received $28,355.88.

1940s civil rights demonstrations 20

Southwestern Bell Telephone Company demonstrations
1014 Pine Street

Famous-Barr department store
Olive to Locust, Sixth to Seventh streets

Scruggs-Vandervoort-Barney
(closed in 1967)
Olive to Locust, Ninth to Tenth streets

Stix, Baer and Fuller
(now Dillard's)
Washington to Lucas, Sixth to Seventh streets

In 1943, the St. Louis chapter of the March on Washington Movement (MOWM), an organization that called for the end to hiring discrimination, worked to obtain jobs for African Americans at Southwestern Bell. A number of black women had applied for jobs as telephone operators, but they had not been hired. On June 12, several hundred men and women picketed the company, and on September 18, two hundred members of the local MOWM paid their telephone bills in pennies at the downtown office. In late fall, as a first step toward integration, Southwestern Bell agreed to open an office with black employees in a black neighborhood.

From December 1943 to January 1944, several black organizations staged a letter-writing campaign, urging downtown department stores to end discrimination at their lunch counters and to hire black women as sales clerks. The stores did not reply, but in April 1944 the St. Louis Board of Aldermen passed a law, introduced by a black alderman, the Reverend Jasper C. Caston, integrating lunch rooms at City Hall and other municipal buildings.

The success of the Caston bill led in May 1944 to the formation of the Citizens Civil Rights Committee (CCRC)—an independent organization that included members of the National Association for the Advancement of Colored People (NAACP), MOWM, and other groups—which organized the effort to open department store lunch counters to blacks. On May 15, 1944, three black women and one white woman sat down at the Stix, Baer and Fuller lunch counter. They were denied service, but the store manager said that if other stores opened their lunch counters to blacks, Stix would follow suit. For the next two months, committee members demonstrated twice a week at the Famous-Barr, Stix, and Scruggs stores. Many white customers offered encouragement; none were observed leaving before they finished their meals. However, when forty black and fifteen white women sat at the Famous and Stix lunch counters on July 8, the stores closed the restaurants. Negotiations continued into 1945. Only Scruggs opened its lunch counter to serve African-American patrons, though its upstairs dining room remained segregated.

In the 1950s, Congress of Racial Equality (CORE) protests helped open the lunch counters at local drugstores and dime stores, as well as Famous and Stix. In May 1961, St. Louis passed its first public accommodations bill, outlawing segregation in all restaurants, hotels, stores, theaters, parks, and playgrounds.

See also: Demonstrations at the U.S. Cartridge plant

Knights of Liberty 21

Seventh and Lucas Avenue (formerly Green Street)

In 1846, at a house on this site, thirteen black men under the leadership of Moses Dickson (1824-1901) organized a secret society called the Knights of Liberty, which would enlist and arm southern slaves for an insurrection to end slavery. Dickson was to remain in St. Louis and coordinate the movement, while the other twelve organized and trained slaves for the revolt. The manual of the International Order of Twelve Knights and Daughters of Tabor, written by Moses Dickson, claimed that:

> It was a gigantic, desperate movement. We expected to arrive at Atlanta, Ga., with at least 150,000 well-armed men. The chief [Dickson] was ready to give the command to move forward in July 1857, but he paused and scanned the signs that were gathering over the Union. The North and the South were having a terrible struggle for mastery of the slave question.

Dickson became convinced that slavery would be ended only by bloody civil war, and he counseled his followers to hold off on their revolt. Meanwhile, he turned the Knights from insurrection to underground action. They assisted slaves to escape from the South through the Underground Railroad. Later, members of the Knights of Liberty fought with Union forces during the Civil War.

After the war, Dickson returned to St. Louis and became an ordained minister in the African Methodist Episcopal church.

African Methodist Church 22

Seventh Street and Washington Avenue

In 1840 the Reverend William Paul Quinn (1788-1873), a leader in African Methodism in the West, introduced the African Methodist Episcopal faith to Alton and Brooklyn, Illinois, and to St. Louis. During the following year, the Reverend Jordan Early and some other members of the new African Methodist Church in St. Louis secured their first place of worship, a small log cabin near the end of Main Street. Afterwards, the congregation obtained a mission building from the Presbyterians at Seventh and Washington. By the late 1850s, it moved to Eleventh and Lucas.

When the Reverend Hiram R. Revels (1827-1901) served as pastor of this church in 1852, he created a clandestine school to teach blacks to read and write. During the Reconstruction period he went south, where he became the first African American to serve as a United States senator. He was selected by the Mississippi legislature to fill the Senate seat once occupied by Jefferson Davis (1808-89), president of the Confederacy.

In August 1872, the congregation dedicated a new building at the same address. The church later moved to the Mill Creek Valley and is now located on Hamilton Avenue as St. Paul African Methodist Episcopal Church.

See also: St. Paul African Methodist Episcopal Church

Missouri Equal Rights League 23

Eighth Street Colored Baptist Church
Eighth Street and Lucas Avenue (formerly Green Street)

The state's first black political activist organization, the Missouri Equal Rights League, was formed at the Eighth Street Colored Baptist church (later Central Baptist Church) in October 1865. Two weeks after the group named an executive committee, it published an "Address to the Friends of Equal Rights" in local newspapers and in pamphlet form. This address expressed the concerns and aspirations of the league's leaders, focusing on the right to vote. The league also circulated a petition throughout the state, asking the legislature to provide suitable schools for black children.

Both James Milton Turner (1839?-1915), who was chosen as the league's secretary, and John Mercer Langston (1829-97) of Ohio, a well-known black orator who was hired by the league, toured Missouri in support of black suffrage and black access to education. League members lobbied the Missouri General Assembly for the black franchise during the 1867 legislative session. However, the legislature's proposed constitutional amendment eliminating the word "white" as a qualification for suffrage was defeated by Missouri voters in 1868. Blacks gained the right to vote with the passage of the Fifteenth Amendment to the U.S. Constitution in 1870.

"Exodusters"

Wood engraving from Frank Leslie's Illustrated Newspaper, *April 19, 1879.*

Colored Refugee Relief Board 24

903 Delmar Boulevard (formerly Morgan Street)

In 1879 thousands of penniless black men, women, and children—known as "Exodusters"—passed through St. Louis on their way to Kansas and other midwestern and western states, where they hoped to find a better life.

They had come from southern states where they had suffered harsh political, social, and economic oppression at the hands of their former slave masters once Reconstruction had ended and the last federal troops had been withdrawn.

During the 1870s, African-American leaders from Virginia to Louisiana to Texas had discussed plans for alleviating the suffering; they formed a committee to investigate conditions and report on them to the United States government. When their appeal went unheeded, the committee asked for land in the West or for an appropriation of money to allow southern blacks to travel to Liberia, but this request was also ignored. A spontaneous mass movement of blacks from the South to the West began in 1879.

Prominent African Americans in St. Louis organized to feed, house, and supply transportation for the impoverished immigrants as they reached the city. Early in the year, John H. Johnson, a young black attorney at the St. Louis Custom House, proposed the creation of a committee to raise money for relief. As the migrants began to arrive by boat in St. Louis in mid-March, Charlton H. Tandy (1836-1919) summoned St. Louis African Americans to assemble at a mass meeting to arrange temporary relief for the migrants. The meeting was held on March 17 at the St. Paul African Methodist Episcopal Church, where the Committee of Twenty-five was appointed under the chairmanship of the church's pastor, the Reverend John Turner. Among those who joined in the effort were the Reverend Moses Dickson (1824-1901) of the African Methodist Episcopal Church, James Milton Turner (1839?-1915), and John W. Wheeler, businessman and later editor of the African-American newspaper, the *Palladium.*

As the number of immigrants increased through the month of March, they were sheltered at St. Paul's, Eighth Street Colored Baptist, and the First African Baptist churches, and in homes in the African-American community; the community also provided food and clothing for the travelers. Until well into April, the migrants depended almost entirely on the St. Louis black community for subsistence, shelter, and passage to the West.

By mid-April, there was a split in the Committee of Twenty-five, which reorganized as the Colored Refugee Relief Board, with offices at the Delmar address. The Reverend Moses Dickson headed the board; the Reverend John Turner was its treasurer. A rival group, incorporated as the Colored Immigration Aid Society on April 14, 1879, with an office at 618 North Levee (now First) Street, was led by James Milton Turner. It intended to raise funds for the establishment of black colonies in the West and to assist blacks in their efforts to leave the South.

In early April, Tandy traveled to the East to solicit political support and financial contributions for the migrants. He appeared in Washington, D.C., New York, and Boston. Although the existence of two relief agencies caused some confusion, donors around the country, especially eastern humanitarians, sent money and clothing.

Site of the burning of Francis McIntosh — 25

Seventh and Chestnut streets

In April 1836, Francis McIntosh (?-1836), a free mulatto from Pittsburgh who worked as a cook on a steamboat, interfered with the arrest of two boatmen who had been fighting. Two law officers took him into custody. But when one of them told him that his sentence would be five years, he pulled out a knife, injured one seriously, and stabbed the other to death. Enraged at the incident, angry townspeople broke into the jail and dragged out McIntosh. They chained him to a tree and burned him to death.

In his memoir, Mayor John Darby (1803-82) wrote that for two or three years after the lynching, strangers and visitors from the East—particularly from Pittsburgh—went to the locust tree, cut pieces from it, and took them away. In January 1838, Abraham Lincoln (1809-65), then a member of the Illinois state legislature, delivered an address in Springfield in which he called the McIntosh lynching "revolting to humanity." Of McIntosh, he said:

> His story is very short, and is, perhaps, the most highly tragic, of anything of its length, that has ever been witnessed in real life. A mulatto man, by name of McIntosh, was seized in the street, dragged to the suburbs of the city, chained to a tree, and actually burned to death; and all within a single hour from the time he had been a freeman, attending to his own business and at peace with the world.

The High School for Colored Students (Sumner High School) — 26

Eleventh Street near Spruce Street

In 1875, after African-American parents in St. Louis complained about inadequate educational buildings for their children, the state legislature directed the city's school board to provide a high school for black children. The board designated a formerly all-white elementary school as the "High School for Colored Children." The twelve-room building on this site became the first high school for African Americans west of the Mississippi. The school was named for Charles Sumner (1811-74), a United States senator from Massachusetts who in 1861 became the first prominent politician to urge full emancipation. He died the year before the school was opened.

For its first two years, the school was staffed by white teachers. In 1877, black teachers were added to the staff, and in 1879 Oscar M. Waring (1837-1911) was appointed principal; he became the first black principal in St. Louis. In 1890, he was instrumental in creating a Normal School at Sumner for the training of black teachers.

At first the school was mainly an elementary school, with most of its students concentrated in the first four grades. In 1880, only 78 of the school's 411 students were doing high school work. Because of small enrollment and the school's rigorous curriculum, the first Sumner graduation took place ten years after the school was established. Emma Vashon (1866-?) and John F. Pope became the first Sumner graduates in 1885.

Sumner High School remained at this location until 1895, when it moved to Fifteenth and Walnut streets.

See also: Sumner High School (second location)
Sumner High School (third location)

Ballad of "Brady and Duncan" 27

715 North Eleventh Street

The folk ballad "Brady and Duncan" grew out of an incident that occurred on October 6, 1890, in a saloon owned and operated by an African-American man named Charles Starkes. Patrolman James Brady (?-1890) and other policemen had come to the saloon to break up a crowd gathering out front. After an officer threatened one of the men, a fight broke out and Brady was shot. Harrison Duncan (?-1894), a black man, was arrested for the murder. He was defended by Walter Farmer, who in 1889 had become the first black to graduate from the Washington University Law School, and by George Royse, a white attorney from Clayton. Despite his protestations of innocence, Duncan was convicted and hanged at the Clayton courthouse in 1894. Just before his death, which preceded Duncan's execution by a few weeks, Starkes admitted that he had shot Brady, but his confession did not become known until after Duncan was hanged.

During the trial and after the hanging, tension between the races ran high in the city. The ballad of "Brady and Duncan" became a protest against police brutality and a song for civil rights.

See also: St. Louis County Courthouse

Ballad of "Stackalee" 28

Northwest corner of Delmar Boulevard (formerly Morgan Street) and Eleventh Street

There are many versions of the folk ballad "Stackalee" (also called Staggerlee, Stackerlee, Stagolee, Stack Lee), but the song probably originated in St. Louis after an incident in Bill Curtis' saloon at Eleventh and Morgan streets on a frosty Christmas night in 1895. Billy Lyons grabbed the "lucky" hat of Lee Shelton (known as "Stack Lee" because he had once been a stoker on the riverboat *Stacker Lee*), who was at the gambling table. Shelton then pulled out his .44 and shot Lyons to death.

Shrine of St. Joseph ■ 29

1220 North Eleventh Street at Biddle Street

The Shrine of St. Joseph is the site of one of the "authenticated miracles" that led to the canonization of Peter Claver

Shrine of St. Joseph

Photo by Stan Miller. Courtesy of the Missouri Historical Society Photograph and Print Collection.

(1581-1654) by the Roman Catholic Church. Peter Claver, the son of a Spanish farmer, went to Cartagena in Central America as a Jesuit priest in 1610. There he dedicated his life to the service of slaves taken from Africa. Claver was canonized in 1888 and in 1896 declared the patron saint of all the Catholic missions among black people.

A relic of the body of Peter Claver is kept beneath the church altar. In 1861, Ignatius Strecker, a soap factory worker, was struck in the chest by a piece of iron and developed tuberculosis. After he was blessed with the relic, however, Strecker began to recover and was restored to full health. This miracle was one of the two required by Rome for canonization. It also led to the enlargement of the church, which was originally built in 1844.

In many predominantly African-American Catholic parishes today, the Knights and Ladies of St. Peter Claver societies, founded in 1909, perform charitable, apostolic, and parochial services and offer social and recreational activities to their members. A number of groups are active in the St. Louis area.

Cochran Gardens ■ 30

Cochran Tenant Management
1112 North Ninth Street

When President George Bush (1924-) visited this development in May 1991, he called it a model of tenant-managed public housing. Cochran Gardens is one of the nation's oldest experiments in tenant management and one of twenty-five public-housing developments across the country that are currently run, at least in part, by tenants. The twelve-building, 761-apartment complex was completed in 1953. It was converted to tenant management by the St. Louis Housing Authority after the rent strike of 1969. The tenant corporation oversees virtually every aspect of life at Cochran, from elevator maintenance to meals for the elderly.

Cochran Gardens

Photo, 1956. Courtesy of the Community Development Agency Collection, the Missouri Historical Society Photograph and Print Collection.

Henry W. Wheeler United States Post Office ■ 31

Tucker and Olive streets

Henry W. Wheeler (1888-1964), a civil rights activist, fought discrimination in St. Louis, especially at the United States Post Office. Born in Arkansas, he came to St. Louis in 1912, and was employed at the Post Office for nearly fifty years. When the all-black National Alliance of Postal Employees was organized after the American Federation of Postal Workers refused membership to African Americans, Wheeler became its leader and led demonstrations against post office policies that discriminated against black employees.

Wheeler worked tirelessly to eliminate segregation in all public places. For seven years he walked a picket line in front of the American Theatre, until it opened to the public on an equal basis in 1955. He was elected a representative to the Missouri legislature in 1956.

Henry W. Wheeler U.S. Post Office

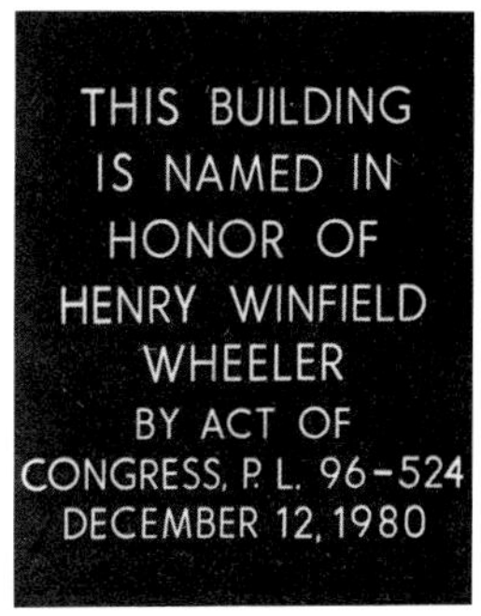

THIS BUILDING
IS NAMED IN
HONOR OF
HENRY WINFIELD
WHEELER
BY ACT OF
CONGRESS, P. L. 96-524
DECEMBER 12, 1980

Plaque. Photo by Lee Harris.

The Central Corridor: Mill Creek Valley, Midtown St. Louis

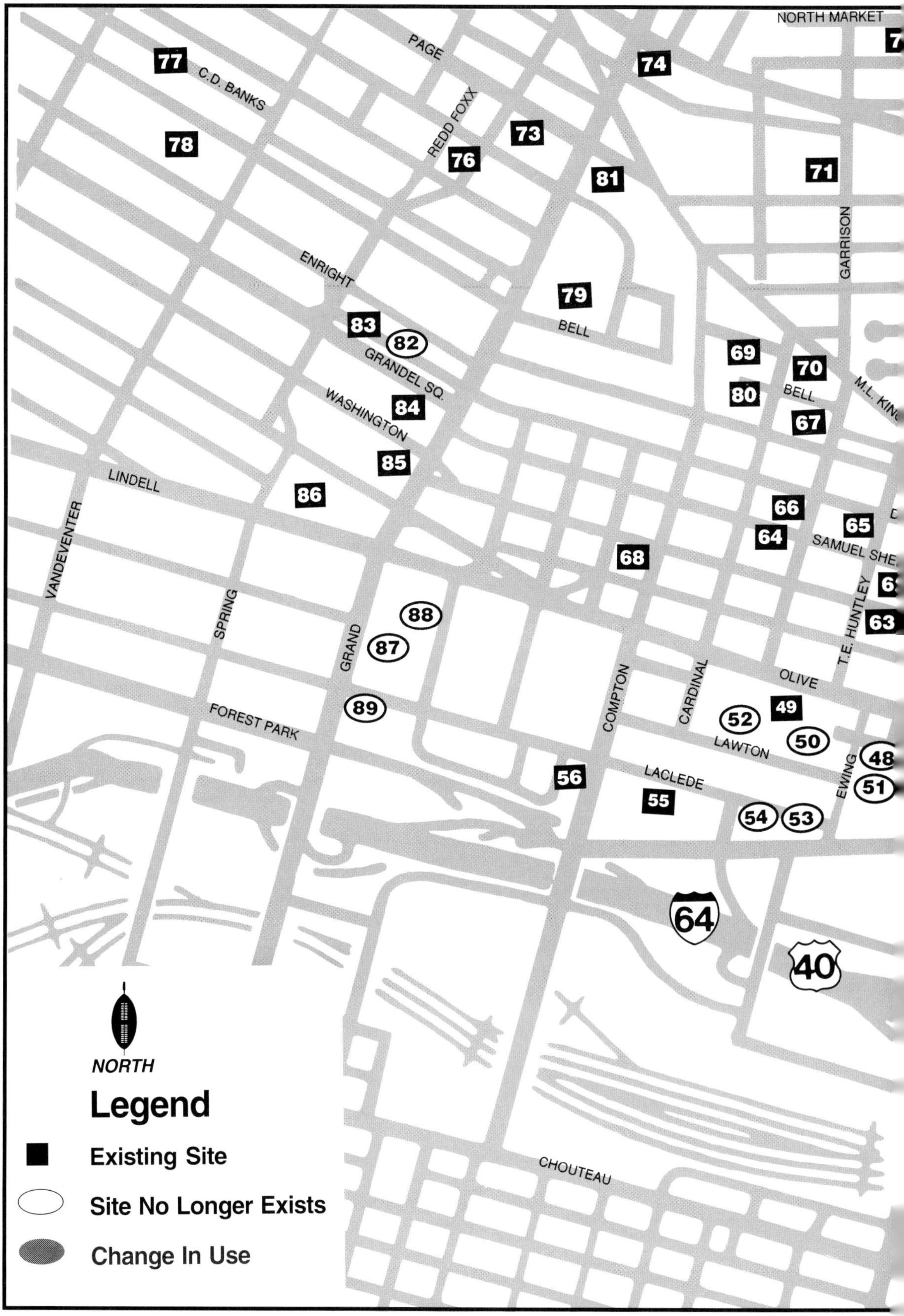

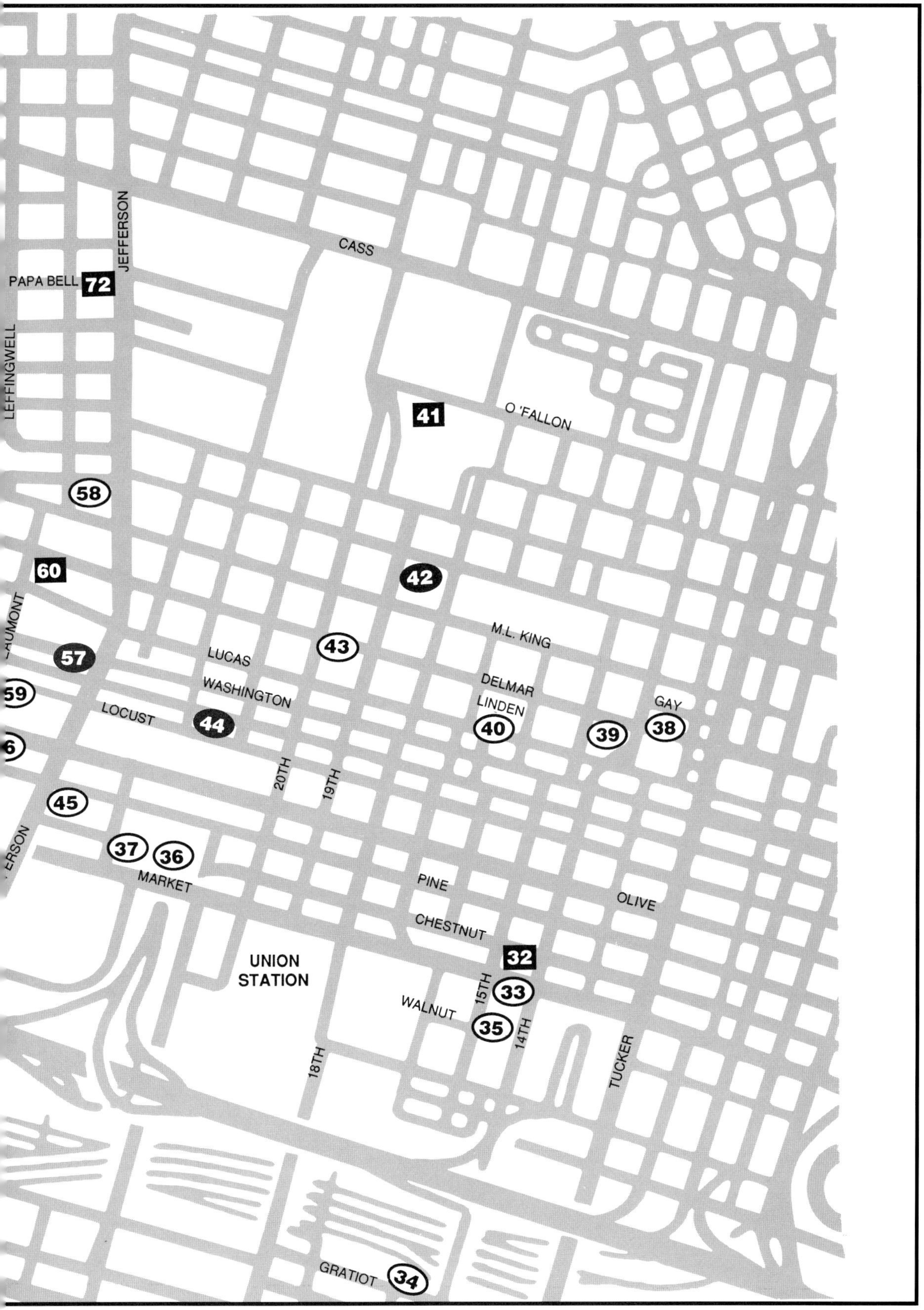

JEFFERSON
PAPA BELL
72
LEFFINGWELL
CASS
41
O'FALLON
58
60
42
BEAUMONT
57
LUCAS
43
M.L. KING
WASHINGTON
DELMAR
59
LOCUST
44
LINDEN
40
39
GAY
38
20TH
19TH
45
JEFFERSON
37
36
MARKET
PINE
OLIVE
CHESTNUT
32
UNION
STATION
15TH
33
WALNUT
35
14TH
18TH
TUCKER
GRATIOT
34

The Central Corridor: Mill Creek Valley, Midtown St. Louis

Entrance to Washington Metropolitan AME Zion Church

Photo by Lee Harris.

The Central Corridor: Mill Creek Valley, Midtown St. Louis

Chapter 2

The central corridor of St.Louis, from Tucker Boulevard (formerly Twelfth Street) on the east to Spring Avenue on the west, had a large, racially mixed, and mostly poor population at the start of the twentieth century. Mansions and tenements, shops, businesses, factories, dance halls, taverns and clubs, restaurants, churches, schools, hotels, and other institutions crowded into this area. Plans for redeveloping the corridor began early in the century as the Civic Improvement League, organized in 1901, called for the creation of a central parkway. The 1920s saw the clearing out of a portion of the area with the creation of the Soldiers' Memorial and Plaza, the construction of Kiel Auditorium, the widening of Market Street, and the addition of Aloe Plaza opposite Union Station.

Mill Creek Valley, which stretched from Twentieth Street to Grand and from Olive to the railroad tracks on the south, had gotten its name from a creek that ran from Vandeventer and Market streets to the Mississippi River. The creek was dammed to provide power for a flour mill, and the resulting lake was called Chouteau's Pond. The pond, later drained, was a popular resort during the early 1800s, and a number of black churches performed baptisms there.

Beginning in the 1850s, Mill Creek Valley was home to a large African-American population. Along with the substantial housing and the cheap tenements that housed black laborers, the area supported Chestnut Valley, a thriving honky-tonk district along Chestnut and Market streets near Twentieth. Scott Joplin (1868-1917) and other musicians played ragtime and jazz music at Thomas Turpin's Rosebud Cafe and other nightspots. Mill Creek and neighboring areas were home to such institutions as the Pine Street YMCA, the Wheatley YWCA, Vashon High School, St. Paul African Methodist Episcopal Church, St. Elizabeth's Catholic Church and School, and Union Memorial United Methodist Church. Such international celebrities as Roy Wilkins (1910-81) and Josephine Baker (1906-75) were born in this part of the city. In 1993, City Hall and the mayor's office, located at Twelfth and Tucker, were turned over to native St. Louisan Freeman Bosley, Jr. (1954-), St. Louis' first black mayor.

After World War II, thousands of rural blacks from the South moved to the area. In 1954, when a massive civic-improvement bond issue was approved that included plans to redevelop Mill Creek Valley, the area's population was roughly twenty thousand people, nearly 95 percent of them black. Demolition of housing and other structures in the valley began in 1959. As thousands of people moved from Mill Creek Valley in the 1960s, mostly into northside and westside neighborhoods, many institutions followed in their wake.

Some institutions remained: Harris-Stowe State College (formerly Vashon High School), Waring School, Central Baptist Church, and Berea Presbyterian Church, among others. New development, such as the renovation of the Scott Joplin House Historic Site and the relocation of the St. Louis Black Repertory Company to Grandel Square, is now helping to revitalize the area.

Soldiers' Memorial

Photo by W. C. Persons, ca. 1935. Courtesy of the Missouri Historical Society Photograph and Print Collection.

Soldiers' Memorial ■ 32

1315 Chestnut Street

"The Unhailed Hero . . . The Black American Soldier in the Great World War" is an exhibit, open since 1981 in the St. Louis Soldiers' Memorial, which honors African-American soldiers from World War I. On display are photographs, weapons, equipment, and uniforms of soldiers in the United States Army's Ninety-second and Ninety-third divisions, which were black units from around the nation. At full strength, they numbered twenty-seven thousand enlisted men.

Also on exhibit are mementos of Dr. William E. Allen, Jr., a retired army lieutenant colonel from St. Louis who served in World War II, and a poster from the Tom Powell American Legion Post No. 77. The Powell Post in St. Louis, chartered in 1919, was the first black veterans' group in the nation. Its name honors Powell, a black soldier from Georgia who died in 1918 in France while transporting messages to the front.

See also: Tom Powell American Legion Post No. 77

The Ballad of "Frankie and Johnny" ○ 33

212 Targee Street (located between Fourteenth and Fifteenth streets, near Market Street)

The best-known version of the song "Frankie and Johnny" is said to be based on a murder that took place on October 15, 1899, in a St. Louis lodging house located at 212 Targee Street. Newspaper accounts from the time report that twenty-two-year-old Frankie Baker (1877?-1950) killed the two-timing "Johnny," seventeen-year-old Albert Britt (1882?-99). Some versions of his death say he was stabbed, while others say he was shot. On the night following the incident, Bill Dooley, a black pianist and songwriter, composed the song that was played in many black saloons, first under the title "Frankie and Albert."

Baker claimed self-defense and was acquitted of Britt's murder. Released by the authorities, she left St. Louis, but the ballad followed her to Omaha, Nebraska, and finally to Portland, Oregon. Her legal attempts to stifle the song and the film portrayals were in vain. Baker died in a Portland mental institution in 1950.

Josephine Baker home ⬭ 34

Gratiot Street near Targee Street

Josephine Baker (1906-75) was born in Mill Creek Valley and grew up on Gratiot Street and at 2632 Bernard Street. After attending Lincoln Elementary School, she began performing for pennies outside the Booker T. Washington Theatre, gradually worked her way into her family's vaudeville act, then joined the chorus line of musical shows. She left St. Louis and by 1921 appeared in New York in an all-black musical written by Eubie Blake (1883-1983) and Noble Sissle (1889-1975). Four years later, she became famous in Paris as the lead exotic dancer in the Folies Bergère revue.

Baker is known for more than her long career on the stage. During World War II she worked with the Free French Army as informant and ambulance driver; she later received the *Croix de Guerre*, France's highest military decoration, awarded for bravery in action. Still later she adopted a "rainbow family"—fourteen children of different nationalities. And she fought courageously against racism. When Baker returned to the United States in 1951, she refused an offer of twelve thousand dollars a week to perform at the Chase Hotel because the hotel would not allow integrated audiences. However, in February 1952, she appeared for free at a rally, in Kiel Auditorium which was attended by six thousand people. The rally, organized by the NAACP and the Teamsters' Union, called for the desegregation of St. Louis schools because of intense overcrowding in black schools.

Josephine Baker

Photo by Nathan B. Young. Courtesy of St. Louis University Archives.

Sumner High School

Photo by Emil Boehl, ca. 1876. Courtesy of the St. Louis Public Library.

Sumner High School (second location) 35

Fifteenth and Walnut streets

In 1895 Sumner High School relocated from Eleventh and Spruce to this larger building. In the 1894-95 school year, 210 pupils were enrolled at Sumner, and the class of 1895 had twenty-seven graduates. As a superintendent's report for the period says:

> The Sumner High School not only imparts a thorough liberal education to its pupils, enabling them to enter the best colleges open to colored students, but it also fills the important place of a training school, which furnishes all the teachers needed by the colored primary schools of the city, thus securing well trained talent for this important work.

The new building was an improvement over the earlier one, but it still lacked an assembly room, a gymnasium, a library, and other facilities. Black parents complained, and in 1910 Sumner moved to its present location in the Ville.

See also: The High School for Colored Children
Sumner High School (third location)

DAVE YOUNG. Night.
MIXERS.
JOHN H. CLARK. Day.
Headquarters for Colored Professionals.
The Rosebud Bar,
TOM TURPIN, Prop.
Pool Room in connection.
Also a first-class cafe in rear. Open all night and day. All Prices. Private Dining-room.
ROSEBUD BAR
2220-22 Market St., St. Louis, Mo.
PHONE: Kinloch D-855.

Advertisement from a 1902 issue of the St. Louis Palladium.

Rosebud Cafe 36

2220-22 Market Street

By 1895, St. Louis had become a national center for ragtime music, and those who played ragtime congregated at the Rosebud Cafe. Its proprietor was Thomas Million Turpin (1873-1922), the son of Tom "Honest John" Turpin and brother of Charles U. Turpin (1870?-1935), owner of the Booker T. Washington Theatre. Thomas M. Turpin was a composer and a source of inspiration for a generation of ragtimers in St. Louis, including his good friend, the pianist and composer Scott Joplin (1868-1917). Turpin's "Harlem Rag," published in 1897, was one of the earliest rags written for the piano.

Other great St. Louis pianists of the time—Joe Jordan, born in Cincinnati; Sam Patterson and Louis Chauvin, both from St. Louis; Tennessee natives Charles Hunter and Charlie Warfield—played ragtime at the Rosebud and at such nearby bars as the Gilt Edge Bar, the Four Deuces Saloon, and the Hurrah Sporting Club.

In February 1904, the Rosebud Cafe sponsored its third annual ball and piano contest in Douglass Hall, 2645 Lawton Avenue. An account published in the *Palladium* newspaper reported:

> It was one of the largest, finest and best conducted affairs of the kind ever held in St. Louis. The hall was packed and jammed [with] many well-dressed, good-looking and orderly people, from all classes of society. . . . Mr. Tom Turpin presented an elegant gold medal to the successful contestant, Mr. Louis Chauvin. Messrs. Joe Jordan and Charles Warfield were a tie for second place. . . . Music was furnished by the matchless World's Fair band.

See also: Booker T. Washington Theatre
Scott Joplin Historic Site

Booker T. Washington Theatre 37

2248 Market Street at Twenty-third Street

The Booker T. Washington Theatre, in operation from about 1912 to 1930, was among the first theaters in the United States built and operated by and for African Americans. It had a seating capacity of one thousand and featured vaudeville and other live entertainment, along with motion pictures. A new show with a different theme—African, cowboy, Egyptian, etc.—appeared each week. Because it was part of the Theatre Owners' Booking Association, the black vaudeville circuit, the theater featured appearances by such black stars as Ethel Waters (1896-1977), Bessie Smith (1894-1937), and Ma Rainey (1886-1939).

The theater's owner and manager was Charles Udell Turpin (1870?-1935), who was also the first St. Louis black to be elected to local political office. His brother was Thomas Million Turpin (1873-1922), the proprietor of the Rosebud Cafe. Running as an independent candidate, Charles Turpin was elected constable in 1910, then re-elected in 1914 and again in 1918. In 1928 he was elected justice of the peace and reelected in 1934. With George Vaughn (1885-1949) and Homer G. Phillips (1880-1931), both attorneys, and Joseph Mitchell (1876-1952), editor of the *St. Louis Argus*, Turpin worked within the Republican party to mobilize black voters. They campaigned for black political candidates and lobbied for black appointments to Civil Service jobs.

Turpin was also a pioneer in motion pictures. He supervised the filming of the reproduction of the Pythian Parade and Encampment in St. Louis in 1917; the black soldiers of the Ninety-second Division at Camp Funston, Kansas; and other events involving African Americans.

See also: Rosebud Cafe

Lucy Delaney home 38

1241 Gay Street

Around 1890, Lucy Delaney (1830?-?) published her autobiography, *From the Darkness Cometh the Light; or, Struggles for Freedom,* in which she described her life as a slave in St. Louis and the successful legal action that her mother undertook to win her freedom. Lucy's mother, Polly Crocket Berry, had been a free black living in Illinois when slave runners kidnapped her and sold her into slavery in Missouri. While in captivity, Polly married and had two children, Lucy and Nancy. Her new owners promised her freedom, but instead they sold her husband "down south" and sold Polly herself to a new owner in St. Louis. Somehow she managed to interest a local lawyer in her case, and he sued for—and won—her freedom.

Meanwhile, Polly's daughter Nancy had managed to escape to Canada, but Lucy was still a slave. When Lucy's owners threatened to sell her south too, Polly sued for Lucy's freedom on the grounds that since Polly had been free in Illinois, her children were therefore entitled to freedom. Lucy had to spend seventeen months in jail awaiting trial, but her case finally came to trial on February 7, 1844. Her attorney was Edward Bates (1793-1869), a prominent St. Louisan who was later appointed attorney general by President Abraham Lincoln; his eloquent pleas helped win her freedom. Afterwards, she became a successful seamstress and in 1849 married Zachariah Delaney, who worked as a porter, laborer, and janitor in St. Louis. In 1890 they lived at the Gay Street address.

Dumas Elementary School (Colored School No. 1) 39

1413 Lucas Street

By the end of the Civil War, five schools for African-American children, with a total attendance of sixteen hundred pupils, existed in St. Louis. They fell under the supervision of a Board of Education for Colored Schools, composed of black community leaders. This board received aid and advice from white members of the Western Sanitary Commission, a St.Louis-based organization that had distributed relief supplies, opened hospitals, and established homes for refugees during the Civil War.

The St. Louis Board of Education took control of public education for black children after the Civil War, when the reconstructed state constitution of 1865 stipulated public support for the education of all children in the city. The first public schools for blacks were established in 1866 in rented rooms so dilapidated that additional funds were needed to make them suitable for classes. These schools absorbed the pupils of the original five schools.

Colored School No. 1 opened at Fifth and Gratiot, No. 2 at Tenth and Chambers in the Chambers Street Baptist Church, and No. 3 at Twenty-fourth and Morgan. These early schools frequently changed location. In 1868, for example, Colored School No. 3 moved to Fourteenth and Christy, and in 1880 to Eleventh between Carr and Biddle; it closed in 1881.

By 1890 there were twelve elementary schools for black pupils. They were all assigned numbers, while schools for white children were named for prominent people. Though the Colored Education Association requested in 1878 that the schools be named for "prominent Negroes," the Board of Education did not approve this request until 1890.

Colored School No. 1 had moved from a number of rented quarters to Lucas and Fourteenth streets by 1880. The school was renamed for the French writer Alexandre Dumas (1802-70), author of several hundred books, including *The Three Musketeers*, *The Man in the Iron Mask*, *The Corsican Brothers*, and *The Count of Monte Cristo*. Dumas' father was French, his mother a native of Haiti. Dumas Elementary School closed in the early 1970s.

Lucy Delaney

Engraving by American Engraving Company. From Lucy Delaney, From the Darkness Cometh the Light; or, Struggles for Freedom *(St. Louis, ca. 1890).*

Madame C. J. Walker home 40

1615 Linden Avenue

Sarah Breedlove McWilliams Walker (1867-1919), a pioneer black businesswoman and millionaire who was better known as "Madame C. J. Walker," was born to former slaves in Louisiana. Orphaned at age five, she married Moses McWilliams at age fourteen. Six years later, she was a widow with a small daughter to support.

In 1887, she moved to St. Louis where she remained for eighteen years, working as a washerwoman for $1.50 a day. For part of this time, she and her daughter lived at 1615 Linden Avenue. During this period, her hair began to fall out. Although she tried various remedies, nothing seemed to help. Then one night, she dreamed about an old man who showed her a mixture to use for her hair; when she awoke, she combined the soaps and ointments in washtubs to create what became known as "the Walker Method." She tried the new formula on herself and her friends, then decided to market it.

After selling the product successfully in St. Louis, she moved to Denver, Colorado, in 1905, where she married a newspaperman

Vaughn Public Housing

Photo. Courtesy of the Community Development Agency Collection, Missouri Historical Society Photograph and Print Collection.

named Charles Walker. She began traveling widely to demonstrate her products, and in 1908 she opened a second office in Pittsburgh. In 1910, she consolidated her enterprise in Indianapolis. Always concerned about the black community, she contributed generously to Tuskegee Institute, to the NAACP, and to black charities. A woman of determination, energy, and vision, Madame C. J. Walker became America's first black woman millionaire.

Vaughn Public Housing ■ 41

1919 O'Fallon Street

The 660-unit Vaughn housing project was dedicated on April 28, 1957. The complex, between Cass Avenue and Carr, Eighteenth, and Twentieth streets, was named for George L. Vaughn (1885-1949), a prominent African-American attorney. The first president of the Mound City Bar Association and editor of the *St. Louis Argus*, Vaughn served for many years on the executive committee of the St. Louis NAACP. In the 1920s, he worked within the Republican party to campaign for black political candidates and black appointments to Civil Service jobs, but in the 1930s, along with other black voters, he questioned his Republican loyalties. With attorneys David Grant (1903-85) and Jordan Chambers (1897-1962), he helped convince many younger blacks to vote Democratic; by 1937, 60 percent of the city's fifty thousand black voters had become Democrats. He became active in Democratic politics, serving as a delegate to the 1948 Democratic national convention and as justice of the peace. Among his accomplishments was the successful litigation of *Shelley v. Kraemer*, the landmark 1948 United States Supreme Court case that put an end to racially restrictive covenants as a legal consideration in the sale of housing.

See also: J. D. Shelley home

Booker T. Washington Vocational High School ● 42

814 North Nineteenth Street

A vocational school for African-American students was opened in 1931 at the Franklin School. In 1934 it was renamed the Booker T. Washington Technical High School. With sixteen classrooms, twelve shop rooms, a gymnasium and auditorium, the school could accommodate eleven hundred students. In 1985 the school became a magnet school, the Center for Management Law and Public Policy.

The school was named for Booker T. Washington (1856-1915), an African-American educator who was born a slave and later became the founder of Tuskegee Institute. From 1895 until his death in 1915, Washington was one of the best known and most influential black men in America.

John William "Blind" Boone site 43
Missouri Institution for the Education of the Blind

Delmar Boulevard (formerly Morgan Street) between Nineteenth and Twentieth streets

John William "Blind" Boone (1864-1927), a nationally known concert pianist, was born in a military camp in Miami, Missouri. His mother, a black woman, was a mess cook and his father was a white bugler for the Union army. When he was six months old, Boone was stricken with "brain fever," probably encephalitis, and a doctor had to remove his eyes to save his life. As a child, he moved to Warrensburg, Missouri, and learned to play the harmonica. From the start, he displayed extraordinary musical ability; throughout his life, he could play complicated pieces after only one hearing.

When he was nine years old, he was sent to the Missouri Institution for the Education of the Blind in St. Louis, which then had six African-American students. At the school he was introduced to the piano and his talent blossomed, though the school limited his practice time and assigned him to the trade department to make brooms. Bored, Boone began leaving the school at night to visit St. Louis music halls. At age twelve, he ran away from the school and wandered around St. Louis, playing on street corners near Franklin and Morgan. Finally, he returned to Warrensburg and acquired a manager, who formed the "Blind Boone Concert Company" and took Boone on tour. For years, Boone traveled the country playing popular music, spirituals, and the classics. After his death, the Boone County Museum established a "Blind" Boone exhibit, and Columbia, Missouri, named a housing development and community center for him.

Booker T. Washington Vocational High School

Photo by David Schultz.

John William "Blind" Boone

Photo. Courtesy of the State Historical Society of Missouri, Columbia.

People's Hospital

Photo by David Schultz.

People's Hospital • 44

2221 Locust Street

The People's Hospital was organized as a small private hospital in 1894. It was incorporated under the name "Provident Hospital" and renamed in 1918. For many years, it was the only place where black physicians and surgeons could treat private patients. Before moving to the Locust Street site, the hospital was located at 3447-49 Pine Street. In 1898, a nurses' program for black women began there. At its peak it was a seventy-five-bed, short-term general hospital. It closed in 1978.

True Reformer Hall 45

Pine Street and Jefferson Avenue

In 1878 a secret organization was founded in St. Louis, the all-white Mystic Order of the Veiled Prophet of the Enchanted Realm of Khorassan. Membership in this society was reserved for the city's social elite. Each year, the Veiled Prophet organized a public parade and a private Veiled Prophet Ball, where a Queen of Love and Beauty was selected.

A counterpart organization for blacks was established in 1905. Abdul Menelik Ben Hassin, the black Veiled Prophet, first appeared at the group's ball that year in True Reformer Hall. A newspaper account describes the scene:

> While the orchestra played and the company was in the midst of a dance, the lights suddenly went out, leaving the hall in total darkness. A moment later they suddenly relighted, revealing the presence of the prophet in the center of the hall. He selected from among the throng Miss Sarah Brown, a popular girl, and crowned her queen, then escorted her to the seat of honor. . . . The entire company then formed a grand march, led by the prophet and his queen. After marching around the hall, Abdul disappeared as mysteriously as he came.

In the mid-1960s, Percy Green (1935-), leader of the civil rights group ACTION, condemned the white Veiled Prophet organization as racist. In 1969, to draw attention to this charge, ACTION members threw themselves into the path of Veiled Prophet parade floats, and Green sprinkled the parade route with tacks. In 1972 white ACTION member Gena Scott, dressed in formal attire, swung from the balcony of Kiel Auditorium on a rope and tore away the Veiled Prophet's crown and veil. In 1974, the Veiled Prophet Ball was moved from the city's Kiel Auditorium to the Chase-Park Plaza Hotel so that what ACTION termed "a racist affair" would not be held in a public facility.

In 1979 the Veiled Prophet organization opened to black membership. Three African-American physicians—Dr. William C. Banton II, Dr. Eugene N. Mitchell, and Dr. R. Jerome Williams—became the first black members initiated into the group.

Moses Dickson home 46

2651 Pine Street

Moses Dickson (1824-1901) was born in Cincinnati, Ohio, and later moved to St. Louis. In 1846 he organized the Knights of Liberty. Through the Underground Railroad, he assisted slaves in their escape to free territory. After the Civil War, Dickson returned to St. Louis and, in 1867, became an ordained minister of the African Methodist Church. He worked for education and suffrage for blacks in Missouri. In 1879, as president of the Colored Refugee Relief Board in St. Louis, Dickson helped relocate thousands of former slaves who had fled from the South.

Dickson is also known as the founder of the fraternal organization known as the International Order of Twelve, Knights of Tabor, and its female counterpart society, the Daughters of Tabor, both established in 1872. The Knights and Daughters of Tabor held their annual convention in St. Louis in 1972 to celebrate the one-hundredth anniversary of the groups. To honor Dickson, they led a parade to the Father Dickson Cemetery in Crestwood. Dickson, originally buried in St. Peter's Cemetery, was reburied in 1903 in Father Dickson Cemetery.

See also: Colored Refugee Relief Board
Knights of Liberty
Father Dickson Cemetery

St. Elizabeth's Parish

Photo. Courtesy of the Archdiocese of St. Louis.

St. Elizabeth's Parish 47

2721 Pine Street

Although Roman Catholic parishes in St. Louis were never officially segregated, African-American Catholics were often excluded from white congregations. Before St. Elizabeth's was established, many black Catholics gathered for Sunday mass in a chapel of St. Francis Xavier Church, then at Ninth Street and Lucas Avenue. In the 1870s, Bishop Patrick Ryan organized a citywide parish for African-American Catholics. The refurbished Vinegar Hill Hall at Fourteenth and Gay streets was dedicated as St. Elizabeth's Church on May 18, 1873. The Oblate Sisters of Providence, an order of black nuns, started a parish school in the 1880s and later opened an orphan asylum on Page Avenue. The orphanage was moved to Normandy in 1896.

In 1912, St. Elizabeth's moved to 2721 Pine Street. Although the Oblate Sisters remained in the old neighborhood, the Sisters of the Blessed Sacrament, an order founded by Mother Katharine Drexel (1858-1955) to work among African-American and Native American peoples, opened a mission in 1914 in the 2700 block of Pine Street, adjacent to the church. In 1916 they established a school that enrolled 125 children.

The *Chronicle* (later the *Interracial Review*), published from the 1920s to the 1940s, was started at St. Elizabeth's. The *Chronicle* became the official organ of the Federation of Colored Catholics. After a history of religious service and social concern, St. Elizabeth's was closed in 1950 and the building razed in 1951.

Black soldiers in front of the Pine Street YMCA

Photo, ca. 1917. Courtesy of the Public Buildings YMCA file, Missouri Historical Society Photograph and Print Collection.

Pine Street YMCA 48

Southeast corner of Ewing and Pine streets

In 1887, a YMCA for African Americans was organized in St. Louis under the leadership of John Boyer Vashon (1859-1924), principal of Colored School No. 10. First called the "YMCA for Colored Men," later known as the "Afro-American Young Men's Christian Home Association," it was accepted as a branch of the Metropolitan St. Louis YMCA in 1912. The new Pine Street YMCA was dedicated on March 23, 1919. Even before its completion, the facility was used for housing and feeding black troops on local stopovers during the last days of World War I.

The YMCA, which advertised itself as "the social center of St. Louis," provided well-appointed facilities that included a swimming pool, gymnasium, meeting rooms, dormitories, and a cafeteria. Leading black businessmen served on the board of directors, and many nationally known black lecturers spoke there. The Pine Street YMCA was demolished in 1960. Its present-day successor is the Monsanto YMCA on Page Avenue.

See also: Monsanto YMCA

Berea Presbyterian Church

Photo, ca. 1956 courtesy of the Community Development Agency Collection, Missouri Historical Society Photograph and Print Collection.

Berea Presbyterian Church

Photo by Lee Harris.

Berea Presbyterian Church ■ 49

3010 Olive Street

Berea Presbyterian Church was organized in 1898 as a black congregation. Of forty-three churches in the Mill Creek Valley before the 1960s demolition, Berea is the only one that did not move. The St. Louis Presbytery's Board of Church Extension asked it to remain, remodel, and enlarge. During the 1960s, Berea became a racially mixed congregation, drawing a number of white families into the church. Civil rights organizations met in the church and members participated in civil rights demonstrations. Today, Berea continues its mission work in the Mill Creek area.

Liberty party ○ 50

Douglass Hall
2645 Lawton Avenue

The Liberty party, a black national political organization, was established in St. Louis in the 1880s. In July 1904, the group held its first national presidential convention at Douglass Hall in St. Louis. Its platform advocated unrestricted suffrage for all American citizens, without distinction or qualification; government ownership of such public carriers as railroads and steamboats; and self-government for the District of Columbia. It called for the addition of two black regiments to the army, the promotion of volunteer and regular officers of the Spanish-American War, and pensions for ex-slaves. Finally, it appealed for suppression of the "lynch law."

Although James Milton Turner (1839?-1915) had seemed likely to be the party's presidential nominee, the convention finally nominated an East St. Louis resident, William T. Scott, for president, and W. C. Payne of Warrentown, West Virginia, for vice president. Scott, an Ohio native, had moved to Cairo, Illinois, in 1863, where he opened a hotel and published the *Cairo Gazette*, a daily newspaper. He had come to East St. Louis in 1902. Shortly after the 1904 convention, Scott resigned from the Liberty party when he could not raise funds to repay a $99.80 fine and meet other expenses. The Liberty party then faded into obscurity.

St. Paul African Methodist Episcopal Church ⬭ 51

2800 Lawton Avenue at Leffingwell Avenue

St. Paul's, a descendant of the African Methodist Church organized in 1841, moved from its second location at Eleventh Street and Lucas Avenue (formerly Green Street) to this site in 1890. At the time of its construction, it was the only church in St. Louis built by and for an African-American congregation. The congregation relocated to 1260 Hamilton Avenue when the church at this address was demolished in the 1960s to make way for the Laclede Town housing development in the Mill Creek area.

See also: African Methodist Church

City Hospital No. 2 ⬭ 52

2945 Lawton Avenue at Garrison Avenue

This 177-bed facility opened to the public and began admitting patients in November 1919. A committee of seventeen black physicians, led by Christopher K. Robinson, owner of a printing company and publisher of the *Clarion* newspaper, had convinced city officials to purchase the vacant Barnes Medical College as a health-care center for black city residents and doctors.

When it opened, City Hospital No. 2 was one of five institutions in the United States that offered hospital training to black physicians. An African American, Dr. Roscoe Haskell, became the hospital's first superintendent. A nursing school was established in 1919 and accredited in 1920.

After it became apparent that the hospital facility was inadequate for the growing black community, the committee was reactivated to work for its expansion or for a new facility. City Hospital No. 2 was replaced by Homer G. Phillips Hospital in 1937.

See also: Homer G. Phillips Hospital

St. Paul African Methodist Episcopal Church

Photo, 1956. Courtesy of the Community Development Agency Collection, Missouri Historical Society Photograph and Print Collection.

City Hospital No. 2

Halftone, 1920. Courtesy of the Homer G. Phillips School of Nursing Collection, Missouri Historical Society Photograph and Print Collection.

Harris-Stowe State College

Photo by David Schultz.

Banner

Photo by Lee Harris.

Roy Wilkins home ○ 53

2818 Laclede Avenue

Roy Wilkins (1901-81), the civil rights leader and executive secretary for the NAACP from 1955 to 1977, was born at this site. He attended the Banneker School in St. Louis before moving to St. Paul, Minnesota, as a young child. Wilkins was the managing editor of the *Kansas City Call* and later joined the NAACP as the editor of *Crisis*, its official magazine. During World War II, he was a special consultant to the Department of War on the training and use of black troops. In May 1945, he served as a consultant to the American delegation that helped to found the United Nations. During the 1960s, Wilkins chaired the Leadership Conference on Civil Rights and acted as consultant to the United States State Department.

Johnson Elementary School ○ 54

2841 Laclede Avenue

In 1945 the Johnson Elementary School opened at this location after Waring School, previously at this site, had relocated to a larger building. As the population of the Mill Creek Valley declined, the school was closed in 1959. The school was named for James Weldon Johnson (1871-1938), poet, author, and diplomat. Born in Florida, he was the author of several volumes of poetry, including *God's Trombones*, a book of folk sermons in verse. With his brother, J. Rosamund Johnson (1873-1954), he also composed the hymn "Lift Every Voice and Sing," which is sometimes called the black national anthem. Johnson served as United States consul in Venezuela and Nicaragua.

See also: Waring School

Harris-Stowe State College ■ 55

3026 Laclede Avenue

Harris-Stowe is located in the building that previously housed Vashon High School, the second—and at one time the largest—black high school in St. Louis. Vashon, which opened here in 1927 as an intermediate school and in 1931 as a high school, is now located at 3405 Bell Avenue.

Harris-Stowe, which moved to the Laclede Avenue site in 1963, represents the merger of two schools. One was Stowe, a teachers' college for blacks that developed from the Sumner Normal Department, established in 1890; later, it took the name of Stowe to honor Harriet Beecher Stowe (1811-96), author of *Uncle Tom's Cabin.* The other was Harris, a teachers' college for white students, which began as the Normal Department of the St. Louis Public High School in 1857 and was later renamed for William Torrey Harris (1835-1909), superintendent of St. Louis Public schools from 1867 to 1880. The two schools merged after the United States Supreme Court outlawed segregated education in 1954. In 1979, Harris-Stowe became part of the state university system. Harris-Stowe has traditionally been the city's primary source of new teachers and the leading producer of black teachers in Missouri.

See also: Vashon High School
Turner Middle School

Oscar Minor Waring Elementary School ■ 56

25 South Compton Avenue

In 1920, the Charles Pope School, built in 1872 at 2841 Laclede Avenue, was renamed for Oscar Minor Waring, a lawyer and teacher who became the first black principal of Sumner High School in 1879. Waring was a gifted linguist who spoke fluent German, Latin, French, Spanish, and Italian. By 1937, the school was overcrowded; portable buildings at the corner of Garrison and Market provided additional space. A large new school was built in 1940. The school closed briefly in the mid-1960s, but it reopened in 1965 as a demonstration school for Harris-Stowe, to serve residents of the newly constructed Laclede Town housing development. Waring became a magnet school in the late 1970s. In 1992 it was in use as the Waring Academy of Basic Instruction, a magnet school with 265 students from kindergarten through fifth grade.

See also: Johnson School

Oscar Minor Waring Elementary School

Photo. Courtesy of St. Louis Public Schools.

Jefferson Bank and Trust Company ● 57

2600 Washington Avenue

From August 30, 1963, until March 31, 1964, Jefferson Bank and Trust Company was the scene of a seven-month-long demonstration, organized by the St. Louis Chapter of the Congress of Racial Equality (CORE), aimed at forcing the bank to hire four black clerical workers. The protests proceeded despite injunctions obtained by the bank to halt them. A number of organizers were arrested, convicted, and sentenced to fines and jail terms. Among those taking part in the protests were Twenty-sixth Ward Alderman William L. Clay (1931-), elected to the United States House of Representatives in 1966; Louis Ford (1935-), who was later a state senator; and community leaders Robert Curtis, who was then president of CORE, Norman R. Seay (1932-), Herman Thompson, Lucian Richards, and Charles and Marian Oldham. The demonstrations finally ended when the bank hired five black clerical employees.

In September 1992, the bank, now at 2301 Market Street, was the scene of demonstrations marking the anniversary of the 1963 protest.

Demonstration by the St. Louis Chapter of the Congress of Racial Equality (CORE)

Photo. Courtesy of the Missouri Historical Society Photograph and Print Collection.

Archer Alexander

Photo, ca. 1865. Courtesy of the Missouri Historical Society Photograph and Print Collection.

William Greenleaf Eliot

Oil painting. Courtesy of the Missouri Historical Society Art Collection.

Wall of Respect or *Up You Mighty Race* mural — 58

2600 Dr. Martin Luther King, Jr., Drive

This mural was painted in 1968 by seven local African-American artists. It depicts several black heroes and is similar to murals created in Chicago and New York during the same period.

Another mural at 2953 Dr. Martin Luther King, Jr., Drive was painted by the Creative Coalition, a group of black artists working with On the Wall Productions, Inc. This painting, on the wall of the building that houses *Proud* magazine and the *Jeff-Vander-Lou News*, includes figures of men and women, heads tilted proudly toward the sun.

Other wall art in the area includes: *The Emergence of Pride*, 2953 Dr. Martin Luther King, Jr., Boulevard; *A Human Race,* 4887 Natural Bridge; and *Wall of Strength,* at Taylor and Kennerly.

Archer Alexander site — 59

Home of William Greenleaf Eliot
Beaumont Place and Locust Street

Archer Alexander, a Virginia-born slave, made his escape in 1863 from the farm in St. Charles County where he worked as overseer. Eluding capture, he made his way to a public market in downtown St. Louis. There Abby Adams Cranch Eliot (1817-1908) found him and hired him as a servant for her family's Beaumont Place home. Her husband, William Greenleaf Eliot (1811-87), was a prominent Unitarian minister who had publicly declared that he would never return a fugitive slave to his master. When Eliot discovered that his newly hired servant was a fugitive slave, he decided to protect him through the turbulent Civil War years—and even managed to save him from his former master's kidnapping attempts.

After the war, Eliot and Alexander remained lifelong friends. In his 1885 biography of Alexander, Eliot wrote: "I never knew a man, white or black, more thoroughly Christian . . . in all conduct and demeanor." Eliot recommended that Alexander serve as the model for a new statue, *Freedom's Memorial*, which sculptor Thomas Ball created for the Western Sanitary Commission in St. Louis. The statue, which depicts President Abraham Lincoln and a newly freed slave, just rising from his knees and grasping a broken chain, was unveiled in Washington, D.C., on April 14, 1876. A copy is in storage at the Steinberg Gallery of Art at Washington University.

Scott Joplin House

Photo by David Schultz.

Scott Joplin House sign

Photo by Lee Harris.

Scott Joplin House State Historic Site ■ 60

2658 Delmar Boulevard (formerly Morgan Street)

Black ragtime composer Scott Joplin (1868-1917), who was born in Texarkana, Texas, lived in St. Louis from 1885 to 1894, and again from 1900 to 1906. From 1901 to 1903, he and his wife, Belle Hayden Joplin, lived in this four-family, 1860s-era structure. It was a fruitful time for Joplin, who composed "The Entertainer," "Gladiolus Rag," "The Cascades," and the first of two ragtime operas. During this period, he also changed careers; formerly an itinerant piano player, he became a composer and teacher, working under the direction of Alfred Ernest, the leader of the St. Louis Choral Symphony Society.

Scott Joplin's home was designated a national historic landmark in 1976. A year later, it was rescued from demolition by Jeff-Vander-Lou, Inc., a neighborhood development corporation. In 1983 the home was donated to the state for restoration. On October 6, 1991, it opened to the public, its turn-of-the-century appearance restored. It now includes a room for musical performances, displays centering on Joplin's life and music, and a gallery for exhibits related to African-American history and culture.

All of Joplin's other residences in St. Louis, as well as the Rosebud Cafe on Market Street and clubs along Chestnut and Market in which he played his music, have been demolished.

Phyllis Wheatley Branch YWCA

Photo by Mario Cavagnaro, 1937. Courtesy of the Missouri Historical Society Photograph and Print Collection.

Phyllis Wheatley Branch YWCA ■ 61

2709 Locust Street

In September 1911, several women who were members of the Union Memorial African Methodist Episcopal Church met at the home of Ada Chapman to discuss the need for a Young Women's Christian Association movement for black girls. With the sanction of the St. Louis YWCA, the Chapman Branch was formed. On April 13, 1912, the branch was renamed for Phyllis Wheatley (1753?-84), a black poet born in Africa and brought to Boston as a slave when she was seven years old. Wealthy tailor John Wheatley gave the young girl to his wife as a personal servant. She quickly mastered the English language, and in 1773 she traveled to Europe, where she entertained literary circles with her poetry.

In 1915, the Wheatley Branch was located in a renovated mansion at 709 North Garrison Avenue. It moved to the Locust Street location in 1941. This building had opened in 1927 as the St. Louis Women's Christian Association.

Central Baptist Church

Photo. Courtesy of the Community Development Agency Collection, Missouri Historical Society Photograph and Print Collection.

Central Baptist Church ■ 62

2843 Washington Avenue at T. E. Huntley Drive

Central Baptist Church, the fourth-oldest black church in St. Louis, organized as the Second Colored Baptist Church in 1846. The Reverend John Richard Anderson (1818-63) petitioned for a letter of dismissal from the First African Baptist Church in June of that year, and by August he and about twenty others had formed the new congregation. They originally met in a hall near Third Street and Franklin Avenue (formerly Cherry Street). Over the years, the church has been known by several names: Eighth Street Colored Baptist Church, Green Street Baptist Church, and finally Central Baptist Church. In 1914 the congregation purchased the former Pilgrim Congregational Church, where the distinguished minister and orator, the Reverend Henry Ward Beecher (1813-87), once preached. In March 1971, the church was destroyed by fire, but within four years the congregation had rebuilt its sanctuary and also bought the educational building across the street.

See also: Bellefontaine Cemetery

T. E. Huntley Drive ■ 63

T. E. Huntley Drive runs between Olive Street and Dr. Martin Luther King, Jr., Drive on what used to be Ewing Street. In 1984, it was named for the Reverend Thomas Elliott Huntley (1903-83), who was pastor of Central Baptist Church from 1942 to 1983.

Banneker Elementary School (Colored School No. 5) ■ 64

2840 Samuel Shepard Drive

Banneker School, originally Colored School No. 5, was opened at Eighteenth and Conde streets in 1866. By 1890 it had moved to Montgomery Street and Leffingwell Avenue, where it was renamed for Benjamin Banneker (1731-1804), an African-American astronomer, mathematician, and architect. Banneker produced an almanac comparable to Benjamin Franklin's *Poor Richard's Almanac*. In 1789, he was appointed to assist Pierre L' Enfant in laying out Washington, D.C. When L' Enfant left town before the work was finished in a dispute over his fee, Banneker had to draw up a new set of plans. His fine work won him widespread praise. The *Georgetown Weekly Ledger* of March 12, 1791, called him "an Ethiopian, whose abilities as surveyor and astronomer already proved that Mr. Jefferson's concluding that race of men were void of mental endowment, was without foundation."

In 1932 the Banneker School moved into the Stoddard School building, built in 1873 at Lucas and Ewing avenues. This building was torn down in 1939 to make way for a new Banneker School on the same site. In the late 1950s, the St. Louis public schools were divided into several subdistricts, with their own elementary schools and junior high schools; each subdistrict was centered around one or two high schools. The Banneker School gained national and international attention as the administrative headquarters of the Banneker District, which consisted of twenty-three elementary schools, mostly in the inner city, including schools within the Pruitt-Igoe and Vaughn housing projects. The district program, headed by Samuel Shepard, Jr. (1907-), incorporated highly successful methods for inspiring children to attend school and for encouraging parents to become involved in schools. When the district was reorganized in 1970, the Banneker District became part of the Central Vashon District. In 1992-93, Banneker housed classes from pre-school through fifth grade, with an enrollment of 365 students.

Colored School No. 5

Photo by Emil Boehl, ca. 1876. Courtesy of the St. Louis Public Library.

See also: Samuel Shepard Drive

Washington Metropolitan African Methodist Episcopal Zion Church

Photo by David Schultz.

Samuel Shepard Drive ■ 65

This street, which runs between Jefferson and Grand avenues on what used to be Lucas Avenue, honors Samuel Shepard, Jr. (1907-), an educator and school administrator. From 1957 to 1976 he directed the Banneker District of the St. Louis Public Schools and pioneered innovative methods of inspiring low-income children to attend and excel in school. He challenged teachers not to use the socioeconomic status of their students as an excuse for poor results; he urged parents to get their children to school and help them study.

Within two years, the number of Banneker graduates who won places in a high school program for gifted students had doubled and the number placed in the lowest achievement group had been cut by more than half. Shepard won the St. Louis Newspaper Guild's Page One Civic Award in 1960, the first African American to receive this honor. He was named superintendent of schools for East Chicago, Illinois, in 1976; he retired from this office in 1979.

Washington Metropolitan African Methodist Episcopal Zion Church ■ 66

613 North Garrison Avenue

The oldest African Methodist Episcopal Zion church in St. Louis, Washington Metropolitan was organized in the 1870s. It occupies the site of the former Union Methodist Church, built in 1880 and designated as a historic landmark by the city of St. Louis in 1974.

The church remained in its city location when much of the surrounding area was demolished for redevelopment. Under the leadership of the Reverend Richard Fisher, the church sponsored the construction of the nearby Lucas Heights and Metropolitan Village housing, more than three hundred units of rental apartments and townhouses, built in the 1980s.

Jordan Chambers Post Office Branch ■ 67

901 North Garrison Avenue

Jordan "Pop" Chambers (1897-1962), for whom this post office is named, was known as the "father of black politics" in St. Louis and the "Negro mayor of St. Louis." During the 1930s, he led the exodus of blacks from the Republican party into Democratic ranks. Chambers was the Democratic committeeman for the city's Nineteenth Ward and constable in the old Tenth District. He was also the owner of The Riviera, a nightclub at 4460 Delmar Boulevard. The Anchor Post Office Station was renamed for him in 1964. The Jordan Chambers Park at Compton and Franklin avenues was also named in his honor in the 1950s.

Washington Tabernacle Baptist Church ■ 68

3200 Washington Boulevard

The Washington Tabernacle Baptist Church, organized in 1902, moved to this site in 1926. Several generations of local black leaders were among its members. Its Gothic Revival stone sanctuary, named a city landmark in 1984, dates from 1879. The building was designed by St. Louis architect John Maurice for the former Walnut Street Presbyterian congregation. Washington Tabernacle was the site of a major civil rights rally in May 1963 when Martin Luther King, Jr. (1929-1968), drew more than three thousand participants to his Freedom Rally, held a few months before the March on Washington.

Carver House Community Center ■ 69

3035 Bell Avenue at Cardinal Avenue

Carver House opened in 1939 in a Bell Avenue mansion, though its origins can be traced to an earlier social center founded by the Wesley House Association in 1919. In 1934 the association moved to 4507 Lee Avenue and decided to turn its old building into a black branch of Wesley House. The new center was named in honor of George Washington Carver (1864?-1943), a prominent black botanist, agricultural chemist, and educator. In 1937, the National Youth Administration and the Federal Works Progress Administration organized training and recreational programs at the center. By 1957, more than forty-three thousand children and adults were participating in its programs each year. The current building opened in 1958. In 1992, Carver House, a United Way agency, served more than 645 households, representing some 2,100 people, with social services, after-school programs, and crisis intervention for families and youth.

First Baptist Church

Photo by W. C. Persons, ca. 1915. Courtesy of the Missouri Historical Society Photograph and Print Collection.

First Baptist Church ■ 70

3100 Bell Avenue at Cardinal Avenue

First Baptist Church traces its origin to the First African Baptist Church, organized in 1818. The church bought its present site in 1917, then later purchased the adjacent four-family flat and converted it into an educational building. The church burned to the ground in 1940 and was reconstructed on the same site within thirteen months.

See also: First African Baptist Church

Dunbar Elementary School

Photo by W. C. Persons. Courtesy of the Missouri Historical Society Photograph and Print Collection.

James "Cool Papa" Bell

Photo. Courtesy of the National Baseball Library, Cooperstown, N.Y.

Dunbar Elementary School ■ 71

1415 Garrison Avenue

The Glasgow School, which had opened in 1912, was renamed in 1937 for Paul Laurence Dunbar (1872-1906), a black poet, novelist, and short-story writer. He was the first black poet after Phyllis Wheatley to achieve an international reputation. At age twenty-one he published his first book of poetry, *Oak and Ivy,* and three years later he produced a second book, *Lyrics of a Lowly Life.* In 1992, the Dunbar School had an enrollment of 390 children from pre-school programs through fifth grade.

James "Cool Papa" Bell Avenue ■ 72

In the 1980s, Dickson Street between Jefferson Avenue and Webster was renamed James "Cool Papa" Bell Avenue. James Thomas Bell (1903-91) was a Mississippi native who moved to St. Louis at age sixteen and played professional baseball in the old Negro National League between 1922 and 1950. His daring baserunning and hitting skills placed him among the best players in the league. He is also said to have been one of the fastest men ever to play baseball. Once he reached second base on a bunt; another time he rounded the bases in a record-breaking 13.1 seconds. In 1974, Bell became the fifth Negro National League player elected to the Baseball Hall of Fame in Cooperstown, New York.

American Muslim Mission

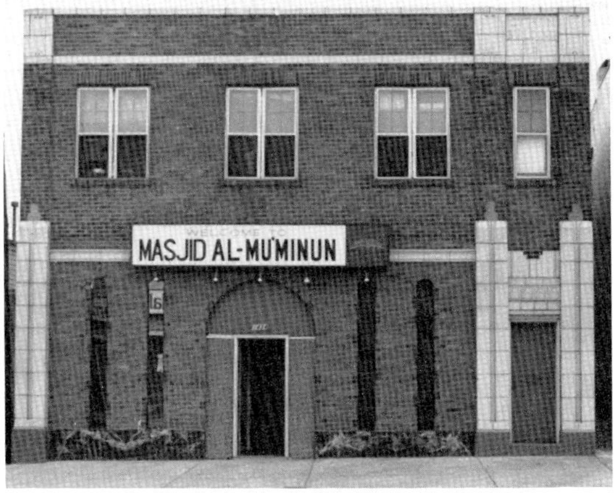

Photo by Lee Harris.

Ferrier-Harris Nursing Home

Photo by David Schultz.

Ferrier-Harris Nursing Home ■ 73

3636 Page Boulevard

Ferrier-Harris Home for the Aged, founded in 1902 as the Colored Old Folks Home, moved to this site in 1943. A group of black women known as the Woman's Wednesday Sewing Club raised funds for the home, which continues to provide facilities for senior citizens in the African-American community. The home is named for Rose Ferrier-Harris, the club's first president. In 1993, it had twenty-seven residents.

American Muslim Mission ■ 74

1434 North Grand Avenue

The Nation of Islam was established in 1930 by W. D. Fard (?-1934) and developed in Detroit by Elijah Muhammad (1897-1975), who later moved to Chicago, where he was arrested for draft dodging. During his imprisonment, he expanded his ministry, teaching black superiority, self-discipline, integrity, honor, self-sufficiency, and racial segregation. In the 1950s, the American Muslims established this mission in St. Louis. They also owned and operated several businesses in the 1900 block of Grand Avenue.

Sentinel newspaper ■ 75

2900 North Market at Glasgow Street

This building houses the *Sentinel*, a weekly newspaper with a circulation of twenty thousand, which was founded in 1968 by Howard B. Woods (1917-76), its publisher and editor. He initiated the "Yes, I Can" dinner as an annual charity event and fundraiser for the *Sentinel*. In 1976, upon the death of her husband, Jane Woods became the publisher of the newspaper, and her son-in-law, Michael Williams, its editor.

Redd Foxx Lane ■ 76

John Elroy Sanford (1922-91), better known by his stage name Redd Foxx, was reared in the 4400 block of Enright Avenue and later in the 2900 block of Bell Avenue. A comedian, he became one of the first African Americans to have a television series of his own when he starred in "Sanford and Son." After Spring Avenue was realigned for construction of the Cochran Veterans' Hospital, a small section remained. In 1973, it was renamed for Foxx.

Mission entrance

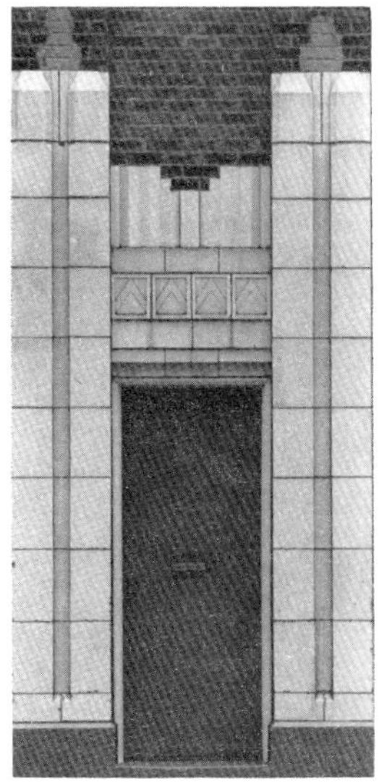

Photo by Lee Harris.

Cole Elementary School

Photo by David Schultz.

C. D. Banks Drive ■ 77

In 1981, a portion of Fairfax Avenue between Vandeventer and Newstead avenues was renamed for Cornelius David Banks (1929-), a youth worker who helped youngsters in local community centers, Scouting programs, and the YMCA. In 1979, Banks became one of five recipients of the national Jefferson Award, presented by the American Institute for Public Service. The award recognized "outstanding public service benefitting local communities."

Cole Elementary School ■ 78

3935 Enright Avenue

Cole Elementary opened in 1931. It was named for Richard H. Cole (1855-1927), a public school teacher and principal at Simmons Elementary School in St. Louis for fifty years. Born in Cincinnati, Cole lived at 4210 West Belle Place in St. Louis. In 1992-93, 340 students from pre-school through fifth grade attended Cole Elementary School.

Vashon High School

Photo by David Schultz.

Vashon High School ■ 79

3405 Bell Avenue

Vashon High School opened as an intermediate school in 1927, and four years later it became the city's second black high school. It was located on Laclede Avenue, now the site of Harris-Stowe State College. The opening represented a major victory for black residents, who had been fighting since 1922 for a high school with a modern physical plant. Previously, black students had to travel to Sumner High School in north St. Louis. In 1963, the school relocated to this address, the former location of the Hadley Technical School. Still in use as a high school, Vashon had a 1992-93 enrollment of 975 students.

Vashon was named for George Boyer Vashon (1824-78), the first black graduate of Oberlin College, and his son John Boyer Vashon (1859-1924), a teacher and principal in the St. Louis public schools. The Vashon Playground and Community Center, at the northeast corner of Market Street and Compton Avenue, was also named for the Vashons.

Well-known graduates of the school include Julius Dix, Lloyd L. Gaines, Lawrence Nicholson, and Virgil Akins (1928-), former world welterweight boxing champion. A St. Louis native, Akins had an amateur career of seventy-nine bouts with nine losses. In 1958 he won the welterweight title by defeating Vince Martinez in a fourth-round knockout. He lost the title six months later to Don Jordan. Akins retired in 1962 because of a serious eye injury.

See also: Harris-Stowe State Teachers College

St. Alphonsus Liguori (Rock) Church

Photo by Emil Boehl, ca. 1890. Courtesy of the Missouri Historical Society Photograph and Print Collection.

Carver Elementary School ■ 80

3325 Bell Avenue

In 1943 Carver School opened in the old Wayman Crow School, which was built in 1882. In 1978 an addition was made to Carver to house a new community school, which had a 1992 enrollment of 275 students from kindergarten through fifth grade. The community school now uses the facilities at Carver and at Vashon High School to provide after-school and evening activities for all ages. The school was named for George Washington Carver (1864?-1943), who emerged from slavery to become a famed scientist, college professor, and inventor. He derived more than 300 products from the peanut and 118 products from the sweet potato.

St. Alphonsus Liguori (Rock) Church ■ 81

1118 North Grand Boulevard

This Roman Catholic Church, established as a parish for Irish immigrants in the late 1860s, is typical of Catholic churches in north St. Louis whose congregations have become predominantly African American. It may be known as the "Rock" church because it was one of the first churches in St. Louis to be built of quarry stone. Housed in a building designed for the Redemptorist Fathers by the Reverend Louis Dold, with much of the work done by the St. Louis firm of Conradi and Schrader, St. Alphonsus today uses African-American traditions in its music and liturgical style. It is known for its outstanding gospel choir.

St. Louis People's Art Center ⬭ 82

3657 Grandel Square

On October 7, 1940, a group of interested citizens met to establish a community art center under the guidelines of the Federal Art Project program. The People's Art Center was intended to be "a means of bringing together people of all racial origins, religious faiths, and economic levels, and all ages, for creative self-expression through a common interest in arts and crafts." The center opened on April 17, 1942, at 2811 Washington Boulevard. Its first exhibition honored the black St. Louis artist E. Simms Campbell (1906-71), a well-known cartoonist and illustrator whose work appeared in such magazines as *Esquire*, *New Yorker*, *Judge*, *Life*, and *Playboy*.

In 1946, the center moved to Grandel Square, now the site of the Urban League parking lot. The center flourished at this location, with local artists and teachers volunteering their teaching skills to support the efforts of the center. By 1954, more than two thousand children and adults from the city and county were enrolled in classes. The program was so successful that larger quarters were needed, and the center expanded to all floors of the building, as well as to the carriage house behind. In 1964, the center moved to the Yalem Human Development Center at 724 Union Boulevard. Financial and administrative problems led to its closing a year later.

Urban League of Metropolitan St. Louis ■ 83

3701 Grandel Square

The St. Louis chapter of the Urban League dates from 1910, the year in which the National Urban League was also founded. It began as the Committee for Social Services Among Colored People, a group of educated blacks and whites, organized to investigate the plight of migrant blacks moving from the rural South to the St. Louis area in search of jobs. The CSSACP began calling itself the Urban League of St. Louis in 1918. A chapter of the Urban League based in East St. Louis merged with the St. Louis group in 1980.

The League was a department of the Provident Association until 1922, when it became a member agency of the Community Fund, now known as the United Way. Its first president was the Reverend John W. Day. The new Urban League set up headquarters at 2234 Locust Street, but soon moved to larger offices at 2434 Market Street. As the first interracial group in the city, the league began a vigorous attack on such problems as segregation, discrimination, and the lack of jobs; it advocated improved housing, cultural, and health-care facilities. Its early initiatives included the founding of a dental clinic in the Lincoln School, a campaign that led to the founding of the Charles Henry Turner Open-Air School for Crippled Children, and the establishment of a neighborhood social service program.

Urban League of Metropolitan St. Louis

Photo, ca. 1960. Courtesy of the Urban League of St. Louis.

In 1925, the League moved to Jefferson and Lucas, then later to 3017 Delmar. Today, the Urban League continues to work for neighborhood betterment; to provide job counseling services and programs for employment, housing, and training; and to take a role in human rights activities. It also operates a community services center at 1408 North Kingshighway, a former Sears department store.

From 1974 to 1981, the former John Berry Meachum Branch of the St. Louis Public Library was housed in the Grandel Square building, which has been the Urban League headquarters since 1981.

See also: East St. Louis race riot of 1917
Vaughn Cultural Center

St. Louis Black Repertory Company

Photo by David Schultz.

St. Louis Black Repertory Company ■ 84

534 North Grand Avenue at Grandel Square

The St. Louis Black Repertory Company, called the "Black Rep," was founded in 1976 by Ronald J. Himes, its producing director. The largest black performing arts company in Missouri, it presents a full season of theater and other entertainment. In time for the 1992-93 season, it moved into new quarters on Grandel Square in the renovated First Congregational Church building, which dates from 1884. This theater, with seating for about 470 patrons, is the first to be built in St. Louis in more than twenty years. The company had previously produced plays in the Twenty-third Street Theater at 2240 St. Louis Avenue, also a renovated church building. Its mission is to provide a platform for theater, dance, and other creative expressions that heighten the community's social and cultural awareness of the African-American perspective.

Vaughn Cultural Center ■ 85

525 North Grand Boulevard

In 1977, the Vaughn Cultural Center was established in a former Sears store at 1408 North Kingshighway Boulevard as a cultural enrichment program of the Urban League. Ermalene Vaughn (1890-1980) contributed funds for its establishment in memory of her husband, Dr. Arthur Vaughn (1888-1974), a prominent physician who served on the St. Louis

The Origin of Freemasonry

Photo by Lee Harris. Courtesy of the St. Louis Public Library.

University medical faculty for more than twenty-five years. The center, which today honors the memory of Mrs. Vaughn as well, strives to increase awareness and understanding of black history and culture by sponsoring cultural events and activities. It also houses a gallery for exhibitions by African-American artists.

Mural by Jessie H. Holliman ■ 86

Masonic Temple Association of St. Louis
3681 Lindell Boulevard

This thirty-eight-foot mural entitled *The Origin of Freemasonry*, located in the lobby of the temple, is one of the few true frescoes in Missouri. It was painted in 1941 by African-American artist Jessie Housley Holliman (1905?-84), a Harris-Stowe graduate and student at the Art Institute of Chicago, Columbia University, and the Washington University of Fine Arts. She taught art for thirty-nine years at the Divoll School and was a freelance fashion illustrator.

Holliman also created two other murals. Her first, *Racial and Industrial Harmony,* was painted in the old Urban League building at 3017 Delmar, which was later demolished. Another mural, *Christ's Fellowship*, located in the Central Baptist Church, was destroyed when the church burned in 1971. The Masonic Temple mural, dedicated by Senator Harry S. Truman in 1941, depicts the events that led to the establishment of Masonic societies.

Negro Jefferson Club ○ 87

Grand Boulevard, at the southwest corner of Pine Street

After the Civil War, most African Americans voted with the Republican party, but by the turn of the century the Democratic party had begun to woo blacks. In St. Louis, Democratic ward boss Ed Butler and his son Jim organized a new machine organization known as the Jefferson Club, run by St. Louis Police Board commissioner Harry B. Hawes. Through his efforts, an auxiliary Negro Jefferson Club was established, with such black leaders as C. C. Rankin, Crittenden Clark, W. H. Fields, and James Milton Turner. In 1901 the club helped elect Democrat Rolla Wells as St. Louis mayor. The Democratic party lost African-American support because some of its members continued to voice anti-black sentiments and promises made to black voters were not fulfilled. In addition, Theodore Roosevelt, Republican president of the United States from 1901 to 1909, courted the black vote during his campaigns and administration. With the help of the African-American vote, Roosevelt became the first Republican candidate since U. S. Grant to win Missouri.

The New Deal programs of President Franklin D. Roosevelt, who held office from 1933 to 1945, and his appointment of African Americans to positions in his administration, helped win blacks to the Democratic party during the 1930s.

Citizens Liberty League 88

Pythian Hall, 3507 Pine Street

On December 17, 1919, a group of prominent African-American St. Louisans organized the Citizens Liberty League at a meeting held in the Pythian Hall. The league was formed to elect blacks to public offices and achieve greater representation by blacks on the various committees of the Republican party. Among the founding members were Aaron W. Lloyd, grand chancellor of the Knights of Pythias of Missouri, president; Crittenden Clark, Washington University law graduate, vice president; Captain Walter Lowe; attorney George L. Vaughn (1824-78); and *St. Louis Argus* publisher Joseph Mitchell (1876-1952). A women's auxiliary league was organized early in 1920. Assisted by the statewide Missouri Negro Republican League, the Citizens Liberty League was able to gain the nomination and election of an African American, Walthall Moore, to the Missouri General Assembly in 1920. Although Moore lost his bid for reelection in 1922, Crittenden Clark was elected as the first black justice of the peace in St. Louis, while Charles U. Turpin and Langston Harrison were elected constables. In 1924, Moore was returned to the General Assembly, and Robert T. Scott was chosen as the first black ward committeeman.

Finley Park 89

Grand Boulevard and Laclede Avenue

The first professional black baseball team in St. Louis was the St. Louis Giants, founded in 1909 as part of the Negro National League. The team played its games in Finley Park, once a Federal League park. Player Bill Drake described his experiences with the Giants in John Holway's 1975 *Voices from the Great Black Baseball League*:

> In 1910 I came here to play with the St. Louis Giants. At that time the team was playing in Finley Park, the old Federal League park, at Grand and Laclede. . . . I was getting $100 a month. Back then that was tops. But that was a fortune when you consider prices. The best room in town only cost $2.50. A T-bone steak was a quarter—biscuits a nickel extra. And if you wanted to eat soul food, why that was even less.

In 1920, the team moved to Giants Park, near North Broadway and Clarence Street. A new group of owners purchased the Giants in 1921, renamed them the St. Louis Stars, and the following year moved them to a field near Compton Avenue and Market Street (near the site of Harris-Stowe State College). The team used this ballpark, called Stars Park, until 1931. Next to it was a trolley barn that cut into left field; right-handed power hitters had an easy time in the foreshortened field. In 1930, Stars Park installed the first permanent lights for night baseball in St. Louis. During the same season, the St. Louis Stars won the Negro National League Championship in a split-season playoff versus the Detroit Stars. In 1939, the team moved to Mound, Illinois.

St. Louis Negro League team photo

Photo. Courtesy of the National Baseball Library, Cooperstown, New York.

North Central City

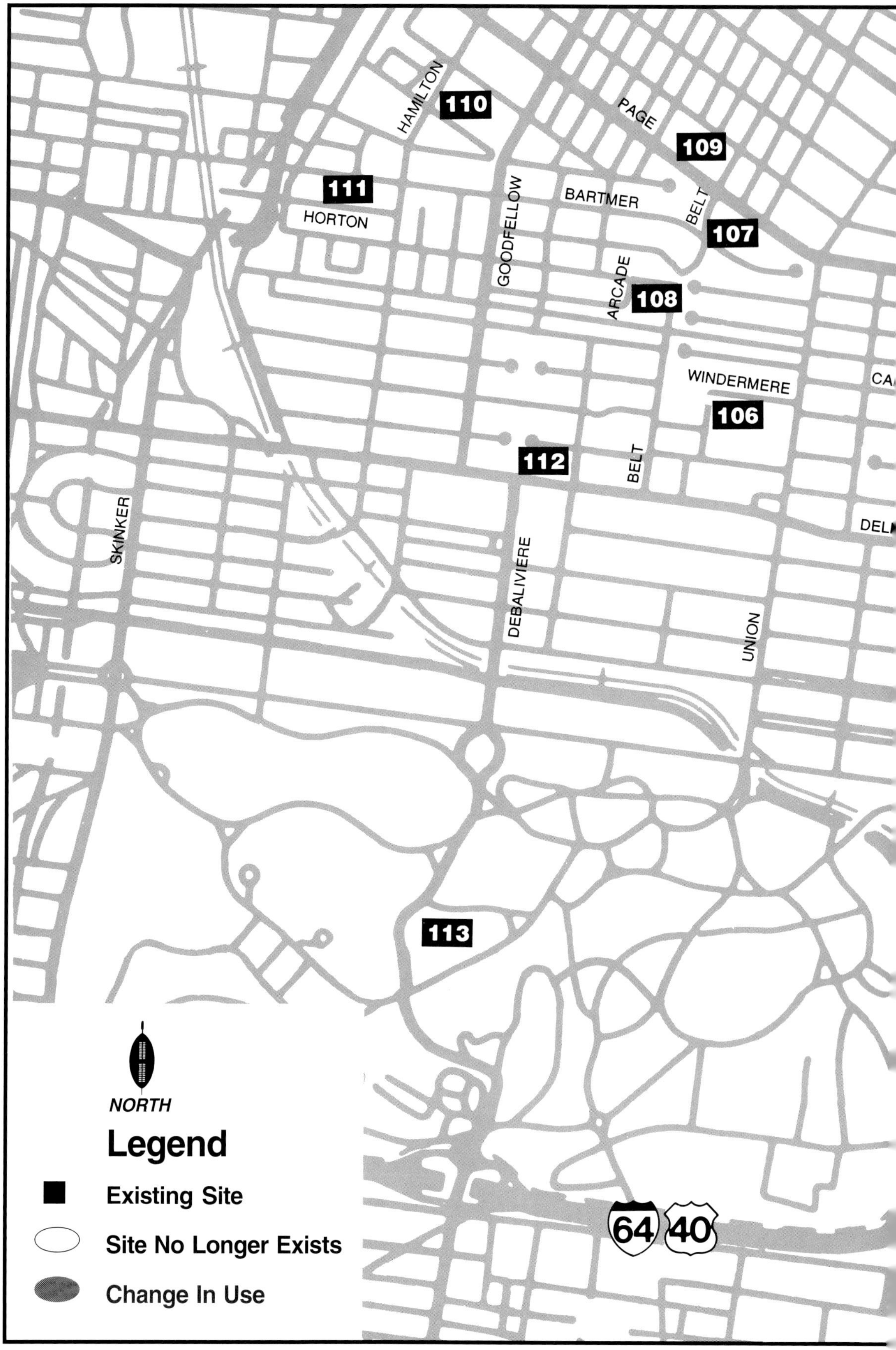

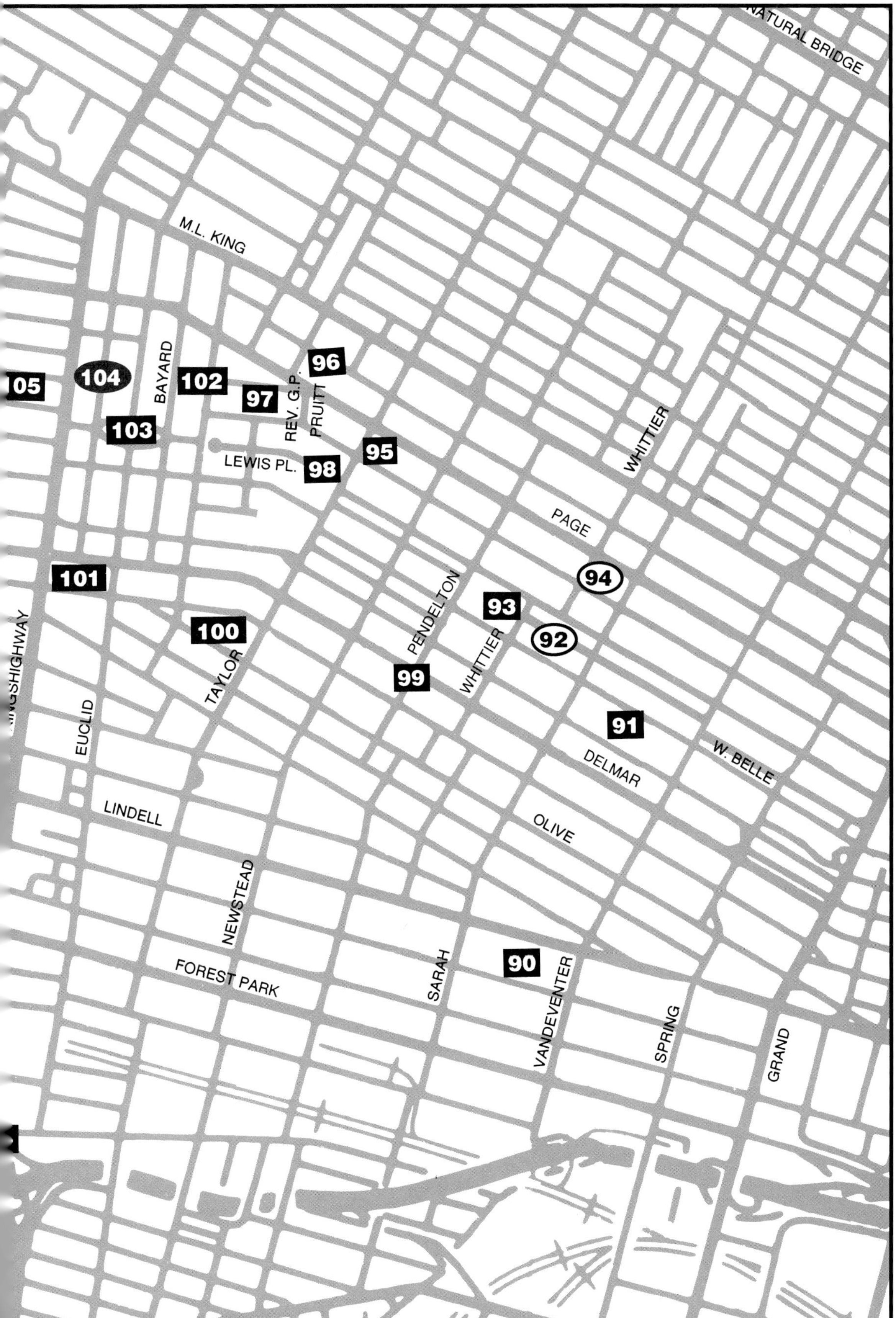
NATURAL BRIDGE
M.L. KING
BAYARD
05
104
102
97
96
REV. G.P.
PRUITT
103
LEWIS PL.
98
95
WHITTIER
PAGE
94
101
100
TAYLOR
93
92
PENDELTON
WHITTIER
99
KINGSHIGHWAY
EUCLID
91
DELMAR
W. BELLE
LINDELL
OLIVE
NEWSTEAD
FOREST PARK
SARAH
90
VANDEVENTER
SPRING
GRAND

North Central City

Martin Luther King, Jr. statue at Fountain Park

Photo by Lee Harris.

The *St. Louis American* newspaper ■ 90

4144 Lindell Avenue

The offices of the *St. Louis American*, the second-oldest black-owned newspaper in St. Louis, are located in this building. The first issue of the paper appeared on March 17, 1928. It was established by A. N. Johnson, a Baltimore newspaperman, and his son-in-law John L. Procope, a St. Louis businessman. Johnson became managing editor, Frederick C. Alston (1895-?) the art director and cartoonist, and Nathan B. Young, Jr. (1896-1993), editorial and feature writer.

The paper grew steadily until the 1929 stock market crash, when several stockholders pulled out and Johnson returned to the East Coast. Young continued to run the paper, with the assistance of a young Lincoln University graduate, Nathaniel E. Sweets (1901-88). Sweets accepted the position of advertising manager for the paper and eventually became business manager and publisher. After Sweets' retirement in 1981, his son, Fred Sweets, sold the family's interest in the paper to Gene Liss, who was then joined by Dr. Donald Suggs and C. W. Cates. In 1984 Suggs purchased Liss' shares in the paper and became the majority shareholder and publisher.

The *American*, a weekly with a circulation of fifty-two thousand in 1992, is known as a leading voice for civil rights, fair housing and employment, and black participation in politics at the local and national level.

The *St. Louis American*

BEHIND THE SCENES PAGE 1B

FACES AND PLACES DROPS IN ON CARNAHAN FUNDRAISER PAGE 10A

BUY IT SELL IT TRY IT FIND IT IN THE ST. LOUIS AMERICAN CLASSISFIEDS

THE ST. LOUIS AMERICAN

OCT., 22 - 28, 1992 — THE BLACK WEEKLY — CAC Audited — VOL. 64 NO. 32

Jones Blasts Housing Efforts, As Report "Gathers Dust"

BY FREDRICK L. MCKISSACK
Of *The St. Louis American*

This past July, the St. Louis Low Income Housing Report, compiled by the Center on Budget and Policy Priorities in Washington, D.C., was released amid much fanfare. The report revealed, among other things, that the availability of low-income housing in the metropolitan area "is in a crisis state due to a sharp decline in recent years in the number of low-cost rental units, stagnant household incomes and cutbacks in federal assistance."

According to the report as of April 1992, 29,000 families in the St. Louis metropolitan area were on waiting lists for government subsidized housing. In addition, seven of every eight poor households pay more than the maximum considered affordable under federal standards.

The Rev. Buck Jones, founder and director of Project Hope for East St. Louis and St. Louis, was among those on a panel here who discussed the report when it was released and urged politicians and community groups not to let it "gather dust."

But last Friday, Jones and members of Project Hope protested outside the offices of the St. Louis Housing Authority, 4100 Lindell Boule-

A member of Project Hope, who has been

The Rev. Buck Jones, director of Project HOPE, claims the Housing Authority is failing in its commitment to provide adequate housing. (Pat Washington photo)

in the report have been implemented.

"They let the report gather dust," Rev. Jones said, ruefully. "The poor are in a severe crisis in this city. We need at least 20,000 new single-family units built in this city this year alone."

Jones said he receives at least 50 calls a week about housing. "We can help maybe two or three at best," Jones said. "The poor just cannot afford housing in

equate Housing for Missourians, which co-sponsored the panel discussion last summer, said Jones' protest may be targeted at the wrong agency.

"I don't feel that they (Housing Authority officials) were either to blame or totally innocent for the situation. I don't know if we can expect them to do anything or even

Swatek Joins Drug Crackdown on Property Owners in City

BY PATRICIA WASHINGTON
Of *The St. Louis American*

Landlords who allow illegal drug activity to continue at their property will now face civil lawsuits in addition to criminal prosecutions.

Circut Attorney Richard L. Swatek announced Wednesday that his office would formally join and participate in "Operation Crackdown", a joint effort of a number of law enforcement and governmental entities whose goal is the elimination of area crackhouses.

Among those already participating in the program are the U.S. Attorney's Office, the U.S. Marshal's Service, the Drug Enforcement Administration, the St. Louis Metropolitan Police Department, St. Louis City government and departments within St. Louis County government.

Swatek said his office would primarily be enforcing the provisions of Section 195.130 of the Missouri Statutes. This law, dating back to 1939, allows the Prosecuting Attorney of any county--or, in St. Louis--the Circuit Attorney, to file a civil suit against any person, including the owner or lessee of a property, using a building for the illegal use, keeping or sale of a controlled substance.

Sawtek said that to his knowledge, this law had never been applied in the city of St. Louis. He called it the perfect tool to use against landlords who continued to rent to drug dealers, knowing the property is being used for illegal purposes.

"We're sending a clear message to the crack dealers and to such landlords," Swatek said. "We've been endangered by these thugs long enough--we can't sit around any longer and let the crack city. Through Operation Crackdown, our office can contribute to the fight against crackhouses."

Richard L. Swatek
St. Louis Circuit Attorney

Swatek emphasized that his office will begin immediately to pursue those landlords who are knowingly renting to drug dealers. He reported that many unscrupulous property owners actually prefer renting to dealers as they pay promptly with cash, and will pay an inflated price for strategic location from which to operate their criminal business.

"We're delighted that the Circut Attorney will be joining our efforts," said U.S. Attorney Stephen B. Higgins. "With the addition of that office to the Operation Crackdown team, a critical dimension is added to our successful program."

Swatek stated that enforcement of the state statute is different from the ordinance recently proposed by the city

Lloyd L. Gaines home ■ 91

3932 West Belle Place

Lloyd Lionel Gaines (1911-39?), a Mississippi native, moved to St. Louis with his family when he was fourteen years old. He graduated first in his class from Vashon High School. After attending Stowe Teachers College, he completed his bachelor's degree at Lincoln University in Jefferson City. He applied to the University of Missouri School of Law; it was the first time that a black had tried to gain admission to the school. The law school rejected his application and suggested that he take advantage of a state statute that provided out-of-state scholarships for blacks.

Gaines approached the NAACP, which assembled a legal team to assist him. His case, *Missouri ex el. Gaines v. Canada*, was rejected by the Boone County Circuit Court and, on appeal, by the Missouri Supreme Court. But on December 12, 1938, in a landmark decision, the United States Supreme Court ruled 7-2 that the University of Missouri School of Law, then a segregated institution, would have to admit Gaines unless the state could offer him equivalent training elsewhere. This ruling was the first in a series of decisions that culminated in the abandonment of the 1896 "separate-but-equal" doctrine of *Plessy v. Ferguson*.

Gaines publicly announced his intention of entering the University of Missouri the following September. During its 1939 session, however, the Missouri legislature passed a bill providing $275,000 to establish a law school at Lincoln University. Lincoln administrators found space in the Poro College building in St. Louis, and the new law school opened with thirty students in September 1939.

Lloyd Gaines was not among them. In March 1939, Gaines paid a visit to Chicago. One evening he left the fraternity house where he was staying to do a brief errand. He was never seen or heard from again.

The Slaughter Athletic Club ○ 92

4145 West Belle Place

William Slaughter (1897-) founded the Slaughter Athletic Club in 1937 in a garage behind his home on West Belle Place. His father, Robert B. ("Pop") Slaughter, managed the club while William worked as a Pullman porter. In 1940, they moved it to the second floor of a Sarah Street building, still located at the northeast corner of the Hodiamont tracks, that had served as the Paradise Dance Hall in the late 1920s and early 1930s. The club's boxing team won St. Louis Golden Gloves trophies in 1938, 1939, and 1940. The Slaughter Athletic Club operated until World War II. William Slaughter served as the first black athletic commissioner of Missouri's state athletic board in 1938.

A number of nationally prominent fighters trained at the club including Archie Moore (1913-), world light- heavyweight champion from 1952 to 1962, and Henry Armstrong (1912-1989), the only fighter ever to hold three world championship titles at the same time. Born Henry Jackson in Mississippi, Armstrong came with his family to St. Louis when he was five years old. He graduated from Vashon High School in 1928, then trained with fighter Harry Armstrong and boxed in amateur league bouts. After a brief, unsuccessful stint on the professional fighting circuit in Pennsylvania, he changed his name to "Armstrong" and started afresh. In 1936 he won the world featherweight championship, along with a reputation as a knockout artist. Two years later, he won the world welterweight title and later that year the lightweight championship. He fought forty-six fights from 1937 to 1939 without one loss and set a world's record for the longest series of knockouts. He was elected to boxing's Hall of Fame in 1954. After his boxing career ended, he became associate minister of Mount Olive Baptist Church, 2912 St. Louis Avenue.

Stevens Middle School ■ 93

1033 Whittier Avenue

This school first opened in 1964 as Stevens Elementary School, serving kindergarten through eighth grade. In 1981 it became a middle school, with grades six, seven, and eight; in 1992-93, it had 408 students. The Reverend George E. Stevens, Jr. (1861-1941), for whom the school was named, was pastor of Central Baptist Church for thirty-four years. He spoke out strongly in favor of civil rights for African Americans and against all forms of segregation or discrimination. He also worked for the improvement of secondary and higher education for blacks. In 1920 he was the first black minister in St. Louis to become a candidate for the Board of Education; he received twenty thousand write-in votes.

St. Joseph High School ○ 94

Page Boulevard and Whittier Avenue

In 1937, two Sisters of St. Joseph established the St. Joseph High School for black Catholics in the old Father Dunn Newsboy Home on Washington Avenue. After a few years, it moved to 3954 West Belle Place and then to its final location in St. Ann's School at Page and Whittier. St. Joseph served all the black Catholic students in St. Louis and St. Louis County until 1947, when Archbishop Joseph E. Ritter (1892-1967) desegregated the St. Louis Catholic schools. One well-known alumnus is Robert Guillaume (1937-), an Emmy-award-winning actor best known for the television series "Benson."

Beckett Playground

Photo by Lee Harris.

Beckett Playground ■ 95

Page Boulevard and Taylor Avenue

This three-acre playground, created in 1959, is named for William Henry Jackson Beckett (1882-1954), a popular and inspirational physical education teacher at Sumner High School. A Philadelphia native and 1906 graduate of Springfield College in Massachusetts, Beckett first came to St. Louis in 1910 as physical education director at Sumner. In 1912, he left for six years to work as executive secretary of the Washington, D.C., YMCA and later as physical trainer for soldiers preparing to serve in World War I. In 1918, he returned to Sumner, where he remained until his retirement in 1952.

Pleasant Green Missionary Baptist Church

Photo by W. C. Persons, 1946. Courtesy of the Missouri Historical Society Photograph and Print Collection.

Pleasant Green Missionary Baptist Church ■ 96

1220 Reverend George Pruitt Place

In 1866, Pleasant Green was established when small groups of members began holding home prayer meetings, under the guidance of the Reverend Thomas E. Napier. The young congregation soon acquired a rented storefront at the corner of Main and Mullanphy streets. During the next two decades, the church moved to several different rented locations. In 1908, the congregation purchased its own building at Eliott and Wash (now Cole) streets. Pleasant Green bought its current sanctuary, a former synagogue at West End Avenue and Page Boulevard, in 1945. For many years, the church held an Easter baptismal ceremony on the banks of the Mississippi River.

Reverend George H. Pruitt Place ■ 97

On August 18, 1985, West End Avenue between Newberry Terrace and Page Boulevard was renamed to honor the Reverend George H. Pruitt (1885-1978), who was pastor at Pleasant Green Baptist Church from 1939 until his death. In 1948 he organized the Acacia Lodge No. 166 of the Masonic Order. He was also a member of the Education Department of the National Baptist Convention U.S.A.

Lewis Place Historic District ■ 98

Lewis Place at Taylor Avenue

Lewis Place, laid out in 1890, was privately owned and developed by the family of William J. Lewis. In 1895, the triumphal gateway, designed by the firm of Barnett, Haynes, and Barnett, was constructed of yellow brick and limestone.

This two-block private place, located north of Delmar Boulevard between Taylor and Walton avenues, is lined with homes built between 1890 and 1928. The street—like many others in St. Louis—was once covered by a racially restrictive covenant that barred blacks from residence in the area. From 1910 to 1945, 378 such covenants were in effect in the city, excluding blacks from many neighborhoods. Most often they had a term of twenty years.

In the 1940s, a group of black St. Louisans, led by Robert Witherspoon (1905-91), decided to fight the Lewis Place covenant. They persuaded fair-skinned blacks to "pass for white" in order to purchase several homes. Then they transferred the deeds to the actual owners of the properties, who voted down the restrictive covenant on the street. Lewis Place Historic District was placed on the National Register of Historic Places on September 15, 1980.

Lewis Place entrance arch

Photo by David Schultz.

Arch detail

Photo by Lee Harris.

Galilee Baptist Church ■ 99

4300 Delmar Boulevard

The church was established in June 1898 in a small house at 609 South Second Street by evangelist Sin Killing Griffin and the Reverends Nicholas and John Williams. In 1907 the church moved to Adams Street and again in 1947 to its present location, the former site of Delmar Baptist Church. Galilee was served for thirty-seven years by the Reverend Isaac C. Peay (1910-), who retired in 1991.

***The Sky's the Limit* mural**

Photo. Courtesy of On the Wall Productions, Inc. © 1979 by Libby Reuter and On the Wall Productions, Inc.

Mural detail

Photo. Courtesy of On the Wall Productions, Inc. © 1979 by Libby Reuter and On the Wall Productions, Inc.

Grand Masonic Temple ■ 100

4525 Olive Street

The Prince Hall Lodge of Masons was established in St. Louis in 1859 and moved to this location in the late 1920s. It was named for Prince Hall (1735-1807), a free black who served in the army during the American Revolution and became the founder of black Freemasonry in the United States. Many of the fraternal and community improvement activities of the Most Worshipful Prince Hall Grand Lodge of Free and Accepted Masons of Missouri and Jurisdiction are still held at this site. Black Muslim leader Malcolm X (1925-65) spoke to an audience in the auditorium in January 1959.

The Sky's the Limit mural ■ 101

Central West Plaza Building
625 North Euclid Avenue

The Sky's the Limit mural, produced by On the Wall Productions, Inc. on the west wall of the Central West Plaza Building, depicts the vitality of the African-American community. It was created in 1979 by artists Robert Fishbone, Sarah Linquist, and Libby Reuter with funding from the Union-Sarah Economic Development Corporation, Inc. (USEDC) and St. Louis Community Development Agency. The mural is accompanied by a poem, "We Rise," by St. Louis poet Shirley Le Flore.

The Central West Plaza Building has been renovated to provide warehouse and commercial space. Across the street, at the corner of Delmar Boulevard and Kingshighway, the Central West Shopping Plaza was developed by USEDC. In 1992, it included a forty-thousand-square-foot building leased to National Supermarkets, F. W. Woolworth, Payless Shoes, and other retail and commercial enterprises.

Captain Charlton H. Tandy home ■ 102

1224 Bayard Avenue

Charlton Hunt Tandy (1836-1919), a Civil War veteran, was captain of "Tandy's Saint Louis Guard," a state militia composed of black volunteers. During the 1880s, he worked to enforce an 1867 court order allowing blacks to ride inside public transportation vehicles. To prevent drivers from passing up black passengers, he grabbed the reins and held the horse until passengers—black and white alike—were allowed to board. Tandy was arrested for this action, but he was supported by Erastus Wells (1856-1944), the streetcar line owner, who paid his fine and said that blacks should be permitted to sit anywhere on the streetcars.

He also became a leader in the movement for public education for blacks. He worked with James Milton Turner (1839?-1915) to raise money for the young Lincoln Institute (now Lincoln University) in Jefferson City; he worked for the appointment of black teachers and principals in the St. Louis public schools; he raised ten thousand dollars to assist poor black immigrants from the South who came to St. Louis; and he pushed for integration of the local postal system. In 1894, he passed the Missouri State Bar examination and established a law practice in St. Louis. He spent his last days as the Republican committeeman for the city's Tenth Ward.

Captain Charlton H. Tandy home

Photo by David Schultz.

Martin Luther King, Jr. statue

Photo by Lee Harris.

Martin Luther King, Jr. statue ■ 103

Fountain Park, east of Kingshighway, between Delmar and Page boulevards

Within Fountain Park is an eleven-foot, bronze statue of Martin Luther King, Jr. (1929-1968), the slain civil rights leader. It was designed by St. Louis sculptor Rudolph Torrini (1923-) with support from the Community Development Agency and the Union-Sarah Economic Development Corporation, Inc. The inscription on the base of the statue reads "HIS DREAM—OUR DREAM." The statue, which was unveiled in 1978, was placed on the National Register on October 18, 1982.

Tom Powell American Legion Post No. 77 • 104

1176-78 North Kingshighway Boulevard

Tom Powell Post No. 77 was formed by fifteen World War I veterans on September 17, 1919. It was named for Private Tom Powell, a Georgia native who had attempted to join the army but was rejected in his home state because blacks could not enlist. Powell travelled to Chicago and joined the Eighth Illinois Infantry Regiment; he was subsequently sent to France, where he was killed in action in 1918. He was awarded the Distinguished Service Cross.

The Tom Powell Post was the first African-American post organized in the American Legion. Its members have served as national committee members and officers. Originally, the post was located at 3907 West Belle, and in 1951 in a larger home at 3514 Franklin. Both have since been demolished. In 1992, the Tom Powell Post sold its Kingshighway location, though its forty-five members still meet in homes and rented halls. The post has an affiliated parade corps, the Junior Drum and Bugle Corps, in which fifty local youngsters participate.

The St. Louis Association of Colored Women's Clubs ■ 105

5029 Cabanne Place

In 1904, the St. Louis Association of Colored Women's Clubs was organized in the home of Marie L. Harrison at 2107 Walnut Street, with the help of Mary Alice Pitts and Susan Paul Vashon (1838-1912). The group's purpose was to look after African-American widows, the elderly, and orphans. As one of its early functions, the association hosted the third biennial convention of its national body, the National Association of Colored Women's Clubs, which met in St. Louis during the 1904 World's Fair. The group's national motto was "Lifting As We Climb."

The St. Louis Association of Colored Women's Clubs

Photo. Courtesy of the Missouri Historical Society Photograph and Print Collection.

In 1948, under the leadership of Mary T. Greer, the association purchased the residence on Cabanne Place as a place for meetings, musicals, teas, and forums. As a service project in 1965, the group placed a plaque (since removed) at the corner of Second and Morgan to commemorate the 1793 Spanish land grant to the free mulatto Esther and the bicentennial of the founding of St. Louis. In 1993, fifteen clubs, with ten to fifteen women each, made up the association, which holds monthly meetings. The group also sponsors a youth division with approximately thirty-five members.

See also: Land grant to Esther

Ntozake Shange home ■ 106

15 Windermere Place

Poet, playwright, and novelist Ntozake Shange (1949-), originally named Paulette Williams, is a New Jersey native who lived on Windermere Place in St. Louis from age six until she was in junior high school. Her father, Dr. Paul Williams, was a surgeon who practiced at Homer G. Phillips Hospital. As an adult, she changed to a Zulu name: Ntozake, which means "she comes with her own things," and Shange, which means "one who walks like a lion." She is the author of *For Colored Girls Who Have Considered Suicide / When the Rainbow is Enuf*, a partly autobiographical collection of poems which expresses her feeling about life, especially life between black men and women. One of these poems, entitled "toussaint," deals with her visits to the St. Louis Public Library and her study of Pierre Dominique Toussaint L'Ouverture, the Haitian revolutionary hero. Shange's 1985 book, *Betsey Brown: A Novel*, deals with the St. Louis black community in 1959 and the upheaval caused by court-ordered integration.

Union Memorial United Methodist Church ■ 107

1141 Belt at Bartmer avenues

Union Memorial is the third-oldest black church in St. Louis. Its history dates back to 1840, but the church was officially founded in 1846. Originally, the congregation worshipped on Broadway between Morgan Street (now Delmar Boulevard) and Franklin Avenue in the home of a slave. Later the church moved to Seventh Street between Cass Avenue and O'Fallon Street, then to Green Street (now Lucas Street), where it was called "Little Rock Church." The church was located in the Mill Creek area before it moved to this site in 1961. In addition to its religious program, this congregation pioneered a training school for area church workers. Many local community leaders have come from this church.

Mitchell Elementary School

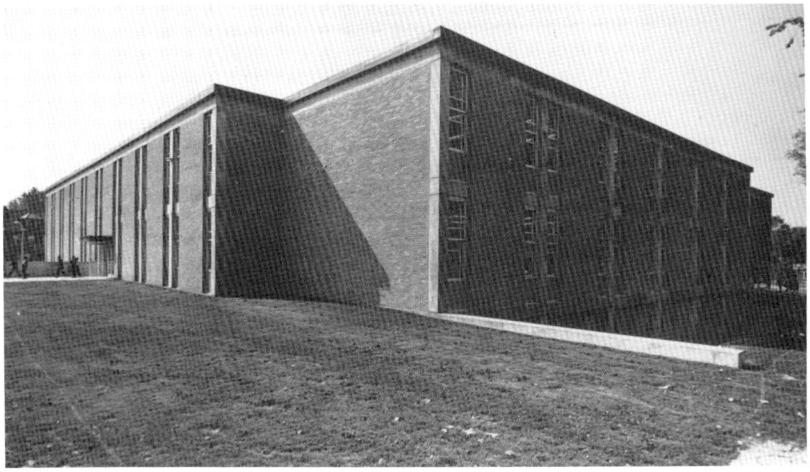

Photo. Courtesy of the St. Louis Public Schools.

Mitchell Elementary School ■ 108

955 Arcade Avenue

Mitchell School, which opened in 1964, was designed with a central courtyard where kindergarten children could play without interrupting the games of older children. It had two branches: one at 5436 Bartmer Avenue, and the other at 1141 Belt Avenue. In 1992-93, the school had 307 students from pre-school through fifth grade. This school was named for two brothers, Joseph Everett Mitchell (1876-1952) and William Mitchell (1878-1945), who were the founders and publishers of the *St. Louis Argus*. Joseph was a Spanish-American War veteran; both brothers worked to achieve better education for blacks and were active in the Pine Street YMCA, the NAACP, and the Urban League.

Monsanto YMCA exercise class

Photo by Lee Harris.

Monsanto YMCA ■ 109

5555 Page Avenue

The Monsanto YMCA was built on the site of the former Page-Park Branch YMCA, the successor to the Pine Branch YMCA. This $2.5 million facility, financed in part by a $1.1 million gift from the Monsanto Company, opened in September 1981. It represented a consolidation of the former Page-Park and North Side YMCAs. The auditorium at the Monsanto YMCA is named for Dr. Arthur Vaughn (1888-1974), a prominent black St. Louis physician.

See also: Pine Street YMCA

St. Paul African Methodist Episcopal Church

Photo by Lee Harris.

St. Paul African Methodist Episcopal Church ■ 110

1260 Hamilton Avenue

St. Paul's is the second-oldest black Protestant church in St. Louis and the oldest African Methodist Episcopal church west of the Mississippi River. It was established in 1841 as the African Methodist Church. The church moved to its present location from the Mill Creek area in the mid-1960s. The congregation has a long history of working for quality education for blacks.

See also: African Methodist Church
St. Paul African Methodist Episcopal Church, Lawton at Leffingwell

Window detail

Photo by Lee Harris.

Cook Elementary School ■ 111

5935 Horton Place

Cook Elementary opened in 1964; in 1992-93 it had 365 students from kindergarten through fifth grade. The Reverend James E. Cook (1900-61), for whom the school is named, was the energetic pastor of Antioch Baptist Church from 1946 to 1961 and the executive director of the Pine Street YMCA. He organized the Pine Street "Y Forum," a series of Sunday gatherings of black families from all economic levels and neighborhoods. He also instituted the "Y Circus" to raise money for his pioneering efforts to offer leadership training for young black males at Camp Rivercliffe near Bourbon, Missouri.

Ruth C. Porter mall and mural ■ 112

Delmar Boulevard at DeBaliviere Avenue

This mall and mural honor Ruth C. Porter (1915-67), one of the founders and the first executive director of the Greater St. Louis Committee for the Freedom of Residence, a group organized in 1961 to break down housing restrictions and integrate housing in St. Louis. She also formed Community Resources, a group working for school integration, and helped to found Kinder Cottage, a church-supported, pre-school program in the West End. In 1958 she won an award from the National Conference for Christians and Jews for promoting interracial understanding. She was named outstanding woman of the year in 1965 by the NAACP. The mural was painted by twenty-two honors arts students under the supervision of On the Wall Productions, Inc.

Ruth C. Porter mural

Photo by Dr. John Wright.

Philippine Constabulary Band

Photo, 1904. Courtesy of the Missouri Historical Society Photograph and Print Collection.

Forest Park ■ 113

Bounded by Kingshighway Boulevard on the east, Skinker Boulevard on the west, Lindell Boulevard on the north and Highway 40 / 64 on the south

The 1,293-acre Forest Park was the site of the Louisiana Purchase Exposition, also known as the 1904 World's Fair. Despite segregated facilities, many African Americans were among the nineteen million visitors to the fair. Many blacks also took part in the fair, among them Scott Joplin, known as the "King of Ragtime," who composed the "Cascade Rag" in honor of the fair; W. H. Loving, an American-born musician and conductor of the Philippine Constabulary Band; and Henry Ossawa Tanner (1859-1937), an outstanding painter. The third Olympic Games were also held at nearby Francis Field, located at Washington University, Big Bend and Forsyth boulevards. George C. Poage (1884-?), who taught at Sumner High School from 1905 to 1914, was the first black to participate in the modern games. He won bronze medals in the four-hundred-meter race and in the two-hundred-meter hurdle race. According to William Crossland's *Industrial Conditions Among Negroes in St. Louis,* the fair attracted a large number of African Americans to settle in St. Louis; many of them opened businesses and became property owners.

For many years, the recreational facilties in Forest Park were segregated, and the Municipal Golf Course was reserved for the use of white golfers only. In May 1922, Albert H. Howard asked the St. Louis Circuit Court to compel Commissioner Fred W. Pape to issue golf permits to him and other black golfers. In 1923, the courts accepted Pape's solution of reserving the golf course for blacks on Mondays from six a.m. to noon. A whistle blew at the end of the period, and black golfers were expected to leave the course. The Monday morning rule was waived in 1940 when the Improved Benevolent and Protective Order of the Elks of the World, called the "largest Negro lodge in the United States," held a golf tournament in the park as part of its convention.

After World War II, as blacks moved into the neighborhoods north of the park, they began to challenge its "separate but equal" facilities. In the late 1940s and early 1950s, restrictions were removed at the golf course, tennis courts, Municipal Opera, and other recreational facilities. In 1945, Richard A. Hudlin, a Sumner High School social studies teacher and tennis coach, brought a lawsuit in an attempt to compete in the city's tennis championship, held in Forest Park. To participate, a player had to belong to a tennis club affiliated with the Municipal Tennis Association; Hudlin, who was black, said that he had been prevented from joining such a club. But the St. Louis Circuit Court ruled that because the tournament was run by the Municipal Tennis Association, a private organization, the court had no power to intervene.

Civil rights demonstration

Photo by Lester Linck, 1965. Ivory Perry lay in front of a car at Tucker (formerly Twelfth Street) and Clark in a September 1965 demonstration. Courtesy of the St. Louis Post-Dispatch.

Civil rights demonstration site ■ 114

South Kingshighway Boulevard and Highway 64/40

In March 1965, civil rights activists Ivory Perry (1930-89) and Ernest Gilkey created a massive traffic tie-up at rush hour on a busy highway exit ramp in St. Louis. The demonstration was designed to awaken the public to the violence then taking place against peaceful civil rights demonstrators in Alabama. First, the two men disabled their truck at the ramp on Highway 40 and Kingshighway, then Perry lay down on the road, blocking the path of oncoming cars. Perry's actions cost him thirty days in the city workhouse and a $250 fine, but they also drew attention to the Alabama situation. On March 25, Perry and nineteen busloads of demonstrators traveled to Alabama to join the Selma-to-Montgomery march, led by Martin Luther King, Jr.

Ivory Perry

Photo by Buel White, 1965. Courtesy of the St. Louis Post-Dispatch.

The Ville, Northwest, Northeast, Riverview

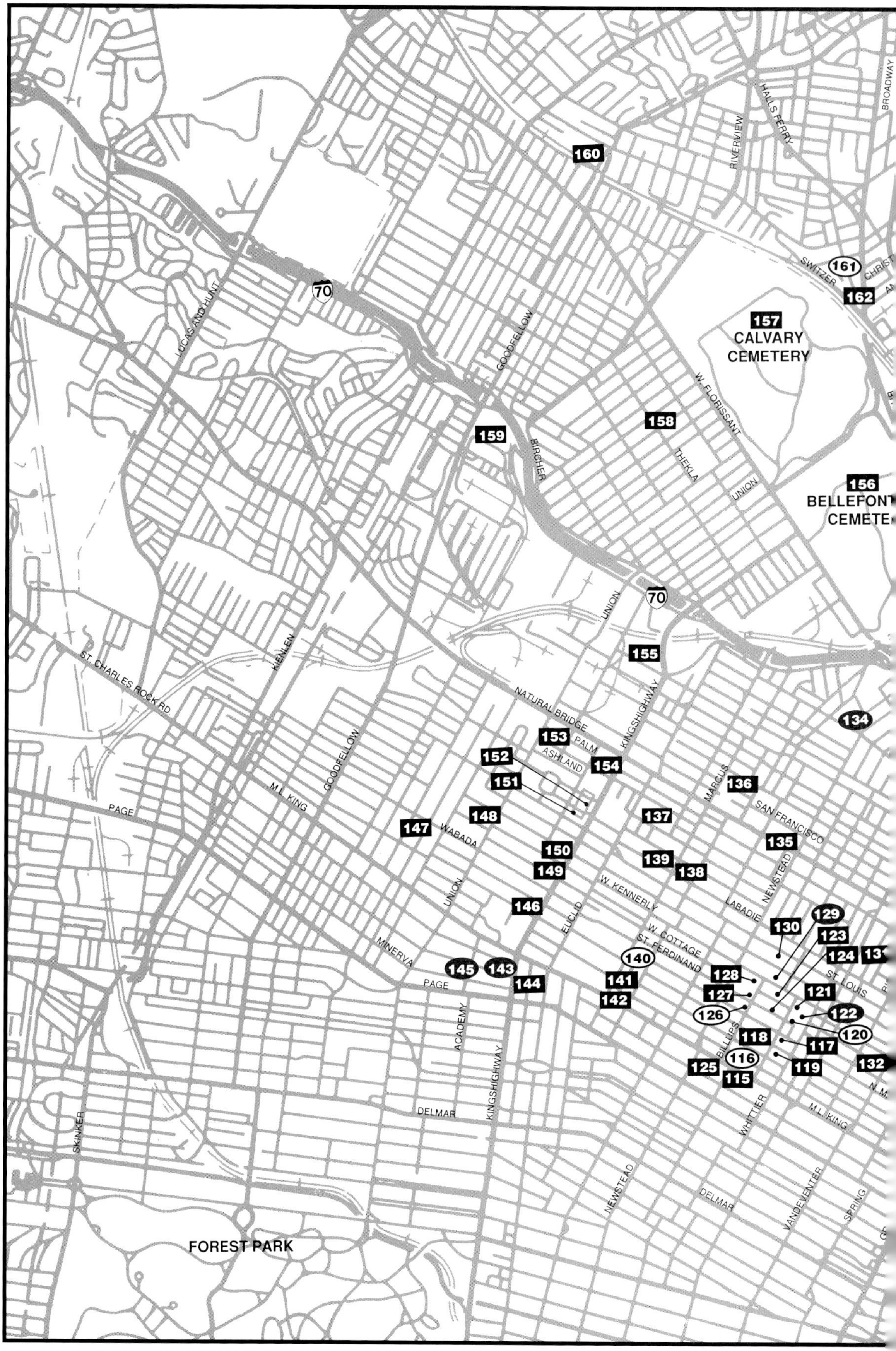

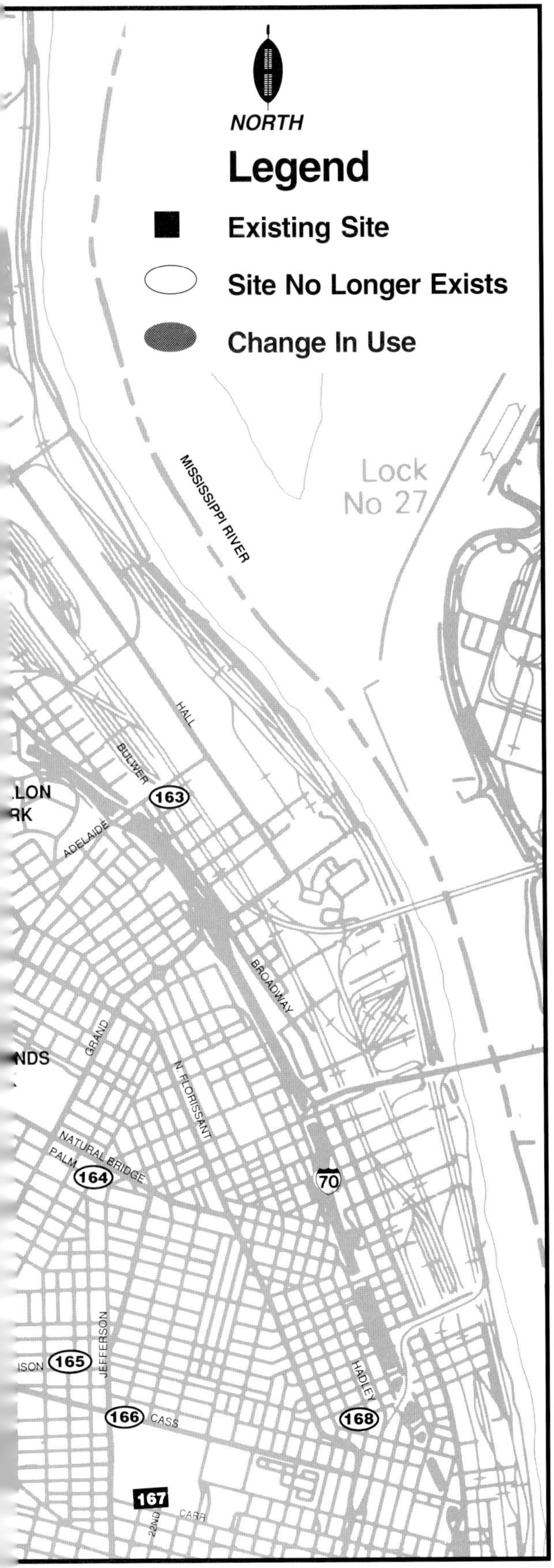
NORTH
Legend
Existing Site
Site No Longer Exists
Change In Use
MISSISSIPPI RIVER
Lock
No 27
HALL
BULWER
163
.LON
RK
ADELAIDE
BROADWAY
NDS
GRAND
N. FLORISSANT
NATURAL BRIDGE
PALM
164
70
ISON
165
JEFFERSON
HADLEY
166
CASS
168
167
22ND
CARR

The Ville, Northwest, Northeast, Riverview

Detail of King Middle School

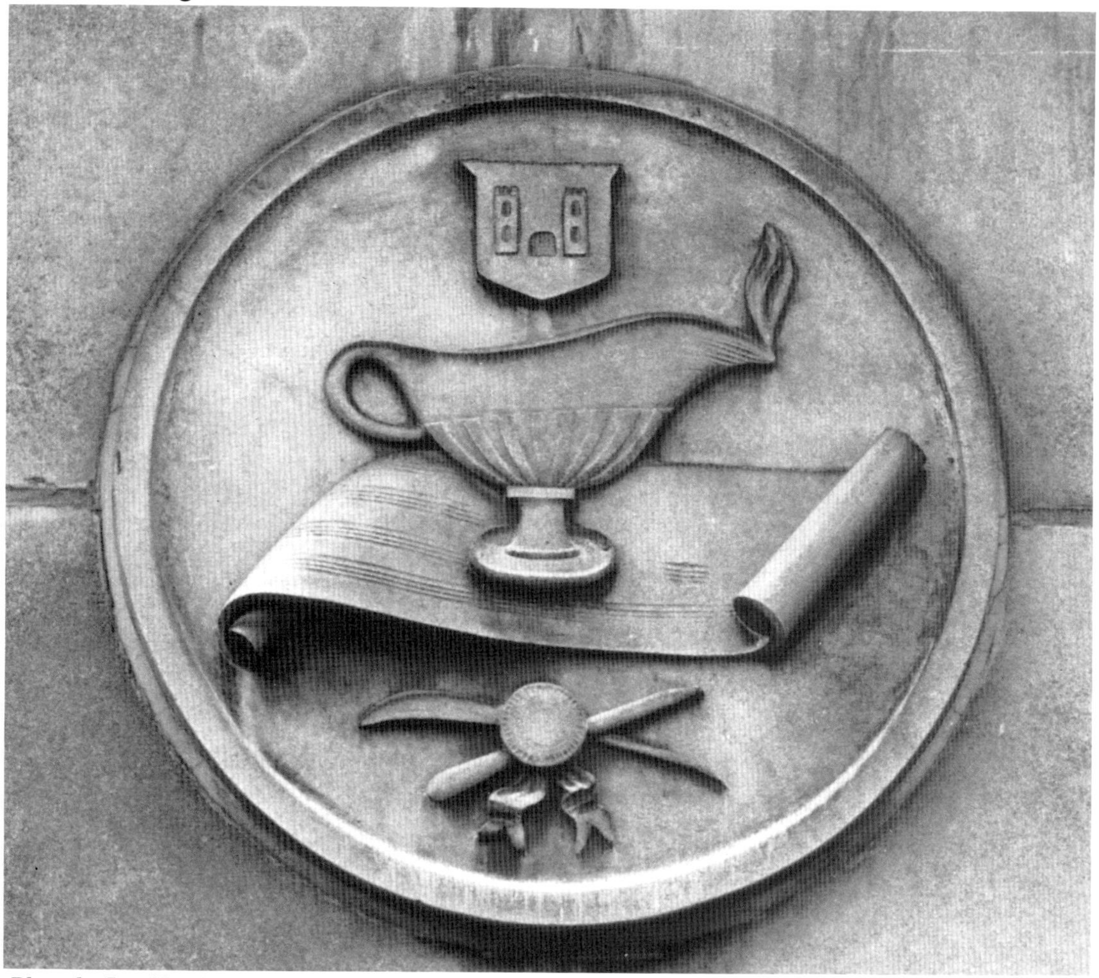

Photo by Lee Harris.

The Ville, Northwest, Northeast, Riverview

Chapter 4

The Ville

During the mid-1800s, Charles Elleards, a horticulturist, built a two-story brick home on Goode Avenue (now Annie Malone Drive) and a large nursery on his estate, which stretched from Goode to Newstead and from Old St. Charles Rock Road (later Dr. Martin Luther King, Jr.,Drive) to Cote Brilliante. A small town known as Elleardsville grew up around the nursery; in 1876 it was annexed to the city.

Over time Elleardsville (shortened to "the Ville") attracted German and Irish immigrants, along with some African-American residents. Its first black institution, Elleardsville Colored School No. 8 (later renamed Simmons School), opened in 1873, and St. James African Methodist Episcopal Church was organized in 1885. At a time when much of the city was covered by restrictive real estate covenants which prohibited blacks from owning or renting residential property, the Ville was open to African Americans. Between 1920 and 1950, the number of black residents in the Ville increased from 8 to 95 percent of the population.

The Ville, now bounded by Dr. Martin Luther King, Jr., Drive, Taylor Avenue, St. Louis Avenue, and Sarah Street, is remembered today as the center of a prosperous black community and the heart of black culture in St. Louis. Such important institutions as Sumner High School, Turner School, Stowe Teachers College, Poro College, the Annie Malone Children's Home, John Marshall Elementary School, St. Philip's Lutheran Church, and Homer G. Phillips Hospital were established in the Ville. Top entertainers such as Albert "Blues Boy" King and B. B. King have performed at area clubs and music halls, among them the Harlem Taproom at 4131 Dr. Martin Luther King, Jr., Drive. The area has produced many prominent social activists, writers, educators, entertainers, and politicians.

Annie Malone Drive ■ 115

Annie Turnbo Pope Malone (1869-1957), for whom this street is named, became one of the world's wealthiest black women in the early 1930s by developing and marketing her beauty culture products for black women. Her business, begun in Illinois, moved to St. Louis when it proved successful. In 1918, she established Poro College at St. Ferdinand and Billups avenues to train beauticians and barbers, secretaries and bookkeepers. Her finance company helped many African Americans buy their first homes, and she engaged in a variety of philanthropic projects. Annie Malone Drive runs between Sumner High School to the west and the former Homer G. Phillips Hospital to the east.

Annie Turnbo Pope Malone

Photo. Courtesy of the Missouri Historical Society Photograph and Print Collection.

Walk of Fame star

Photo by Lee Harris.

Grace Bumbry

Photo. Courtesy of the St. Louis Walk of Fame.

Antioch Baptist Church

Photo by David Schultz.

James Milton Turner home ⬭ 116

1516 Annie Malone Drive

James Milton Turner (1839?-1915) was born a slave in St. Louis County. His father bought his family's freedom when Turner was three years old. Turner attended Oberlin College. In 1865, he became secretary of the Missouri Equal Rights League. After the Civil War, he had a distinguished career as a leader in the movement to establish new schools for blacks throughout the state. From 1871 to 1878, he served as United States minister to Liberia. In the 1880s, he took on the legal problems of freedmen living in Oklahoma Territory, who were denied their tribal and political rights by the Native Americans who had once enslaved them. He is buried in the Father Dickson Cemetery in Crestwood. The Turner Playground at West Belle and Sarah avenues is also named for him.

See also: Father Dickson Cemetery

Grace Bumbry home ■ 117

1703 Annie Malone Drive

Grace Melzia Bumbry (1937-), an internationally acclaimed opera star known for her fine mezzo-soprano voice, is a St. Louis native and Sumner High School graduate who grew up in the Ville. At an early age she sang in the choir of the Union Memorial Methodist Church. As a student at Sumner High School, she studied voice with Kenneth Billups. In 1954, she gained national attention when she sang an aria on Arthur Godfrey's "Talent Scouts" television program. Her performance won her a scholarship to Boston University. She made her Carnegie Hall debut in 1962 and in the same year sang at a gala White House dinner given by President John F. Kennedy (1917-63). The following year she made her London debut in Covent Garden. She has since sung in operatic roles across the United States and Europe and made recordings on several major labels.

Antioch Baptist Church ■ 118

4213 West North Market Street

One of the oldest Protestant churches in the Ville, Antioch Baptist was organized in March 1878 in a member's home on Wash Avenue (now Whittier Street) in Elleardsville. By 1880 the congregation had moved to a frame building on Lambdin Avenue near Kennerly. Antioch was incorporated on May 6, 1884, and the congregation purchased a second building on Kennerly Avenue from the Baptist Home Mission Board of New York. In 1909 the Antioch congregation bought the Goode Avenue Methodist Episcopal Church at Goode Avenue (now Annie Malone Drive) and West North Market Street. Eleven years later, the growing membership erected a new sanctuary next door. They razed the old church in 1954 and constructed an educational building. The Reverend James E. Cook (1900-1961), a well-known community leader, was the pastor of Antioch Baptist Church from 1946 to 1961.

St. Philip's Lutheran Church ■ 119

2424 Annie Malone Drive

This church, a descendant of the Carr Street Mission, was organized in 1926 on Goode Avenue (now Annie Malone Drive). In 1966, the congregation discussed leaving the area but chose instead to reaffirm its commitment to the Ville by constructing its new church building on the same site. It is the largest Lutheran congregation in the St. Louis black community.

Chuck Berry birthplace ○ 120

2520 Annie Malone Drive

Rock 'n' roll great Chuck Berry (1926-) was born Charles Edward Anderson in the bedroom of a three-room cottage on Goode Avenue (now Annie Malone Drive). Later his family moved to other nearby locations, including 4420 Cottage Avenue and 4019 Labadie Street. As a student at Sumner High School, he was a member of Antioch Baptist Church. Now a member of the Rock and Roll Hall of Fame, Berry is known for his many hit songs, including "Roll over Beethoven," "Maybelline," "Memphis," "Nadine," "Johnny B. Goode," and "Reelin' 'n' Rockin'."

St. Philip's Lutheran Church

Photo by David Schultz.

Chuck Berry

Photo. Courtesy of the St. Louis Walk of Fame.

Walk of Fame star

Photo by Lee Harris.

Annie Malone Children and Family Service Center

Photo by David Schultz.

Annie Malone Children and Family Service Center ■ 121

2612 Annie Malone Drive

This center was founded in 1888 by Sarah Newton as the St. Louis Colored Orphans' Home. It was originally located at 1427 North Twelfth Street on ground purchased after the Civil War by black soldiers, who tried unsuccessfully to establish a soldiers' home on the site. In 1905, the home moved to 4316 Natural Bridge; then, on May Day 1922, it moved to its current location at Annie Malone Drive (formerly Goode Avenue) and Kennerly Avenue. A ten-thousand-dollar donation by Annie Malone helped to fund the construction of the new facility. The home was renamed for Annie Malone in 1946. She is still honored each May with a parade sponsored by the home, which serves neglected and abused children, offers family therapy, and houses medical and social services for the community. Recently, the center rehabilitated the former nurses' residence of Homer G. Phillips Hospital as housing for an independent living project.

Homer G. Phillips Memorial Hospital

Photo by W. C. Persons, ca. 1938. Courtesy of the Missouri Historical Society Photograph and Print Collection.

Homer G. Phillips Memorial Hospital • 122

2601 Whittier Street

At the time of its dedication on February 22, 1937, Homer G. Phillips Hospital was the largest and best-equipped institution in the world dedicated to the care of "the indigent sick and Negro population" and also to the training of black doctors. It was named for Homer G. Phillips (1880-1931), an attorney who led the battle to include funding for the hospital in a 1923 bond issue. Phillips did not live to see the hospital's completion; he was shot to death while waiting for a bus in a never-solved murder at Aubert Avenue and Delmar Boulevard on June 18, 1931.

As one of the few fully equipped facilities in the country where black medical professionals could receive training, Homer G. Phillips Hospital became nationally known. It offered internship programs certified by the American Medical Association in internal medicine, pediatrics, urology, general surgery, obstetrics and gynecology, otolaryngology, pathology, ophthalmology, radiology, and neuropsychiatry. It also offered nurses' training through its associated School of Nursing. Amid community uproar, Homer G. Phillips Hospital closed in 1979. Several hundred police officers were needed to keep the peace as the last patients were removed from the hospital. The building, designed by Albert A. Osberg, was added to the National Register of Historic Places in 1982.

Sumner High School

Photo. Courtesy of the St. Louis Public Schools.

Tandy Community Center and Park ■ 123

4206 West Kennerly Avenue

Tandy Community Center is named for Captain Charlton Hunt Tandy (1836-1919), who led the movement to end segregation of public streetcars and the fight for public education for blacks. Tandy Community Center opened in 1938 with reading rooms, a swimming pool, a basketball court, boxing, and industrial arts. The center serves as headquarters for the Silver Gloves Boxing Tournament, an annual event sponsored by the Department of Parks, Recreation and Forestry. The 5.6-acre park on the east side of the center was the home of the Tandy Baseball League. Tennis star Arthur Ashe (1943-93) used to practice on the tennis courts at the end of the park. The nearby Tandy Medical Building at 3737 North Kingshighway Boulevard was also named for Charlton Tandy.

See also: Charlton H. Tandy home

Sumner High School (third location) ■ 124

4248 West Cottage Avenue

Sumner High moved to its present location in 1910. African-American citizens had petitioned the Board of Education to move the school away from the saloons and pool rooms near its Fifteenth and Walnut location and into more spacious, modern quarters. Nationally acclaimed architect William B. Ittner designed the Georgian Revival building, which an article in the *American Architect* called "one of the few schools of this character in the country."

In 1890, a Normal School (the predecessor of Stowe Teachers College and later Harris-Stowe State College) was added to the curriculum. It provided a year's training beyond high school and supplied African-American teachers for the area's black schools. In 1925, Sumner Normal School was designated as a college, though it remained in the Sumner High School building. The 1929 graduating class at Sumner Teachers College was the first to receive the bachelor's degree in education.

Sumner remains a cornerstone of the Ville neighborhood, where it serves some seventeen hundred high school students each year. The school was completely renovated in an $8.3 million, two-year project, finished in 1991. Its well-known graduates include tennis champion Arthur Ashe (1943-93); rock 'n' roll musician Chuck Berry (1926-); opera star Grace Bumbry (1937-); United States Representative William L. Clay (1931-); teacher and historian Julia Davis (1891-1993); Harris-Stowe State College President Henry Givens, Jr.; comedian Dick Gregory (1932-); veteran KMOV-TV news anchorman Julius Hunter; opera star Robert McFerrin; performer Tina Turner (1939-); and St. Louis attorney and former national NAACP chairperson Margaret Bush Wilson. The Sumner High building was added to the National Register of Historic Places in 1988.

See also: High School for Colored Children
Sumner High School (second location)
Harris-Stowe State College

Billups Avenue (formerly Pendleton Avenue) ■ 125

This street honors Kenneth Brown Billups, Sr. (1918-85), a native St. Louisan and graduate of Sumner High School. A well-known musician and teacher, Billups taught vocal music from 1943 to 1949 at Douglass High School in Webster Groves; later, he became director of the Sumner High School music department and supervisor of music in the St. Louis Public Schools. Active in the community, he was founder and director of the Legend Singers, director of the Chancel Choir at Antioch Baptist Church, and president of the National Association of Negro Musicians. He received the Urban League Award of Merit in 1979 for his contributions to local music.

Billups Avenue runs west of Sumner High School on a section that was formerly part of Pendleton Avenue, extending from Kennerly Avenue on the north to Dr. Martin Luther King, Jr, Drive on the south.

Site of Poro College 126

Southwest corner, St. Ferdinand and Billups avenues

As a high school chemistry student in Peoria, Illinois, Annie Turnbo Pope Malone (1869-1957) developed a scalp product that was supposed to help grow and straighten black women's hair. In 1902 she moved to 2223 Market Street in St. Louis to manufacture her product line, which she copyrighted four years later under the name "Poro." The business expanded to larger quarters at 3100 Pine and in November 1918 to a new building at St. Ferdinand and Billups avenues.

At this site, beauticians from around the country received training in Poro products, while salespeople learned techniques for marketing them. Poro,

Poro College

Photo by George Dorrill. Courtesy of the Irv Shankman–Allied Photocolor Collection, the Missouri Historical Society Photograph and Print Collection.

known as a college though it granted no degree, also served as the most popular meeting place for the city's many black social and civic organizations. Its building, which occupied an entire city block, was three stories high, with a rooftop garden. It included an instructional department in cosmetology, a beauty parlor, an auditorium, general offices, a cafeteria, a dining room, a sewing shop, guest rooms, a dormitory, and two emergency rooms for first-aid treatment.

The Poro system achieved renown not only in the United States, but internationally in the Caribbean, Africa, and the Philippines. In the 1920s, Malone employed nearly two hundred people in her business, including many Sumner High School students. Following the St. Louis tornado of 1927, thousands were sheltered, clothed, and fed through Poro College, which served as a principal relief unit of the American Red Cross. In July 1930, the college moved to Chicago. The building became a hotel; in later years it housed the Lincoln University School of Law. In 1965, St. James African Methodist Episcopal Church bought the Poro building and razed it, replacing it with the James House, a residential facility for senior citizens.

See also: Lloyd Gaines home
Annie Malone Drive

St. James African Methodist Episcopal Church

Photo by David Schultz.

St. James African Methodist Episcopal Church ■ 127

4301 St. Ferdinand Avenue

The church was organized in 1884 to serve blacks moving into the Ville. The first church, a frame structure, was built at St. Ferdinand and Pendleton; the present sanctuary was built in 1950-51. Today, St. James works closely with the Vaughn Cultural Center in supporting community events.

The James House, a senior-citizen apartment complex across the street from the church, was started by the church in the late 1960s as a "turnkey project," sponsored by the Office of Housing and Urban Development. The church raised forty-five thousand dollars toward the construction cost of $2.7 million. The complex is located on the site of Poro College.

The Turner Middle School

Photo by David Schultz.

The Turner Middle School ■ 128

2615 Billups (formerly Pendleton) Avenue at Kennerly Avenue

This school building, designed by George W. Sanger and constructed in 1940 on what was then Pendleton Avenue, was originally the home of Stowe Teachers College, the city's one-time training institution for black teachers. The college developed from the Sumner Normal Department, established in 1890, which later took the name of Stowe to honor Harriet Beecher Stowe, whose novel, *Uncle Tom's Cabin*, aroused sentiment against slavery.

Originally the college was housed at Simmons Elementary School, but between 1937 and 1939, pressure mounted to provide a better facility. Meetings were held at the Kennerly Avenue Church to urge the Board of Education to appropriate money for a new building, and finally the board approved the construction of a new college opposite Tandy Park. Stowe College was combined with Harris Teachers College in 1954, when the United States Supreme Court's *Brown v. Board of Education of Topeka, Kansas* decision ended segregation in public schools. The building now houses a middle school which in 1992-93 had 344 students in grades six through eight. It is named for renowned black scientist Charles Henry Turner (1867-1923), who published in a number of scientific journals.

See also: The Turner Middle School Branch
Harris-Stowe State College

The Turner Middle School Branch

Photo by David Schultz.

The Open-Air School

Photo, 1935. Courtesy of the St. Louis Public Schools Audio-Visual Department.

The Turner Middle School Branch • 129

4235 West Kennerly Avenue

Turner Middle School Branch, formerly named Charles Turner Open-Air School for Crippled Children, was the first school of its kind for blacks in the United States. Founded in 1925, it was equipped with ramps and railings instead of stairways to serve its disabled students. An open-air department, for children exposed to tuberculosis, had French doors that stayed open throughout classes, requiring teachers and children to dress warmly. Children were referred to the school by doctors and parents; they attended free of charge. After the 1954 Supreme Court desegregation decision, the school remained open, but it was finally phased out in 1960-61. The school building now serves as an annex for Turner Middle School.

The school was named for noted entomologist Charles Henry Turner (1867-1923). In 1907 he became the first black to receive a Ph.D. from the University of Chicago. From 1908 to 1922, he served as instructor and head of the science department at Sumner High School. His discoveries were published internationally in leading scientific journals.

Simmons Elementary School ■ 130

4318 St. Louis Avenue

Simmons Elementary School, formerly known as Elleardsville Colored School No. 8, was the first black institution in the Ville. It opened in 1873 in a two-room frame building on Claggett Street (now St. Louis Avenue) with an enrollment of fifty-three pupils. By 1877, black teachers had replaced white teachers, and in 1891 the school was renamed in honor of William Johnson Simmons (1849-90), a Baptist minister, author, and founder of the American National Baptist Convention. A new brick building, designed by architect William B. Ittner, replaced the original structure in 1899, with additions in 1911 and 1930. A branch, no longer in operation, was established in 1958 at 4430 Labadie Avenue. In 1992-93, the school had 420 students in grades six through eight.

Simmons Elementary School

Photo. Courtesy of the St. Louis Public Schools.

Simmons Elementary School

Photo by David Schultz.

Northwest

Bishop Scott Lane ■ 131

Bishop Phillip Lee Scott (1908-87) was pastor of Lively Stone Church of God at 4015 St. Louis Avenue and Bishop Scott Lane. The street, named in his honor one year before his death, covers much of what used to be Warne Avenue. It is bounded by Natural Bridge Avenue to the north and Dr. Martin Luther King, Jr., Drive to the south.

Williams School ■ 132

3955 St. Ferdinand Avenue

Williams Elementary School opened in 1964. It was named for Frank L. Williams (1865-1953), principal of Sumner High School from 1908 to 1928 and curator of Lincoln University. Williams was an active YMCA worker who served as board member of the Pine Street Branch YMCA for nearly thirty years and on the national YMCA Council during the mid-1930s. He was the moving force behind the establishment of New Age Federal Savings and Loan Association in 1915. This financial institution provided loans for blacks when other lenders would not. In 1992-93, Williams was a middle school with more than four hundred students, and an overflow in its Branch No. 1 location at 2611 Warne Avenue. A Branch No. 2, now closed, was established in 1953-54 at 4146 Garfield Avenue. The school's special focus is aviation and aerospace, and it has established partnerships with several local military establishments and corporations that are involved in defense work.

Incident at Fairgrounds Park

Photo by Ed Meyer, June 19, 1950. L. S. Curtis and his sons seek entrance to the Fairgrounds Park swimming pool. Courtesy of the Missouri Historical Society Photograph and Print Collection.

Fairgrounds Park ■ 133

Natural Bridge and Grand avenues

This 129-acre park, once the site of the St. Louis Agricultural and Mechanical Fair, also had a race track, built in 1885, which was the scene of yearly horse competitions. In 1903, former slave Tom Bass (1859-1934), owner of a famous stable in Mexico, Missouri, won the gelding class in the saddle horse competition with his horse, Jack O'Diamonds. During a career that spanned nearly fifty years, Bass bred, trained, or rode the greatest show horses in the world. President-elect William McKinley (1843-1901) and President William Howard Taft (1857-1930) visited Bass' horse farm; Bass rode in the inaugural parade of President Grover Cleveland (1837-1908) and on two occasions performed before President Calvin Coolidge (1872-1933). He developed the Bass bit to prevent abuse to horses during training.

This park was also the scene of a 1949 racial incident that took place after Mayor Joseph Darst (1889-1953) ordered the opening of the city's swimming pools and playgrounds to blacks. When fifty black youths attempting to enter the Fairgrounds Park pool were violently attacked by some two hundred teenaged white boys, Mayor Darst rescinded his integration order. A week after the incident, he appointed a Council on Human Relations, which voted in April 1950 to recommend the gradual opening of public swimming pools to blacks. The minority dissented, favoring an immediate end to segregation in all St. Louis recreational facilities. In July 1950, the United States District Court ordered the city of St. Louis to admit blacks to all open-air swimming pools.

Central Medical Center ● 134

4411 North Newstead Avenue at Carter Avenue

Central Medical Center was incorporated in 1983 and located on the one-time site of Christian Hospital as a medical facility to serve the north side. In 1991, it employed four hundred people and provided medical care to many African Americans who were without medical insurance. After persistent financial problems, the hospital closed in May 1993.

Julia Davis Branch Library

Rendering. Courtesy of the St. Louis Public Library.

Julia Davis

Photo. Courtesy of the St. Louis Public Library.

Julia Davis Branch Library ■ 135

4415 Natural Bridge Avenue

The St. Louis Public Library departed from tradition in 1974 when it named a new branch library for a living person, Julia Davis (1891-1993). A well-known educator and historian, Davis graduated from Dumas Elementary School, Sumner High School and Normal School, and Stowe Teachers College; she taught in the St. Louis public schools from 1913 to 1961 and spent thirty-five years at Simmons Elementary School. At the time of her retirement in 1961, she established the library's Julia Davis Fund for the purchase of books, manuscripts, and other materials related to the African-American contribution to world culture. This Julia Davis Research Collection on African-American History and Culture has since grown into a major research collection.

At the dedication of the branch library, then located at 4666 Natural Bridge Avenue, Davis said that "the purpose of the collection at this library and the main library is to perpetuate the learning and sharing of authentic information concerning the contributions of peoples of African descent to the world culture."

The Julia Davis Branch Library opened at its new location, 4415 Natural Bridge Avenue, on February 14, 1993. Land for the new branch, the first branch of the St. Louis Public Library system to be constructed since 1974, was donated by Commerce Bank of St. Louis. The fifteen-thousand-square-foot building, designed by architect Russell Lewis, features a 125-seat auditorium and space for fifty thousand volumes. Computers and educational software packages are available for public use. The Julia Davis Collection, formerly housed at Central Library, has been moved to the new branch.

Eugene "Tink" Bradley Playground

Photo by David Schultz.

W. C. Handy

Photo, ca. 1938. Handy (seated with cane), is seen here at Old Rock House. Courtesy of the Missouri Historical Society Photograph and Print Collection.

Eugene "Tink" Bradley Playground ■ 136

Marcus and San Francisco avenues

Eugene O. "Tink" Bradley (1919-81), for whom this playground is named, was alderman for the Twenty-first Ward from 1965 until 1981. He was acting president of the St. Louis Board of Aldermen from November 1979 through November 1980, the first black to serve in this post. A graduate of Vashon High School and Lincoln University, Bradley was active in the community as board member of the St. Louis Urban League and president of the Lincoln University Alumni Association. On the aldermanic board, he served as chairman of the Ways and Means Committee and was a vocal supporter of Homer G. Phillips Hospital.

Handy Park ■ 137

Euclid and Ashland avenues

This park is named for W. C. Handy (1873-1958), well known as the "Father of the Blues." A noted composer, he was also a performer, choral and orchestral conductor, and musical historian. He wrote a symphonic piece, "Afro-American Hymn: Blue Destiny," along with more than 150 other compositions.

In 1893, Handy arrived in St. Louis by boxcar to seek his fortune. Lonely, hungry nights on the cobblestone levee taught him the sights and sounds of the riverfront; years later they inspired his most celebrated song, the "St. Louis Blues," published in 1914. He once explained that, in writing the song, he took "the humor of the coon song, the syncopation of ragtime, and the spirit of the Negro folk song and called it blues." Sophie Tucker introduced the song successfully into her vaudeville act, and its record and sheet-music sales quickly boomed, making Handy famous. As Handy put it, "I was forty the year the 'St. Louis Blues' was composed, and ever since then my life has . . . revolved around that composition." The song has since been played around the world.

J. D. Shelley home ■ 138

4600 Labadie Avenue

In 1990, the Shelley house became a National Historic Landmark. It had played an important role in a 1948 United States Supreme Court decision, *Shelley v. Kraemer*, that ended restrictive real estate covenants based on race. In 1939, J. D. Shelley, his wife, and six children bought a house at 4600 Labadie that had a fifty-year covenant barring its sale to "persons not of Caucasian race."

Louis W. and Ethel Lee Kraemer, white residents of the neighborhood who lived at 4532 Labadie Avenue, promptly brought suit against the Shelleys on behalf of the Marcus Avenue Improvement Association. This association, supported by the Real Estate Board of St. Louis, had been established in 1910 to prevent blacks from purchasing homes in the area from Newstead Avenue on the east to Kingshighway on the west, and from the south side of Natural Bridge on the north to Easton Avenue on the south.

James T. Bush, Sr., the black real estate broker who had sold the property to the Shelleys, assumed responsibility for their defense. He formed the Real Estate Brokers' Association of St. Louis, which financed the Shelleys' case. The Shelleys were represented by well-known black attorney George L. Vaughn. First the St. Louis Circuit Court refused to issue an injunction to prevent the Shelleys from taking possession of the house, but the Missouri Supreme Court reversed this decision. In 1948, the United States Supreme Court ruled that constitutional rights guaranteed by the Fourteenth Amendment had been violated in this case and that restrictive covenants limiting access to property on the basis of race were not legally enforceable.

Plaque at J. D. Shelley home

Photo by Lee Harris.

J. D. Shelley home

Photo by David Schultz.

Sonny Liston site ■ 139

4708a Labadie Avenue

Charles "Sonny" Liston (1932-70), world heavyweight champion, was an Arkansas native who moved to St. Louis as a child. When he was eighteen years old, he robbed a service station and was imprisoned in the Missouri State Penitentiary, where he learned to box. He was released to the custody of Frank Mitchell, the owner of the *St. Louis Argus*, who lived at the Labadie Avenue address. Liston won the 1952 Golden Gloves title and then turned professional, though he had trouble securing fights because of his lengthening police record and his alleged ties to organized crime. In 1962 and 1963, he defeated Floyd Patterson twice for the heavyweight title. However, Muhammad Ali later won the title from Liston in two controversial bouts. In 1970 Liston died in Las Vegas of a drug overdose.

Scovel Richardson home 140

4635 North Market Street

In October 1941, Scovel Richardson (1912-82), a black associate professor at Lincoln University School of Law, bought this property, which was covered by a restrictive covenant that did not expire until December 1942. In making the purchase, he had the help of a white straw party and a black agent employed by the white-owned Dolan Real Estate Company. By carefully timing their closing date and deed transfer, Richardson and his wife were able to move into the house late in the week, knowing that their white neighbors would notice their presence over the weekend.

As expected, the Marcus Avenue Improvement Association confronted the Dolan Real Estate Company, which had a subpoena served the next Monday. Richardson's legal strategy was to use a series of demurrers, each one causing long delays before the hearing, which did not take place until the following March. In the meantime, the Richardsons were harassed by threatening phone calls, stink bombs, searchlights flashing through their windows, and snoopers around their home. The restriction on the Richardson house expired in December 1942. In December 1944, *Dolan v. Richardson* finally came to trial, but the case was thrown out of court because the restriction had expired and the plaintiffs had no grounds upon which to sue.

Scovel Richardson, a graduate of the University of Illinois and Howard University School of Law, went on to serve as dean of Lincoln University School of Law from 1944 to 1953. He became the first black admitted to the St. Louis and American Bar Associations and the first black attorney in Missouri to be named a member of the American Law Institute. In 1953, President Dwight D. Eisenhower (1890-1969) appointed Richardson as the first black member of the United States Parole Board; he was named the board's chairman in 1954. After four years on that board, he was unanimously confirmed by the United States Senate as a judge on the United States Custom Court. He received the Urban League Citation for Progress in Human Relations and Civic Achievement in 1953.

Dick Gregory Place ■ 141

Richard "Dick" Gregory (1932-), a St. Louis native and graduate of Sumner High School, is a comedian, author, and entrepreneur. He has interrupted his successful stage career several times to fight for civil rights and the interests of blacks. In April 1977, Wagoner Street was renamed Dick Gregory Place in his honor. It runs between Dr. Martin Luther King, Jr., Drive and North Market Street.

The *St. Louis Argus* office

Photo by Dr. John Wright.

The *St. Louis Argus* newspaper ■ 142

4595 Dr. Martin Luther King, Jr., Drive

The *Argus*, a weekly tabloid with a circulation of forty thousand, is located in this building. It was founded around 1912 by Joseph Mitchell, his brother William Mitchell, and his brother's wife, Nannie Mitchell. With Joseph Mitchell as managing editor, the newspaper championed better schools, educational opportunities, and full civil rights for African Americans. After the death of William Mitchell in 1945, his widow, Nannie Mitchell-Turner, became business manager and later president-treasurer of the Argus Publishing Company. The paper has remained a forum for African-American concerns under the direction of her son, Frank Mitchell, the present publisher; Eugene Mitchell, her grandson; and the paper's editor, Donald Thompson. It is the oldest black newspaper in Missouri and one of the oldest in the United States. The name "Argus" refers to a creature in Greek mythology that had one hundred eyes and never slept.

New Age Federal Savings and Loan ● 143

1401 North Kingshighway Boulevard

This institution, the oldest minority-owned financial institution in the state and among the oldest in the nation, was organized in 1915 by Frank Williams (1865-1953), principal of Sumner High School. Because of changes in federal regulations that governed savings and loans, it was forced to close in 1991. It provided loans to the black community during periods when blacks were denied financing by other institutions.

National Association for the Advancement of Colored People ■ 144

1408 North Kingshighway Boulevard

The St. Louis branch of the NAACP was organized in 1914 as the result of a mass meeting held at St. Paul African Methodist Episcopal Church. J. E. Spingarn (1875-1939), a founder of the group's national organization, came to speak to the audience. This meeting generated so much interest that another was held the next morning at Union Memorial Methodist Church. The St. Louis group agreed to form a permanent organization and applied for a charter, which was approved by the national organization in March 1914. The group's 625 charter members included James Milton Turner, Charlton H. Tandy, and Annie Turnbo Pope Malone.

One early issue confronting the group was residential segregation. An organization called the United Welfare Association, composed of associations representing white neighborhoods that were near all-black areas, staged a successful petition drive in 1916 to put a residential segregation law on the ballot. The NAACP worked diligently to oppose the ordinance, but on February 29 it passed by a citywide vote of 52,220 to 17,877. Under the terms of the new law, a person of one race could not move to a block on which 75 percent of the residents were of another race.

But the new ordinance never went into effect. Shortly after it was passed, a federal judge in St. Louis issued a temporary injunction to postpone its enforcement until the United States Supreme Court had ruled on a similar segregation ordinance in Louisville, Kentucky. In 1917 the United States Supreme Court declared the Louisville ordinance unconstitutional in *Buchanan v. Warley*, and the St. Louis judge made his injunction permanent. However, a legally enforceable alternative—restrictive real estate covenants—continued to spread the practice of segregated housing.

St. Martin de Porres Elementary School ●145

Academy and Minerva avenues

In September 1977, three Catholic elementary schools consolidated to become a new school, St. Martin De Porres, located in the old St. Mark's School building. The school closed at the end of the 1988-89 school year, and most of the students moved to Bishop Healy Elementary School.

Martin de Porres (1579-1639), the saint for whom this school is named, was one of South America's foremost humanitarians. He was born in Lima, Peru, the son of Juan de Porres and Ana, a freed Panamanian. In 1594, he became a Dominican lay brother and served the order in various capacities, chiefly in caring for the sick. He founded an orphanage and hospital; he also ministered to the African slaves in Peru. Canonized in 1962 by Pope John XXII, he is known as the patron of interracial justice.

See also: Bishop Healy Elementary School

King Middle School ■ 146

1909 North Kingshighway Boulevard

King Middle School is located in a building that formerly housed William Cullen McBride High School. The city purchased the building from the Archdiocese of St. Louis in 1971 and opened it in 1972 as a public school, with special education programs. It became a middle school in 1982. The school is named for Martin Luther King, Jr. (1929-68), the black civil rights leader who was awarded the Nobel Prize for Peace in 1968. King was killed in 1968 while standing on a motel balcony in Memphis, Tennessee, where he had gone to give support to the striking garbage collectors. In 1992-93 King Middle School had 350 students in grades six through eight.

King Middle School

Photo by David Schultz.

Detail of King Middle School

Photo by Lee Harris.

Langston Middle School ■ 147

5511 Wabada Avenue

The Langston School opened in 1964. A protected area beneath the building, which is constructed on piers, serves as a covered playground. In 1992-93, Langston Middle School had 380 students in grades six through eight, with ungraded special education classes.

This school was named for John Mercer Langston (1829-97) and his son, Arthur D. Langston (1855-1908). John Langston, born to a slave mother and white father in Virginia, graduated from Oberlin College before the Civil War. Refused admittance to law schools in New York and Cincinnati, he returned to Oberlin to study theology and graduated again in 1853. Next he studied law under Philemon Bliss of Elyria, Ohio, and was the first black admitted to the Ohio bar. During a distinguished career, he served as: law professor and acting president at Howard University, United States minister to Haiti, president of Virginia Normal and Collegiate Institute, and the only black Virginia congressman in the Fifty-first Congress.

Arthur D. Langston, also an Oberlin graduate, earned a bachelor's degree in 1877 and a master's degree in 1885. He was an influential teacher in the St. Louis Public Schools from 1877 until his retirement from Dessalines School, which he served as principal.

See also: Missouri Equal Rights League

Clayton Missionary Baptist Church

Photo by David Schultz.

Bishop Healy Elementary School

Photo by David Schultz.

Clayton Missionary Baptist Church ■ 148

2801 North Union Boulevard

In 1893 Clayton Missionary Baptist Church was organized on Brentwood Boulevard in Clayton, Missouri. Twelve years later, the sixty-seven-member church, then located in a small, shingled building surrounded by open fields, called the Reverend W. L. Rhodes as its pastor. He served the church for sixty-eight years. The congregation built a new building in 1907. In 1961, the church relocated to 2801 North Union Boulevard.

Bishop Healy Elementary School ■ 149

2727 North Kingshighway Boulevard

James Augustine Healy (1830-1900), for whom this school is named, was consecrated Bishop of Portland, Maine, in 1875. He was the first black American to become a Roman Catholic bishop. Healy was the son of an Irish immigrant and an African-American mother; he and two brothers all became priests. One of his brothers, the Reverend Patrick Francis Healy, S.J., Ph.D. (1834-1910), served from 1874 to 1882 as the first black president of Georgetown University, Washington, D.C. Another brother, Alexander Sherwood Healy (1836-75) also became a Sulpician priest. Bishop Healy Elementary School opened in 1922 as Blessed Sacrament School; the name was changed in 1971. In 1992-93, Bishop Healy had some 340 students from kindergarten through eighth grade.

All Saints Episcopal Church ■ 150

2831 North Kingshighway Boulevard

All Saints Episcopal Church, the first Episcopal church for African Americans in St. Louis, was established in 1847. It began as a small mission, the Mission of Our Savior, at 1220 Morgan Street (now Delmar Boulevard). In June 1875 the mission moved to a building at Sixth and Cerre streets, and was renamed the Mission of the Good Samaritan. In 1883 the name changed to All Saints Episcopal Church, and the congregation moved to a large building at Twenty-second Street and Washington Boulevard. It moved again in 1906 to the former Messiah Unitarian Church at Garrison and Locust avenues, purchasing the building for thirty-five thousand dollars. The church suffered severe storm damage in 1909, but the congregation repaired the sanctuary and resumed services five months later. To accommodate its rapidly increasing membership, the church moved to its present location in 1957.

Tyus Court ■ 151

Tyus Court runs between Norwood Street and Kingshighway Boulevard. It is named for Leroy Tyus (1915-), a Tennessee native who spent more than forty years in state and local politics. He served as Missouri state representative for the Twentieth Ward (Sixty-third District) from 1950 to 1961. While in office, he introduced an unsuccessful bill to integrate all state public schools; he also successfully co-sponsored a bill for fair employment practices. Tyus served as constable for the Third district and as Twentieth ward committeeman from 1960 to 1982.

Gateway National Bank

Photo by Dr. John Wright.

Hayes Lane ■ 152

Hayes Lane runs between Greer Street and Tyus Court on what used to be called East Norwood Drive. It was named for Robert Hayes (1942-), once known as "the world's fastest human." He won two gold medals at the 1964 Olympic Games, where he became the first person to run one hundred meters in ten seconds. From 1965 to 1974, he was a wide receiver and offensive end for the Dallas Cowboys.

Gateway National Bank ■ 153

3412 Union Boulevard

Gateway National Bank, incorporated in 1965, was the first bank established by blacks in St. Louis. It was the eighth institution to be chartered nationwide with substantial black representation among its founders. At the time of its incorporation, it had $200,000 in capital, with a surplus $200,000 and $100,000 in undivided profits. After a period of decline during the late 1980s, the bank is once again profitable, with earnings of $20,000 in 1992 and assets of $16.8 million. It is still the only black-owned bank in St. Louis.

Frederick N. Weathers Post Office

Photo by Dr. John Wright.

Swimming at the Mathews-Dickey Boys' club

Photo. Courtesy of the Mathews-Dickey Boys' Club.

Mathews-Dickey Boys' Club

Photo by David Schultz.

Frederick N. Weathers Post Office ■ 154

3415 North Kingshighway Boulevard at Palm Avenue

In 1986, this post office was named for Frederick N. Weathers (1906-), a St. Louis businessman, community leader, and longtime political figure in the Democratic party. He served as board member of the Urban League for twenty years, of the YMCA (Page Park, Pine Street, and Monsanto branches) for twenty-three years, and of the NAACP for ten years. In 1988 he received an award from the NAACP for developing its life membership structure. As Democratic committeeman of the Eighteenth Ward for twenty-eight years, he worked toward the promotion of blacks in city government. From 1979 to 1980, he served on the St. Louis Board of Police Commissioners and was instrumental in adding an affirmative action clause to the charter.

Mathews-Dickey Boys' Club ■ 155

4245 North Kingshighway Boulevard

Each year, Mathews-Dickey Boys' Club serves some forty thousand youth, ages six to eighteen, from throughout the St. Louis metropolitan area. The club got its start in 1961, when Martin L. Mathews and Hubert "Dickey" Ballantine began five neighborhood baseball teams, which played in Handy Park. A clubhouse soon opened in a small storefront building; in 1981, the club dedicated its current $2.5 million facility. The present club site covers twelve acres on the west side of Kingshighway at Penrose Avenue. It includes a gym, game and craft rooms, boxing ring, meeting rooms, club offices, and general purpose rooms. The site also includes lighted soccer, football, and baseball fields; tennis courts; and general recreation areas. Along with extensive athletic programs, the club offers individualized tutoring for youth, as well

Bellefontaine Cemetery gravestone

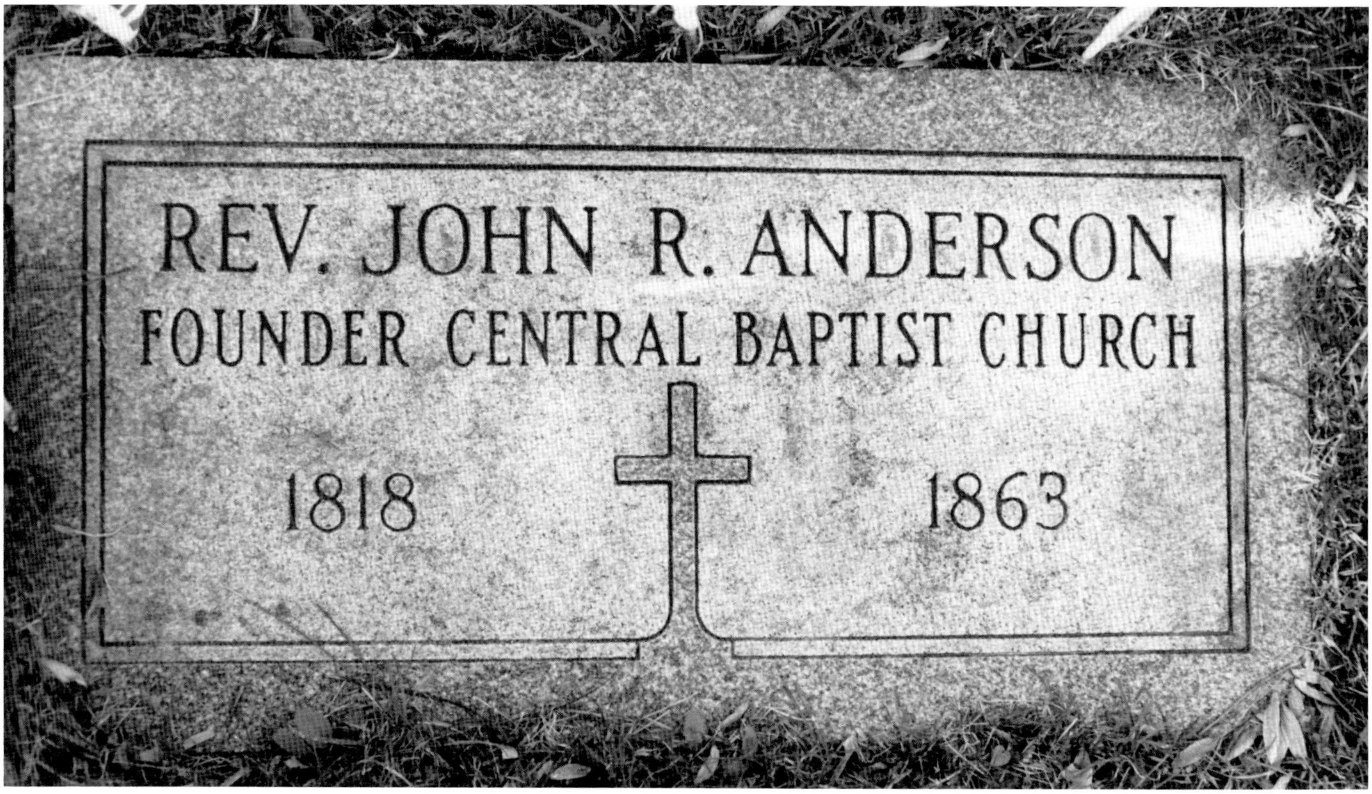

Photo by Lee Harris.

as CLIP (Computer Literacy Instructional Program). A girls' program at Mathews-Dickey was begun in 1986, and in 1989 a nineteen-thousand-square-foot wing was added to the club to house six classrooms, a teaching/demonstration kitchen, and the Jackie Joyner-Kersee Auditorium.

Bellefontaine Cemetery ■ 156

4947 West Florissant Avenue

In this cemetery, incorporated in 1849, two prominent ministers lie buried: the Reverend John Berry Meachum (1789-1854), founder and first pastor of the First African Baptist Church, and the Reverend John Richard Anderson (1818-63). Born in Shawneetown, Illinois, Anderson learned to read as a child in St. Louis at a Sunday school established by the Reverends John Mason Peck and James Welch. As a young man, he worked for the Reverend Elijah Parish Lovejoy in Alton and was an eyewitness to his murder. In 1847 he was called to serve as associate pastor of Second Colored Baptist Church and became pastor two years later.

Maps of the cemetery are available in the cemetery office.

See also: Freedom School
First African Baptist Church

Bellefontaine Cemetery gravestone

Photo by Lee Harris.

Dred Scott

Oil painting by Louis Schultze. Courtesy of the Missouri Historical Society Art Collection.

Calvary Cemetery ■ 157

5239 West Florissant Avenue at Union Avenue

A Catholic cemetery established in 1857, Calvary contains the remains of a notable black woman and two widely known black men. Pelagie Aillotte Rutgers (ca.1802-1867), one of the city's wealthiest property owners, is buried in the cemetery near her husband, Louis. Also at Calvary is the grave of Thomas Franklin (1848-1938), trusted valet to three St. Louis archbishops. Born a slave in New Orleans, Franklin came to the city in 1873 and became a servant to Archbishop Peter Kenrick (1806-96). He accompanied the archbishop on his rounds and regularly helped him serve mass. Later, he served Archbishops John J. Kain and John J. Glennon (1862-1946). He lived at 3512 Bell Avenue.

Dred Scott (1799?-1858), the former slave whose suit for freedom brought him national renown, was first buried in the old Wesleyan Cemetery (near the present intersection of Grand and Laclede avenues). When the cemetery was abandoned in 1867, he was reburied by his final owner, Taylor Blow (1820-69), in an unmarked grave at Calvary Cemetery. On July 24, 1957, a granite headstone, donated by a granddaughter of Taylor Blow, was placed on the grave and dedicated on September 17, 1957, the ninety-ninth anniversary of Scott's death. On May 30, 1992, a plaque inscribed "in memory of a simple man who wanted to be free—Dred Scott" was dedicated with little fanfare by the African Historical and Genealogical Research Society. The plaque was donated by Eddie Randle and Sons Funeral Home.

Maps of the cemetery, with directions to these sites, are available at the cemetery office.

See also: Old Courthouse
Madame Rutgers estate

Cardinal Ritter College Preparatory High School ■ 158

5421 Thekla Avenue

This school was established in 1979; it was then the only Catholic high school in north St. Louis. In 1984, it was recognized as an exemplary school by the United States Department of Education. In 1992-93 it served 320 students in grades nine through twelve. More than 90 percent of its students go on to college. The school is named for Cardinal Joseph E. Ritter (1892-1967), who ordered desegregation of the St. Louis Archdiocesan Catholic schools in 1947, seven years before the Supreme Court decision that led to the desegregation of public schools.

Demonstrations at the U.S. Cartridge plant • 159

4300 Goodfellow Boulevard at Bircher Boulevard

In the 1940s, the U.S. Cartridge plant was the site of demonstrations aimed at increasing the number of defense-related jobs for St. Louis African Americans. In May 1942, A. Philip Randolph (1889-1979), president of the Brotherhood of Sleeping Car Porters, visited St. Louis to start a local unit of the March on Washington Movement (MOWM), which called for the end to discrimination in all government, military, and national defense jobs. With Theodore McNeal, head of the St. Louis Brotherhood local, and David Grant (1903-85), a black St. Louis attorney, Randolph formed a committee of fifteen men and eight women to work toward increasing the number of African Americans employed at local defense plants.

In the spring of 1942, six hundred blacks—most of them common laborers and porters—were employed at the U.S. Cartridge plant, out of a total of twenty thousand workers. In late May, 150 of the blacks, who had just completed a construction project, were dismissed from their jobs. On June 20, four hundred men and women marched to the plant, carrying signs that included the MOWM slogan, "Winning democracy for the Negro is winning the war for democracy." They demanded higher wages for black porters, employment for black women, and admission to training schools for defense jobs. Subsequently, the plant hired fifty black women as matrons, advertised for "colored male workers," and gave black porters their first pay raises of five and ten cents per hour. White workers were automatically given raises after 30, 90, and 120 days of employment. By the fall of 1942, eight hundred blacks were employed at the plant; the number continued to increase throughout the year. The plant, however, segregated the black workers in a separate building.

On May 10, 1943, when black foremen were transferred to a new building to replace white foremen who had been promoted, thirty white women walked off their jobs. The company, fearing a strike, replaced the black foremen with whites. On May 12, black employees threatened a strike unless the black foremen were reinstated. After negotiations, plant managers agreed to open more skilled jobs and training courses to blacks. On June 3, thirty-six hundred black workers walked off their jobs when management hired a white foreman over an eligible black. After several days, the strike ended and the plant hired and trained more blacks, promoted thirty-two blacks to foremen, and opened up new jobs for blacks. Most of the black workers continued to work in segregated conditions.

In September 1943, partly as a result of the St. Louis MOWM actions, Mayor Aloys P. Kaufmann (1902-84) appointed seventy-two citizens to a race relations commission. Theodore McNeal speculated in a 1970 interview that MOWM activities had resulted in sixteen thousand jobs for St. Louis African Americans.

Cardinal Ritter College Preparatory High School

Photo by David Schultz.

New Northside Missionary Baptist Church ■ 160

8645 Goodfellow Boulevard

In 1992, New Northside celebrated the ninetieth anniversary of its founding by the Reverend George W. Clemons. In 1902, he pitched a tent in the 2900 block of Semple Avenue and held revival services there. The church he established, then called Semple Avenue Baptist Church, was the first black Baptist church west of Kingshighway. Soon the growing congregation built a sanctuary at 3033 Semple. Members were baptized in a pool located at the rear of the church.

In 1957, the church rebuilt its facility. A few months later disaster struck: The north side of the building collapsed due to a construction error. The church was torn down, and the congregation held services in a storefront in the 5400 block of St. Louis Avenue. By 1959, a new sanctuary on Semple was completed and the church's name was changed to New Northside Baptist Church.

In 1975, the congregation moved to its current location on Goodfellow; ten years later, it expanded on the same site. In 1990, New Northside opened a child development center.

Aldridge Elementary School (Colored School No. 11) ○ 161

Switzer and Christian avenues

Ira Aldridge (1805?-67), for whom this school was named, was an internationally famous black actor. The son of a Presbyterian minister, he began his career as a teenager with cameo roles in plays presented at the African Grove Theater in New York. Later he studied acting in England and became a star in Shakespearean roles. He made his debut in *Othello* at London's Covent Garden on April 10, 1833. For the next thirty years he performed throughout Europe; he was awarded medals by the kings of Prussia and Austria in recognition of his talent. Aldridge, who became a naturalized British subject, planned an American tour soon after the Civil War, but he died before he could carry it out.

Aldridge Elementary School, then called Baden Colored School, opened in a two-room building on this site during the late 1870s. In 1890, the school was renamed for Ira Aldridge. It closed in 1908.

North Corinthian Baptist Church ■ 162

447 Antelope Street

North Corinthian was organized in June 1860 in the part of St. Louis called Baden or "German Town." The church was originally a frame building on a lot twenty-four feet wide by fifty feet long. In 1903, the church extended its property to the east. In 1909, the church building burned to the ground; the present building was erected in 1912.

Garnet Elementary School

Photo by Emil Boehl. Courtesy of the Missouri Historical Society Photograph and Print Collection.

Garnet Elementary School 163

5339 Bulwer Avenue near Adelaide Avenue

This 120-seat school opened in 1877 as Colored School No. 9 at Bellefontaine Road and O'Fallon Avenue in north St. Louis. By 1885, the Garnet School had moved to Bulwer Avenue near Adelaide Avenue; portable buildings were added in 1906-07. The school closed in 1938.

In 1890, it was renamed for the Reverend Henry Highland Garnet (1815-1882), a former slave who became a minister and active member of the American Anti-Slavery Society. In 1843, at the National Convention of Colored People in Buffalo, New York, he issued a radical call for slaves to revolt. The convention voted down his motion, which was opposed by another influential leader, Frederick Douglass. Pastor of several prominent churches in New York City and Washington, D.C., Garnet also spent several years as a missionary in Jamaica. In 1881, he became United States minister to Liberia.

National Day of Lamentation 164

Entertainment Hall, 2358 Palm Street

A national "Day of Lamentation" was declared on May 31, 1892, to protest crimes of violence against African Americans, particularly lynchings. Early in the day, services were held in African-American churches throughout St. Louis. Later, a mass meeting drew fifteen thousand black citizens to Entertainment Hall. Prominent men, among them Walter Farmer, James W. Grant, James Milton Turner, Moses Dickson, John W. Wheeler, and George B. Vashon, spoke at the meeting. They later circulated a resolution that denounced the brutality and lawlessness of mob action.

Northeast

Curtis Elementary School 165

2824 Madison Avenue

The Penrose School was built in 1894 and renamed in 1943 for two black pioneer brothers: Thomas A. Curtis (1862-1943), a dentist, and William P. Curtis (1866-1945), a physician. A branch at 2825 Howard Street was built in 1949; the school closed in 1973.

Thomas Curtis first practiced in Alabama, where he had ranked second in the state board examination; in 1896 he moved to St. Louis, where he practiced for more than forty-five years. A civil rights activist, he also served as board member of the People's Hospital and the Pine Street YMCA and vestry member at All Saints Episcopal Church. He helped organize the Urban League and the St. Louis branch of the NAACP, which he served as its first black president. In 1910 he helped found the *St. Louis Argus*.

William Curtis, a physician educated at Howard University, came to St. Louis in 1894. He helped establish the Provident Hospital (later called People's Hospital) and became its first president. Like his brother, he worked to organize the Urban League of St. Louis; he also was an active member of the First African Baptist Church.

Curtis Elementary School

Photo. Courtesy of the St. Louis Public Schools.

Pruitt-Igoe Housing Project

Photo. Courtesy of the Missouri Historical Society Photograph and Print Collection.

Pruitt-Igoe Housing Project 166

Jefferson and Cass avenues

With the passage of federal legislation in 1937 and state legislation in 1939, St. Louis embarked on a program of building low-rent housing. The most ambitious aspect of the program was the Pruitt-Igoe Housing Project, just north of the central business district. The Pruitt Apartments, named for Captain Wendell O. Pruitt (1920-45), St. Louis-born World War II flying ace, were completed in 1954 at a cost of $21.7 million; they were a complex of twenty eleven-story buildings, originally intended for black tenants. The Igoe Apartments, named for former United States Congressman William I. Igoe (1879-1953), were completed a year later for $14.4 million; they comprised thirteen eleven-story buildings for white tenants. Pruitt-Igoe opened with racial quotas; in practice, however, almost all of the 11,500 residents of the thirty-three buildings were black.

Initially, Pruitt-Igoe attracted attention because it was supposed to be one of the largest and best-designed public housing projects of the post–World War II period. But the buildings were poorly planned and badly managed. Elevators stopped on every other floor, there were no restrooms on the ground floor, and the thousands of children who lived there had no planned recreation space.

The complex, which quickly became a center for crime, turned into a national scandal. As United States Congressman William Clay (1931-) once put it:

> Pruitt-Igoe was doomed the day it left the drawing boards. You can't concentrate almost three thousand low-income families in forty-three high-rise buildings and expect them to survive in an area that provided no shopping facilities, no health service, inadequate transportation, a minimum of job opportunities, and almost nonexistent schooling, playground, and recreational facilities.

All the buildings were demolished during the mid-1970s.

Colored School No. 2

Photo by Emil Boehl, ca. 1876. Courtesy of the St. Louis Public Library.

Pruitt Military Academy ■ 167

1212 North Twenty-second Street

Captain Wendell Oliver Pruitt (1920-45), for whom the school was named, was a St. Louis native and graduate of Sumner High School. In World War II, Captain Pruitt distinguished himself as a member of the Thirty-second Fighter Group and the Ninety-ninth Squadron. For his skill and courage in combat, he was decorated with the Distinguished Flying Cross and the Air Medal with four oak-leaf clusters. He died while training new pilots at Tuskegee Air Force Base in Alabama. Pruitt is pictured in the *Black Americans in Flight* mural at Lambert-St. Louis International Airport.

In 1944, when Pruitt was honored at City Hall, he said: "My highest hope and the highest hope of the others [black soldiers] is that we will find the Four Freedoms realized here when we return." The "freedoms" he referred to were the ones identified by President Franklin Delano Roosevelt: the freedom of expression, the freedom of every person to worship God in his or her own way, the freedom from want, and the freedom from fear.

The school named in his honor was founded in 1954-55 as Pruitt Elementary School and later became Pruitt Tutorial School, which closed in the early 1980s. The school reopened in 1984-85 as Pruitt Military Academy, a magnet school. In 1992-93 it had some 425 students in grades six, seven, and eight.

Dessalines School (Colored School No. 2) ○ 168

1745 Hadley (formerly North Twelfth) Street

This school, originally called Colored School No. 2, opened in 1866 at Tenth and Chambers streets. In 1871 it moved to North Twelfth and Webster streets. It closed in the early 1970s.

General Jean-Jacques Dessalines (1758-1806), for whom the school was named, was a former slave, Haitian officer, and aide to Toussaint L'Ouverture (1743-1803), father of the Haitian Revolution of 1791. He took control of the Haitian army after Toussaint L'Ouverture's death, and under his defiant motto, "War for war, crime for crime, atrocity for atrocity," he rallied the troops and forced the French into retreat. The French left the island, and Dessalines proclaimed the second republic in the Western Hemisphere. Disgusted with the loss of his colony, Napoleon became increasingly disenchanted with all his possessions in the Western Hemisphere. In 1803 he sold the Louisiana Territory, which included St. Louis, to the United States.

Turner Elementary School • 169

Lilac and Leeton avenues

The one-room Turner Elementary School was opened in 1923 by the Riverview Gardens School District, then known as the Science Hill School District No. Seven, to serve the black students of the district. Parents of nineteen black children from the Prospect Hill area of Riverview had met with the superintendent to request the school. In the late 1930s a second room and teacher were added. During the 1940s, enrollment dipped slightly after some of the homes in the Prospect Hill area were razed to make room for an expansion of the nearby Portland Cement Plant. In 1946, a new one-room school was constructed to replace the old building. It was furnished mostly with cast-off materials and used equipment. One teacher was assigned to the school and taught everything from basic skills to sewing.

Just after the 1954 Supreme Court school desegregation decision, the Riverview Gardens School Board appointed a committee of parents and administrators to develop a plan for integrating the black students into the school system. The board voted to maintain Turner as a black school for one more year because of district overcrowding, but when it voted in 1955 to continue the segregation at Turner, the NAACP and some residents protested. The board reversed its decision. During the 1955-56 school year, the district's sixteen black elementary students were integrated into the system. Turner was closed and is currently used for district storage.

Turner Elementary School

Photo by Dr. John Wright.

South St. Louis, Carondelet, South County

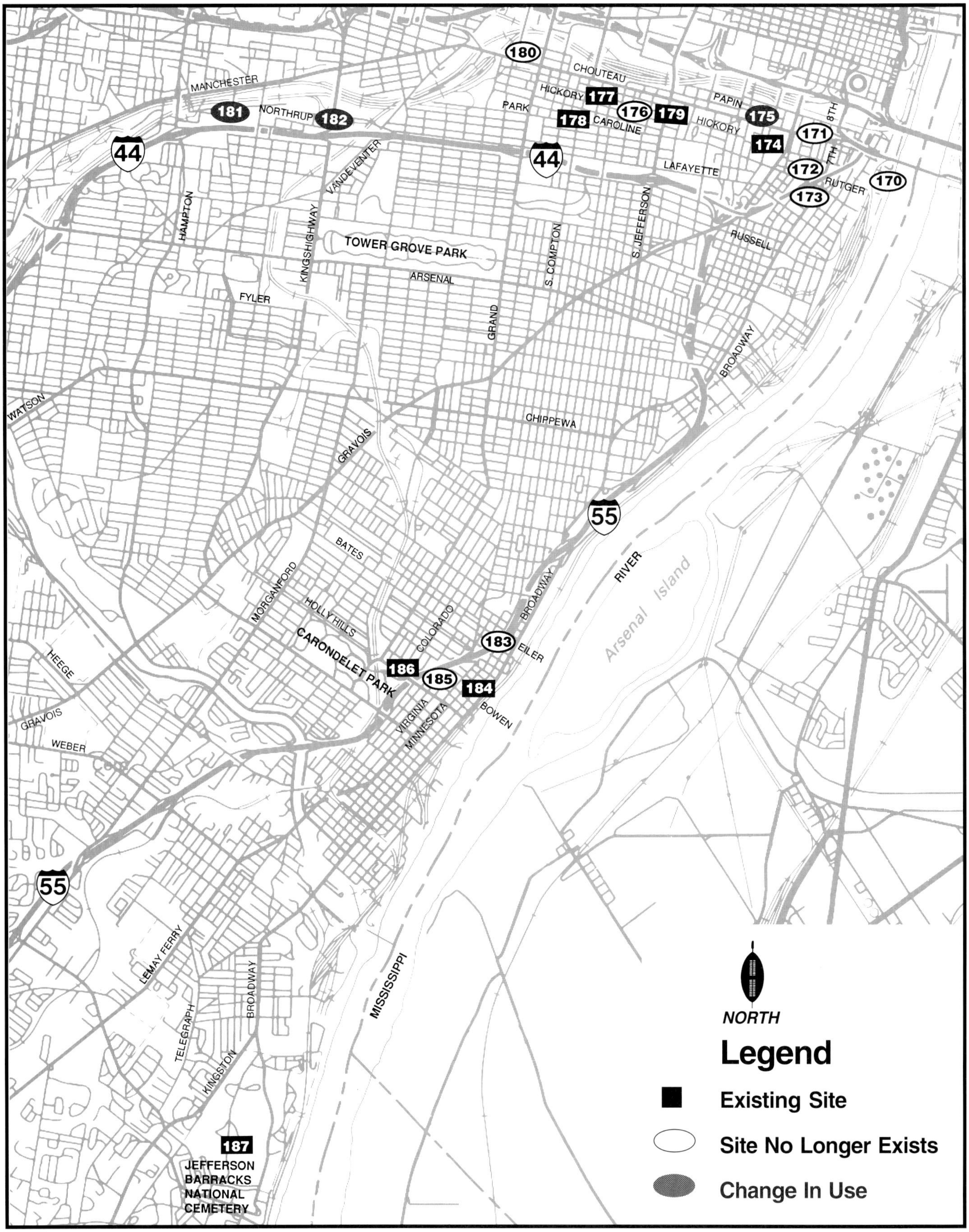

Hooverville

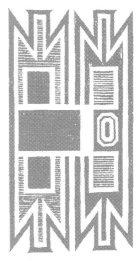

Photo. Courtesy of the Western Historical Manuscript Collection, University of Missouri-St. Louis.

Hooverville 170

Area on the levee south of the MacArthur Bridge (formerly the Municipal Bridge) at Chouteau

From 1929 to 1936, during the Great Depression, St. Louis had the nation's largest "Hooverville," a shantytown derisively named for President Herbert Hoover. In 1933, an estimated five thousand destitute men, women, and children were living in this squatter colony that stretched for miles along the Mississippi River. This settlement was one of the few racially integrated areas in St. Louis. The last shack was torn down by Works Progress Administration workers in 1936. In the 1950s and 1960s the area was redeveloped for highways and industry.

John C. Frémont headquarters

Residence and Headquarters of General Frémont. *Graphite on paper, by Alexander Simplot, 1861. Courtesy of the Missouri Historical Society Art Collection.*

John C. Frémont headquarters 171

Eighth Street and Chouteau Avenue

John C. Frémont (1813-90) first passed through St. Louis during the late 1830s as a young army lieutenant assigned to the United States Topographical Engineers. He met and married Jessie Benton (1824-1902), daughter of Senator Thomas Hart Benton, who became an aggressive promoter of her husband's career. Between 1842 and 1849, Frémont made four famous expeditions to the West, two of them with black guides from Missouri. On Frémont's second expedition, his scout was Jacob Dobson, a free black and servant to Senator Thomas Hart Benton (1782-1858); Dobson later became an attendant in the United States Senate. In 1856, Frémont ran for president on the ticket of the new Republican party.

In 1861, President Abraham Lincoln appointed Major-General Frémont as commander of the army's Department of the West. He established his headquarters in a mansion, formerly owned by Joshua B. Brant, on Chouteau Avenue. Throughout the night of August 29, Frémont worked at his desk; in the morning, he read his wife an emancipation proclamation, in which he placed the state under martial law. All anti-Union Missouri citizens would have their property confiscated and their slaves freed. Those found with arms in the northern half of the state would be court-martialed; if they were found guilty, they would be executed.

President Lincoln, who did not know that Frémont was preparing the proclamation, feared that the proposed executions would result in bloody retaliation by anti-Union forces. He acted quickly to rescind Frémont's order and, on November 2, he relieved Frémont of his one-hundred-day command.

Madame Rutgers estate ⬭172

North half of Seventh Street, bordered by Rutger Street, Broadway and Park avenues

Pelagie Aillotte Rutgers (ca. 1802-67), a member of St. Louis' mid-nineteenth century black elite, had substantial real estate holdings in the St. Louis area. Her home was known as the "Rutgers Mansion." Born in St. Louis, she was christened Pelagie Aillotte but called Eliza by her mother, a slave. Her first husband was St. Eutrope Clamorgan (1799-1822), son of Jacques Clamorgan (?-1814), St. Louis fur trader, merchant, and explorer. In 1825, she married Louis Rutgers, the mulatto son of a Dutch immigrant, and acquired her property through marriage. During the 1840s, the value of her real estate increased greatly, and Madame Rutgers became a major St. Louis landholder who rented commercial buildings and tenements on her land to white businessmen. Estimates of her wealth ran as high as five hundred thousand dollars, making her the richest black in St. Louis and advancing her into the first rank of wealth in the city. For example, she is said to have owned a piano worth two thousand dollars. Madame Rutgers and her husband are buried in Calvary Cemetery.

By the mid-nineteenth century, the growth of St. Louis enriched many free blacks who owned and operated boarding-houses, ran produce stores, and practiced various trades. Many of them were descendants of mulattos, freed during the Spanish period, whose fortunes came from inherited real estate. Cyprian Clamorgan's 1858 pamphlet, "The Colored Aristocracy of St. Louis," indicated that members of this black elite lived in the area generally bounded by Seventh and Rutger, Fourth and Pine.

See also: Clamorgan Alley
Calvary Cemetery

Madame Rutgers estate

Rutger and Main Streets, St. Louis, 1863. *Graphite on paper, by Paulus Roetter, 1863. Courtesy of the Missouri Historical Society Art Collection.*

Colored School No. 12 ⬭173

Columbus (now Eighth) and Barry streets

Colored School No. 12, also known as the Arsenal Colored School, was opened in 1880 at Columbus and Barry streets, in the present-day LaSalle Park area. By 1885, the school had moved to Seventh and Hickory streets. Five years later, it was renamed for Crispus Attucks (1723?-70), believed to be a runaway slave who was killed by the British at the Boston Massacre. The school closed at this location by 1910.

Another St. Louis public school, established in the former L'Ouverture school building, was also named for Attucks. This Attucks School was located at 2612 Papin Street, with branches at 2135 Chouteau and 2022 Papin. It opened during the 1950-51 school year and closed in 1971.

Walk of Fame star

Photo by Lee Harris.

Leon and Michael Spinks home ■ 174

Darst-Webbe Housing Complex
1241 Hickory Street

Boxing champions Leon (1954-) and Michael Spinks (1957-) grew up in St. Louis, first in the Pruitt-Igoe Housing Project and later at Darst-Webbe. In 1976, both brothers won Olympic gold medals in Montreal. In February 1978, Leon defeated Muhammad Ali for the World Boxing Association heavyweight crown, though he lost the championship in a rematch. He won the North American Boxing Federation cruiserweight title in 1983. Michael won a 1981 decision over Eddie Mustafa Muhammad to win the world light-heavyweight title. Twice, he beat former heavyweight champion Larry Holmes to win the International Boxing Federation heavyweight title. After suffering his only professional loss, a first-round knockout by Mike Tyson in 1988, Michael ended his career with an overall record of 31-1.

St. Mary's Infirmary ● 175

1536 Papin Street

In 1933, the Sisters of St. Mary opened their previously all-white hospital, founded in 1877, to a staff of black physicians; at the same time, they also admitted African-American patients. St. Mary's provided professional education for African-American doctors and nurses; a nursing school was established in 1933. Review courses and other postgraduate training for black physicians were given by the staff of St. Louis University School of Medicine. St. Mary's Infirmary closed in 1966.

Maya Angelou site ○ 176

2714 1/2 Caroline Street

Actress, author, and educator Maya Angelou (1928-) was born Marguerite Johnson to Bailey and Vivian Baxter Johnson. At the time of her birth, the family was living in St. Louis on Hickory Street. In her 1970 autobiography, *I Know Why the Caged Bird Sings*, Angelou described her childhood. At age three, after their parents' marriage had disintegrated, she and her brother were sent from their California home to live with their paternal grandmother, the owner of a general merchandise store in Stamps, Arkansas.

Five years later, the children moved back to St. Louis, where they lived for six months with their maternal grandparents, Percy and Flora Baxter, on Caroline Street. Angelou enrolled briefly at L'Ouverture School. Next, she and her brother moved in with their mother and her boyfriend, who abused Angelou; afterwards, the children returned to Arkansas. As an adult, Angelou worked as an actress, journalist, author, and civil rights activist. In 1993, she was Reynolds professor of American Studies at Wake Forest University in Winston-Salem, North Carolina. On January 20, 1993, she read her poem, "On the Pulse of Morning," commissioned for the occasion, at the inauguration of President William J. Clinton in Washington, D.C.

L'Ouverture School (Colored School No. 4) ■ 177

3021 Hickory Street

In 1866 Colored School No. 4 opened on Cozzens Street near Pratt Avenue (now Jefferson Avenue). In 1885 it moved to 2612 Papin Street where it was renamed L'Ouverture in 1890. In 1945, L'Ouverture Branch No. 1 at 2135 Chouteau opened in a portable six-room building. Later, L'Ouverture Branch No. 2 opened at LaSalle and Caroline avenues. Although the main school building was severely damaged by fire in November 1945, it was used together with the branches until 1950.

The postwar housing shortage caused a delay in the building of the new L'Ouverture school. Fifty-three families lived in tenements on the new school site. Since little or no housing was available for them to rent, they fought eviction for almost two years. Finally, a compromise was reached, and the new school at 3021 Hickory Street opened in 1950. In 1992-93, the L'Ouverture School was used as a middle school with 480 students.

The school is named for Pierre Dominique Toussaint L'Ouverture (1743-1803), a Haitian patriot who led a 1791 revolt against the French and set in motion events that culminated in the Haitian revolution and independence. In 1799, he became ruler of the island of Hispaniola, including the Spanish colony of Santo Domingo (now the Dominican Republic) and the French colony of Saint-Dominique (now Haiti). He resisted Napoleon, who wanted to restore French rule to Haiti. Outmaneuvered by the French, Toussaint L'Ouverture surrendered in 1802. He was transported to France, where he died in prison in 1803. His commanders once again battled the French; in 1803, French colonial rule in Haiti ended. On January 1, 1804, Haiti proclaimed its independence.

Colored School No. 4

Photo by Boehl & Koenig, ca. 1876. Courtesy of the St. Louis Public Library.

Drawing class at L'Ouverture School

Photo, ca. 1900. Courtesy of the St. Louis Public Schools.

The loss of Haiti, as well as the imminence of a new war with Great Britain, squelched Napoleon's plans for a French empire in North America, and in 1803 he sold all of Louisiana, including St. Louis, to the United States for fifteen million dollars.

Mount Zion Missionary Baptist Church

Photo by David Schultz.

Du-Good Chemical Laboratories

Photo by David Schultz.

Mount Zion Missionary Baptist Church ■ 178

1444 South Compton Avenue

The Mount Zion Missionary Baptist Church was organized in 1859 as the Mount Zion Baptist Church, served by the Reverend Wyatt Scott. The congregation, which began meeting in the homes of its members, was first housed in a log cabin located east of Jefferson at Papin Street. The church then moved to 2624 Papin Street, a site that was sold to the Board of Education for construction of the L'Ouverture School. In the 1920s the church moved to 2765 LaSalle Street and in 1992 to its present location. The church supports an elementary school and day care center.

Du-Good Chemical Laboratories ■ 179

1215 South Jefferson Avenue

On this site in 1948, Lincoln I. Diuguid (1917-), a science instructor at Harris-Stowe State College from 1949 to 1982, opened one of the first chemical laboratories owned and operated by a black American. The company provides microanalytic services and makes Du-Good products: cleaners and cosmetics marketed to the black community. Diuguid, who has a Ph.D. in organic chemistry from Cornell University, has trained more than one hundred black and white scientists who have worked in his laboratory.

Wheatley School (Colored School No. 7) ⬭ 180

4239 Papin Street

Colored School No. 7 opened around 1880 in the area known as Rock Springs, which was incorporated into St. Louis in 1876. In 1890 the school was renamed for Phyllis Wheatley (1753-84). Born in Senegal, West Africa, she arrived in Boston at the age of seven or eight, then was bought off the slave block by John Wheatley, a wealthy merchant and tailor. Wheatley and his wife Susannah reared the girl more as a daughter than a slave and gave her the name Phyllis. The young girl soon astonished everyone by speaking, reading, and writing fluent English.

Wheatley's first published poem in 1770 attracted much local attention. At age 20 she was acclaimed a prodigy in both America and Europe. Voltaire praised her for her "very good English verse." In 1773, she visited England, where her book, *Poems on Various Subjects Religious and Moral*, was published.

The Wheatley School was last used in the 1972-73 school year; the Board of Education sold the building in 1974.

Wheatley School (Colored School No. 7)

Photo by Emil Boehl. Courtesy of the Missouri Historical Society Photograph and Print Collection.

Clay mines area of the Hill • 181

Kingshighway Boulevard, Hampton Avenue, Manchester Road, Fyler Avenue

African Americans, along with settlers of English, German, French, and Irish descent, were early residents of the Hill section of St. Louis, now the city's principal Italian neighborhood. Blacks came to the area in the 1880s to work in the local clay mines. Most lived in the Fairmount District around the mines, where by 1890 terra cotta and brick industries had sprung up along the Frisco and Missouri-Pacific railroad tracks. Two settlements formed the nucleus of the community: one near the Pattison Avenue Baptist Church, 5232 Pattison Avenue, which was organized in 1897; the other was organized near the Pentecostal church on Sublette near Manchester. By 1903, more than three hundred black laborers worked in factories in the Hill area.

Clay miners

Photo. The St. Louis Regional Commerce and Growth Association, St. Louis: Its Neighborhooods and Neighbors, Landmarks and Milestones *(St. Louis, 1986).*

Vashon Elementary School (Colored School No. 10) • 182

5324-26 Northrup Avenue

The school, originally Cheltenham Colored School or Colored School No. 10, opened in 1877 and closed in 1908. It served the African-American children who lived in the Hill area of St. Louis. From 1879 until at least 1881, the school was located on Davis Street near Manchester Road, in an area known as Cheltenham. During the 1890s it moved to Northrup Avenue. In 1892, eighty-nine students attended the school. The school was renamed in 1890 for George Boyer Vashon (1824-78), a black scholar and jurist. His son, John B. Vashon (1859-1924), served as one of the principals of the school.

Carondelet

Carondelet was first settled by Clement Delor de Treget, a Frenchman, in 1766 and named for Baron de Carondelet, then governor of the Louisiana territory. This Creole settlement, located about five miles south of St. Louis on the Mississippi River, was incorporated as a separate village and annexed by St. Louis in 1870. The borders of the Carondelet area are the Mississippi River, Grand Avenue, the River Des Peres, and Bates Avenue.

The early residents of Carondelet were mainly French; few black residents were listed in the census records for the city's first century. The 1850 Carondelet census, for example, listed twenty-six slaves among the population. After the Civil War, the population grew in response to the employment needs of the many nearby riverfront industries. Black people moved to the area and worked in the iron works, blast furnaces, and later in steel mills. Others worked as farmers or domestics, while some worked in professional or business positions.

A number of businesses owned by African Americans were located along Broadway, Colorado, and Iron streets. Some identified from early city directories are Major Brown's barbershop at 7000 Broadway; George Britton and Virgil McKnight's barbershop at 6311 Broadway; Eliza Shores' dressmaking shop at 7008 Broadway; Purnell's ice and coal company at 6105 Colorado; Henry Schwartz's scrap iron and rag business on Broadway; Charles Bradley's scrap iron and rag business, 6101 Colorado; Cab Daggs' cleaning and shoe shine at 7411 Broadway; and Cornelious Brown's cleaning and shoe shine at 7009 Broadway.

By 1880, Carondelet's black population had risen to 450. Most African-American residents were not concentrated in one area; however, a black settlement did exist on the banks of the Mississippi, from the foot of Dover Street to the foot of Quincy. The black population continued to grow until the 1920s, when it began to decrease.

The Jefferson family, early settlers of Carondelet

Photo. Courtesy of the Carondelet Historical Society.

St. John's Methodist Church 183

113 Eiler Street

St. John's Methodist Church was the first black church built in Carondelet. It was constructed in 1869 on land donated by a member of the Blow family; its first pastor was the Reverend Moses Dickson. St. John's burned the same year in which it was built, and the site is now an empty lot.

Quinn Chapel African Methodist Episcopal Church

Photo by Donald Dates.

Quinn Chapel African Methodist Episcopal Church ■ 184

225 Bowen Street at Minnesota Avenue

The congregation of Quinn Chapel formed in the 1870s as the Carondelet African Methodist Episcopal Church. In 1880, the church purchased a building from the city of St. Louis that had been constructed in 1869 as Carondelet's North Public Market but had never been occupied. In 1882, the chapel was dedicated to William Paul Quinn (1788-1873), the first missionary bishop of the African Methodist Episcopal Church and founder of the African Methodist Church in St. Louis in 1840.

The chapel has now served its congregation for more than one hundred years. A new tower was built in 1899 to accommodate the gift of a church bell, which is inscribed "A Fulton of Pittsburgh, Pa., 1847," and was originally used on a steamboat. In 1908, the congregation added a parsonage. In 1974, the building was placed on the National Register of Historic Places.

See also: African Methodist Church
St. Paul African Methodist Episcopal Church

Martin R. Delaney School (Colored School No. 6)

Photo by Emil Boehl, ca. 1890s. Courtesy of the Missouri Historical Society Photograph and Print Collection.

Corinthian Baptist Church

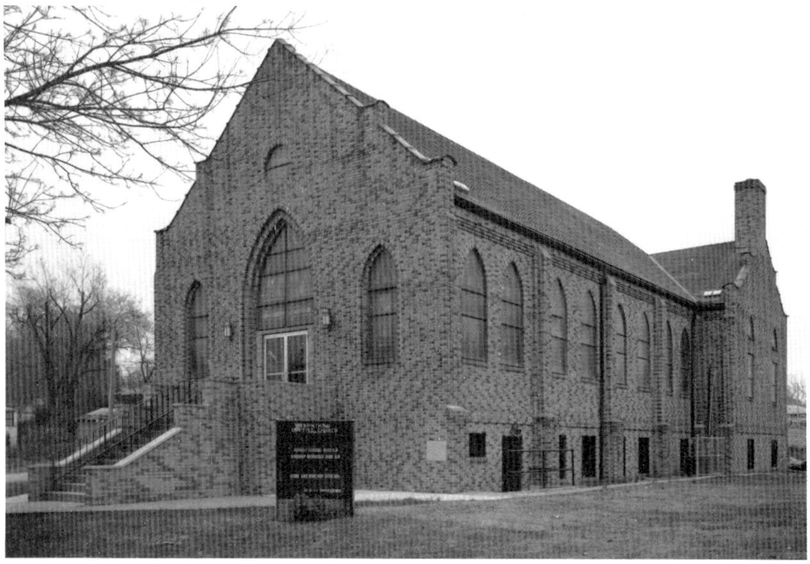

Photo by David Schultz.

Martin R. Delaney School (Colored School No. 6) 185

6134 Virginia Avenue

In 1870, the St. Louis Board of Education authorized the school administration to rent one room in Carondelet for African-American students. But rented quarters proved hard to find, so in 1873 Colored School No. 6 was built at Fifth and Market Streets (now Virginia Avenue and Bowen Street). In the 1890s, it was renamed for Martin R. Delaney (1812-85), a black physician and publisher who was the grandson of a slave brought from West Africa. He was active in the Underground Railroad. Delaney studied medicine at Harvard College and became a Union officer in the Civil War.

A new brick school was built in 1911; however, most students soon moved from the area and attended other schools in central or north St. Louis. The Delaney School was renamed the Virginia Avenue School in 1935 and opened to white students, while the remaining black children in the neighborhood attended the Delaney Portable Center at Minnesota Avenue and Bowen Street, near the Quinn Chapel. The Virginia Avenue School was rededicated in 1953 and renamed the Maddox School. The building still stands, but it no longer serves as a public school. The cornerstone is legible and reads "Delaney School."

Corinthian Baptist Church ■ 186

6326 Colorado Avenue

Around 1875 the Reverend George W. West came to Carondelet to establish a church. Prayer meetings were held in the home of Richard Walker at South Broadway and Bowen (formerly the Carondelet Police Station and Courthouse). The group formed the Second Baptist Church and moved to a building on Kraus Street.

The congregation split around 1890, and a faction broke away to organize St. Luke's Baptist Church. Second Baptist then moved to the Hildebrandt Building near Robert Avenue and finally to 619 West Stein. The two groups rejoined in 1895, took the name Corinthian Missionary Baptist, and erected a frame building. In 1950, a new brick building was opened and dedicated on Colorado Avenue.

Jefferson Barracks National Cemetery ■ 187

101 Memorial Drive

The Fifty-sixth U.S. Colored Infantry was organized in St. Louis in August 1863. Much of its service was in garrison duty, although the men saw action at points in Arkansas and Mississippi. Their unit was stationed at Helena, Arkansas, from March 1864 to September 1866.

During two-and-a-half years of service, the Fifty-sixth Infantry lost 674 men: 25 of them killed or mortally wounded in action and 649 dead from disease.

The remains of 175 men from the Fifty-sixth Infantry were interred at Quarantine Station, Missouri, near Koch Hospital in St. Louis County. Their graves were marked by a marble obelisk inscribed "To the Memory of 175 Non-Com. Officers and Privates of the 56th U.S.C. Infty. Died of Cholera in August 1866." In 1939, the remains were removed to the National Cemetery and the obelisk was placed on Grave 15009 in Section 57 through the joint efforts of the War Department and a citizens' committee chaired by Joseph E. Mitchell, publisher of the *St. Louis Argus*. On May 30, 1939, a dedication and memorial ceremony was held to honor the men. The obelisk is now flanked by graves 15008 and 15010, each inscribed "56th U.S. Infantry—Unknown."

A total of 1,068 members of the U.S. Colored Infantry were buried in the Jefferson Barracks National Cemetery by 1870. Most are unidentified, though five of the soldiers are known: Hamilton Allen, Moses White, George English, Lewis Montgomery, and Scott Glasby. They all died in August 1866 and are buried in Section 22 of the cemetery.

Plaque with inscription

Photo by Lee Harris.

Marble Obelisk

Photo by Lee Harris.

Pagedale, Wellston, Beverly Hills, Hillsdale

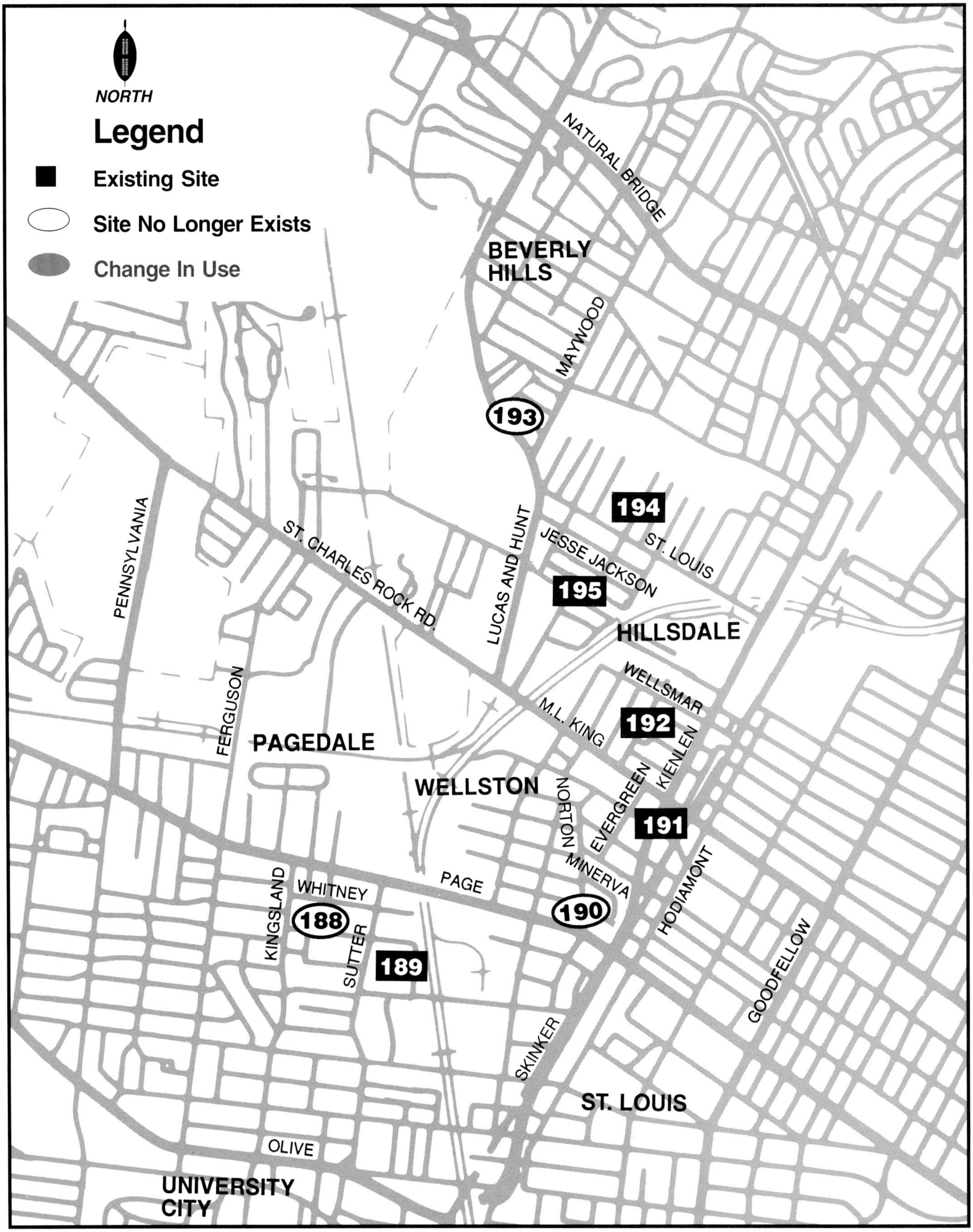

Pagedale

Nicolas Craig homestead ⬭188

Southeast corner of Kingsland and Whitney avenues

Whitney Avenue is a one-block-long street located between Kingsland and Scutter avenues. Nicolas Craig and his family, the first blacks in the community, settled on Whitney Avenue around the turn of the century, when the area was still considered "country." As a boy of twelve, Nicolas had run away from slavery in Kentucky and come to Missouri. He approached a farmhouse near Hannibal, Missouri, and asked for a drink of water. The woman who gave him the drink proved to be his mother, who had been sold as a slave when he was a small boy.

During the 1940s and 1950s, many black professionals moved to Whitney Avenue and it became a center for social affairs. Its residents included Morris Henderson, one of the past presidents of the county branch of the NAACP, and the late Wirt D. Walton, a Harris-Stowe instructor who composed the school's anthem.

Daughter of Nicolas Craig

Photo by Nathan B. Young. Courtesy of the St. Louis University Archives.

Wellston

Eskridge High School ■189

1200 Sutter Avenue

In 1978, Eskridge High School (formerly Millard M. Halter High School) was renamed for Melvin Ray Eskridge (1963-78), an African-American student who had become seriously ill with cancer while he was a freshman at the school. Despite his failing health, he insisted upon attending school as long as possible. After his death, the Wellston Board of Education and the school administration decided that it would be fitting to honor him for his courage and determination. At the dedication ceremony, Melvin Eskridge was described as "a distinguished scholar, citizen, musician, and humanitarian." In 1992-93, Eskridge had some 220 students in grades nine through twelve.

DuBois Elementary School

Photo by Dr. John Wright.

DuBois Elementary School 190

6117 Minerva Avenue

DuBois Elementary School was constructed in 1950 by the Wellston School District for its African-American students. This four-room school, now closed, was named for William E. B. DuBois (1868-1963), black educator and author, who studied at Fisk University and the University of Berlin. He received three degrees from Harvard College and in 1897 became the first black ever to receive a Ph.D. His doctoral dissertation, *The Suppression of the African Slave Trade*, was the first published work in the Harvard Historical Studies. In 1905, DuBois and other black leaders met in Niagara Falls and formed "The Niagara Movement" to work for full freedom of the press and freedom of speech, as well as equal economic and educational opportunities for blacks. But the movement never won widespread popular support and by 1910 it had ended. However, it was a precursor of the NAACP, organized in 1909 in New York City, which DuBois also helped to found.

Lloyd Brown Center ■ 191

1414 Evergreen Street

This center, which opened in 1978, is named for Lloyd Brown, Sr. (1912-72), the first black elected official in Wellston. Mayor Johnny Henderson, Wellston's first black mayor, chose to honor Brown because of his extensive community involvement. He served on the Wellston School Board from 1963 to 1967 and on the City Council from 1967 until his death. The center now houses a Head Start program, senior citizen programs, basketball and boxing facilities for youth, and a variety of other community activities.

Bishop Elementary School ■ 192

6310 Wellsmar Avenue

Bishop Elementary School is named for Curtis Bishop (1911-), Wellston School District's first black principal of an integrated school. A Kentucky native, Bishop received his bachelor's degree from Kentucky State University and his master's degree from Washington University. From 1947 to 1950, he taught in the St. Charles Public Schools. In 1953 he became teacher/principal at Wellston's DuBois Elementary School, a position he held until the school closed in 1957. He next taught math at Wellston Junior High and was named assistant principal in 1962. In 1969 he was appointed principal of Spensmar Elementary School and remained in this post until his retirement in 1976. Because of Bishop's many contributions to the district, the Wellston Board of Education renamed Spensmar to honor Bishop in 1975. In 1992-93 the school had 333 students in grades one through eight, with two special education classes.

Bishop Elementary School

Photo by Lee Harris.

Curtis Bishop

Photo. Courtesy of Curtis Bishop.

Beverly Hills

Turner Elementary School ⬭ 193

Lucas and Hunt Road, north of Maywood Avenue

Turner Elementary School served the black students in the Normandy School District from the turn of the century to the early 1920s. The school was named for James Milton Turner (1839?-1915), one of the most important African-American leaders in Missouri after the Civil War. He was a leader in the movement to establish schools for blacks across the state. As minister to Liberia from 1871 to 1878, he was also America's first black diplomat.

James Milton Turner

Photo. Courtesy of Lincoln University.

Hillsdale

Greenwood Cemetery ■ 194

6571 St. Louis Avenue

This cemetery was established on January 19, 1874, by Herman Krueger as a burial place for black farm workers from the Hillsdale area. It remained in the Krueger family until the mid-1970s. Since then, it has changed hands three times. The oldest grave sites, many of them marked by concrete planters manufactured by Greenwood workers during the 1920s, are at the far north end of the cemetery.

Jesse Jackson Avenue ■ 195

This street, previously called Curtis Avenue, runs east from Lucas and Hunt to Cherry Avenue. It was renamed in 1983 for the Reverend Jesse Jackson (1941-), minister and civil rights activist.

Kinloch, Berkeley, Ferguson, Robertson, Black Jack

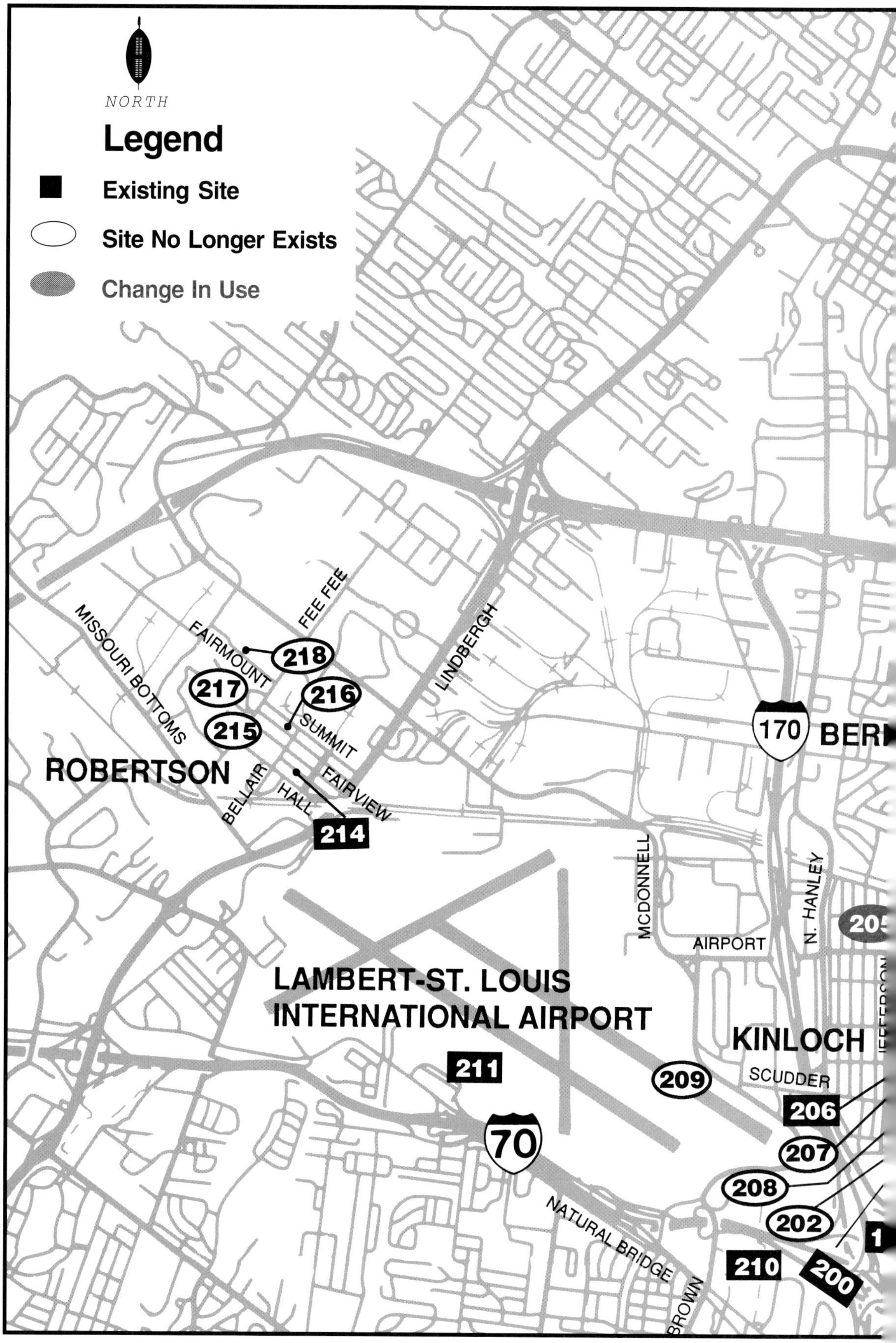

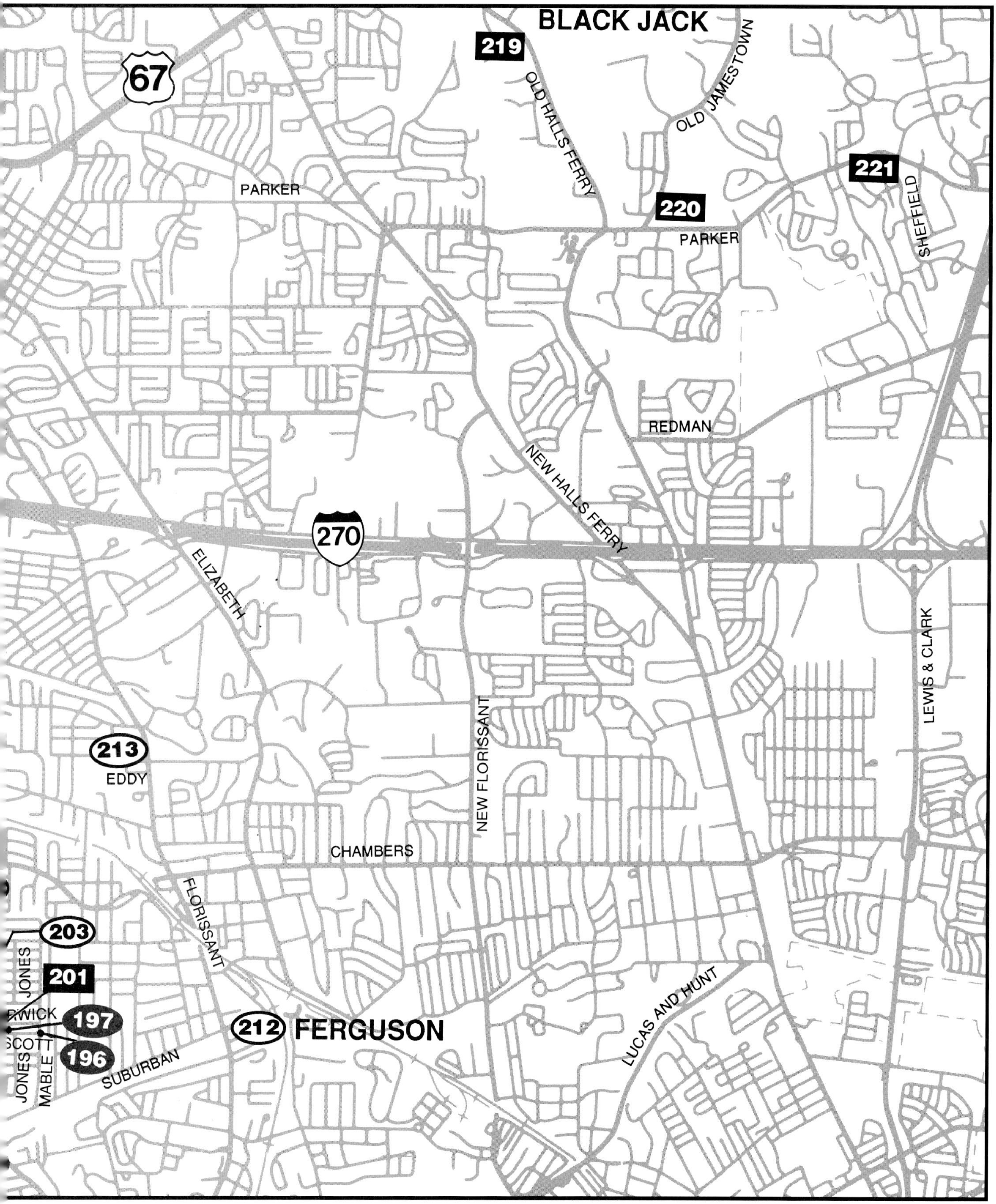
BLACK JACK
219
67
OLD HALLS FERRY
OLD JAMESTOWN
221
PARKER
220
PARKER
SHEFFIELD
REDMAN
NEW HALLS FERRY
270
ELIZABETH
LEWIS & CLARK
NEW FLORISSANT
213
EDDY
CHAMBERS
FLORISSANT
203
JONES
201
RWICK
197
SCOTT
196
JONES
MABLE
SUBURBAN
212
FERGUSON
LUCAS AND HUNT

Universal Negro Improvement Association members

Photo. Courtesy of Dr. John Wright.

Kinloch, Berkeley, Ferguson, Robertson, Black Jack Chapter 7

Kinloch

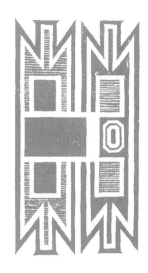

Because the early history of Kinloch is obscure, it is unclear when blacks first arrived in the area. Some believe that the area was on the route of the Underground Railroad before the Civil War. A few escaping slaves may have stayed behind to establish small farms. Kinloch Park was developed in the 1890s as a commuter suburb for whites, though a small portion of land was reserved for blacks who came to work as servants. Just how the black migration started is not clear, but it is reported that a "Mrs. B___" and her husband purchased a piece of property through their friendship with the white owner. When neighbors discovered that the new owners were black, they immediately sold their lots and moved; other white families would not move in. The lots were then opened to blacks. Within a few years, thirty or more black families came to occupy five or six blocks in the extreme southeast portion of the area. Some blacks moved to Kinloch after the 1917 East St. Louis race riot; many others were black soldiers returning from service in World War I.

In March 1937, fearing that the black population would take control of the school district, white Kinloch residents voted to split the district and establish Berkeley as a separate city. Until the 1960s Kinloch remained relatively isolated, with only two roads running into the city. It was bounded by a major roadway on one side, a creek on another side, and fences running the length of the community on the other two sides. In August 1948, Kinloch was incorporated as a fourth-class city and Missouri's first all-black city. By the end of 1992, Lambert-St. Louis International Airport had bought 776 homes in Kinloch as part of its noise abatement program. Once the houses are all demolished, the land will be rezoned for commercial or industrial use.

Vernon Elementary School •196

5764 Mable Avenue

Vernon was established in 1927 by the Ferguson School District to serve the black students living in Kinloch on the east side of Mable Avenue. The original two-room facility eventually grew to four rooms, which were used until the school closed in 1967. Its students were sent to the Central, Vogt, and Lee Hamilton elementary schools. The old building was leased to the Kinloch School District for use as an administration building. It was abandoned in 1975 when the Kinloch District merged with Ferguson-Florissant and Berkeley.

Kinloch Elementary School •197

5650 Jones Avenue

Kinloch Elementary opened in 1961 as Smith School, named for Sylvester L. Smith, a former superintendent of the Kinloch School District. Currently the school is known as the Kinloch Center. The Ferguson-Florissant School District uses it for a Child Development Center and community and social services offices.

Kinloch Church of God in Christ

Photo by David Schultz.

Kinloch Church of God in Christ ■ 198

8122 Hugo Avenue

Kinloch Church of God in Christ was organized in 1914. The congregation first met under an apple tree in a King Street front yard, and work began on the sanctuary the next year. In 1949, fire damaged the church, and another building was erected on what is now the parking lot west of the church. The congregation moved to its present facility in 1952. It is now the Tabernacle of Faith and Deliverance.

Kinloch Public Library

Photo. Courtesy of Dr. John Wright.

Kinloch Public Library ● 199

5591 Martin Luther King Boulevard

Kinloch Public Library, built by the Works Progress Administration, opened in 1941 in the Robert Building at Lix and Warwick avenues. This community-owned library was managed by a 126-member association, and it was open to all residents of Kinloch and Robertson. When the St. Louis County Library District was organized, the Kinloch Public Library became its first branch, located in the Folwell Building on Warwick Avenue. The library moved into its Martin Luther King Boulevard location after it outgrew the Folwell facility.

Kinloch Fire Department ■ 200

5684 Martin Luther King Boulevard.

This small fire department, one of two black fire departments in St. Louis County, was organized as a volunteer force in January 1936. Even though it became tax-supported in 1944, it was still operated by volunteers for some time. Originally, only those residents who purchased fire tags were provided with fire protection. For many years, the community had just one fire hydrant, which was located at Lix and Wesley avenues. Until the 1960s, when the community installed forty fire hydrants, firemen had to carry tanks to transport water. In 1953, a bond issue was passed which provided funds to build the present firehouse.

Holy Angels Parish and Our Lady of the Angels School ■ 201

8122 Scott Avenue

Holy Angels is one of the oldest, continuously operating black parishes in the St. Louis Archdiocese. In 1925, the Reverend A. J. Garvey, S.J., the missionary pastor for Robertson, a predominantly black community located west of Kinloch, first held services for fifteen people in the old Wade Funeral Chapel on Carson Road. The earliest church was the former St. John and St. James Church in Ferguson, which was moved to Kinloch and erected on Lix Avenue across from the present firehouse. Mass was offered for the first time on Christmas Day, 1925. In the fall of 1927, the church moved to its present location; the current building was erected in 1951.

In the summer of 1931 the Reverend Otto J. Moorman, S.J., founded a school and had it staffed by the Sisters of Notre Dame. The school's initial enrollment of forty students from kindergarten through eighth grade soon grew to 147 as students came from as far away as Wellston, St. Louis, and Robertson. In 1954, Holy Angels School (later renamed Our Lady of the Angels School) moved from its frame facility to its present brick building. Members of the Oblate Sisters of Providence, an order of black nuns, were assigned to the school in 1955 and remained as teachers until 1972.

An Oblate Sister of Providence

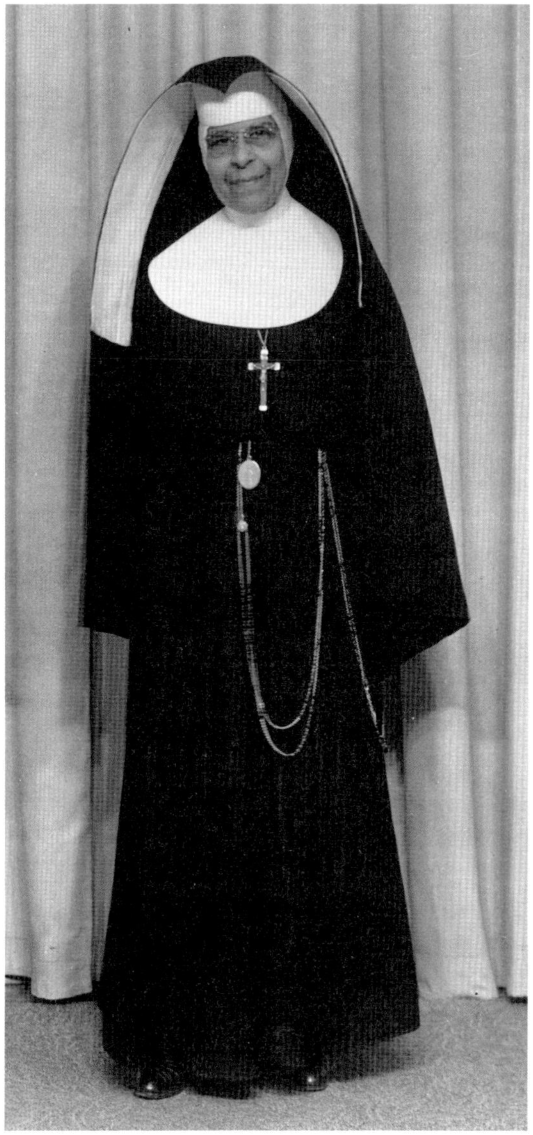

Photo. Courtesy of the St. Louis Review.

UNIA, Division 198

Photo. Courtesy of Dr. John Wright.

UNIA members

Photo. Courtesy of Dr. John Wright.

Black Star Line stock certificate

No. 31219

Shares Two

AFRICA THE LAND OF OPPORTUNITY

INCORPORATED UNDER THE LAWS OF THE STATE OF DELAWARE

BLACK STAR LINE, INC.

CAPITAL STOCK $10,000,000
SHARES $5. EACH

This Certifies that Elijah Woodson is the owner of Two Shares of the Capital Stock of BLACK STAR LINE, INC. full paid and non-assessable transferable only on the books of this Corporation in person or by Attorney upon surrender of this Certificate properly endorsed.

In Witness Whereof the said Corporation has caused this Certificate to be signed by its duly authorized officers and its Corporate Seal to be hereunto affixed this Eleven day of March A.D. 1921

Secretary-Treasurer. President.

J. Meyers Inc. 391 B'way

Photo. Courtesy of Dr. John Wright.

The Universal Negro Improvement Association and African Communities League, Division 198 202

Warwick Avenue

This organization was founded in Jamaica by Marcus Garvey (1887-1940), who came to America in 1916. National membership soon grew to about two million. The organization set up a chain of cooperative grocery stores, restaurants, steam laundries, tailoring and dress-making shops, millinery stores, and a publishing house. Garvey, who hoped to establish a black nation in Africa, also sold shares in a short-lived steamship firm, the Black Star Line, Inc.

Division 198 was established in the late 1920s in Kinloch as a "social, friendly, humanitarian, charitable, educational, instructional, constructive and expansive" society. Its objectives were to promote racial pride, support an independent Africa, and foster black-owned businesses. Its motto was "One God, One Aim, One Destiny," and its colors were red for blood, black for the race, and green for hope.

Dunbar Elementary School ⬭ 203

Scudder Avenue and Dr. Martin Luther King, Jr., Boulevard

Dunbar Elementary, which opened in 1914, with an addition built in 1932, was the oldest school in use for black students in St. Louis County when it closed in 1976 after the merger of the Ferguson-Florissant, Berkeley, and Kinloch school districts. In 1936, Dunbar also served briefly as a high school under the auspices of the W.P.A. Emergency Education Program. The building was demolished in 1979. Paul Laurence Dunbar (1872-1906), for whom the school was named, was a black poet and writer who earned an international reputation for his focus on African-American themes.

Kinloch High School ⬭ 204

5929 Witt (formerly Lix) Avenue

The first high school program for Kinloch's black students began in Dunbar Elementary School in 1936. High school classes met from 3:00 P.M. until 7:00 P.M.; elementary students used the building in the mornings and early afternoons. Both the decision to build a black high school and the school's proposed location angered white Kinloch residents, who tried several times to split the district. In 1937, they succeeded in forming their own separate city, Berkeley. Kinloch High School, which had been built in 1936 for whites, became Berkeley High School.

Black Kinloch residents elected a board of education and began building a new Kinloch High School, which opened in 1938 as the third high school for blacks in St. Louis County. An annex was added in 1967. The school remained in use until 1976, when the Kinloch, Ferguson-Florissant, and Berkeley school districts merged. Kinloch School District produced Missouri's first six black superintendents of schools.

Dunbar Elementary School

Photo, ca. 1945. Courtesy of Dr. John Wright.

John F. Kennedy Junior High School ⬬ 205

5990 Monroe Avenue

Kennedy Junior High opened in 1964 and became one of the first in the nation to be named in honor of the late president. As Board President John O'Guin explained: "The Board was meeting when the President was slain and chose to name the school in his honor because it was felt that the President had done a lot for the American people and the Negro in particular." In 1976, the building was closed as a result of the merger of the Ferguson-Florissant, Berkeley, and Kinloch school districts. The city of Kinloch acquired the building for its City Hall and Administration Building, and it is still used for that purpose.

Paul Laurence Dunbar

Photo. Courtesy of the St. Louis Public Schools.

First Missionary Baptist Church of Kinloch ■ 206

5844 Monroe Avenue

First Missionary Baptist, the oldest church in Kinloch, was organized in 1901. Before the congregation had its own building, services were held in members' homes. The first church was built at 5836 Washington Avenue. By 1919 the congregation had outgrown its facility; using volunteers and only one paid worker, the group managed to erect a new building at 5835 Jefferson Avenue. The church continued to prosper, and in 1949 the members built a new brick edifice at 5944 Monroe Avenue. Fire destroyed it on September 26, 1950, but within five years the congregation had rebuilt the church at its present site.

Young Women's Christian Association ⬭ 207

5810 Monroe Avenue

The Kinloch YWCA was founded by a group of Kinloch women known as the "Home Group," who saw the need for a recreation center for Kinloch children. A building was erected on this site and dedicated in January 1953. The Kinloch Center became an official branch of the YWCA of Metropolitan St. Louis in 1969; its many employees through the years included Ruth C. Porter, who was active in fighting injustices in education and housing in Kinloch.

See also: Ruth C. Porter mall and mural

First United Methodist Church ⬭ 208

5775 Jefferson Avenue

First United Methodist, the second-oldest church in Kinloch, was organized in 1904 as the First Methodist Episcopal Church. It was an offshoot of an older church, Union Memorial Methodist Church in St. Louis.

See also: Union Memorial Methodist Church

Berkeley

Scudder Avenue Colored School ⬭ 209

Scudder Avenue and Brown Road

Originally built for children of wealthy whites, Scudder Avenue School was designated for blacks after becoming the property of the Kinloch District in 1902. The two-room structure held two grades, though the enrollment seldom exceeded thirty pupils. The school closed in 1914 when the Dunbar Elementary School opened in Kinloch.

Washington Park Cemetery ■ 210

3300 Brown Road, near Highway 70 and southeast corner of Lambert-St. Louis International Airport.

Washington Park, a thirty-acre cemetery established in the 1920s, is the largest black cemetery in the St. Louis area. Until the 1980s, families were allowed to mark gravesites with homemade monuments; now all markers must be made of granite. Because of nearby MetroLink light-rail construction, a major project began in 1992 to relocate some twenty-five hundred graves from the cemetery grounds.

Among the well-known St. Louisans buried in Washington Park is John Feugh (1851-1939), who was the personal servant of Henry Shaw (1800-89), founder of the Missouri Botanical Garden, and later a valued employee at the Garden itself. A Georgia native, Feugh came to St. Louis in 1879 and found work at Shaw's downtown office. When Shaw moved out to his country home on the Garden grounds, Feugh went with him and lived in a house on the grounds for thirty-five years. At Shaw's direction, he hauled and planted many of the Garden's trees. In 1889, Feugh was made caretaker of the Garden museum, where he became known to thousands of visitors.

Black Americans in Flight Mural ■ 211

Lambert-St. Louis International Airport, lower concourse east of the baggage claim area

This fifty-one-foot mural, created by artists Spencer Taylor and Solomon Thurman, chronicles the achievements of blacks in aviation since 1917. The five-panel mural was unveiled on August 13, 1990, near Siegfried Reinhardt's mural depicting the history of manned flight. Protests over the lack of any black fliers in Reinhardt's mural led to the painting of this companion piece, which includes seventy-five portraits, ranging from Eugene Bullard, a black fighter pilot for the French Flying Corps in World War I, to three black astronauts: Guion Bluford (1942-), Mae Jemison (1956-), and Ronald McNair (1950-86). The work also includes Captain Wendell O. Pruitt (1920-45) and other Tuskegee Airmen who flew in the Ninety-ninth Fighter Squadron during World War II. Tuskegee Airmen from St. Louis who were still living in 1993 included: Clarence Bradford, Everett Bratcher, John Briggs, Carl Carey, Page Dickerson, Otis Finley, Jr., Victor Hancock, William Holloman, James B. Knighten, Lewis Lynch, Christopher Newman, Henry Peoples, Clarence Shivers, and Charles White.

See also: Pruitt Military Academy

***Black Americans in Flight* mural**

Photo. Courtesy of Lambert–St. Louis International Airport.

Vernon Elementary School

Photo. Courtesy of the Ferguson Historical Society.

Mount Olive Missionary Baptist Church

Photo. Courtesy of the Ferguson Historical Society.

Ferguson

Vernon Elementary School ⬭212

East side of Florissant Road approximately one hundred yards south of Maline Creek

In 1887, the Ferguson School District bought one acre of land on the east side of Florissant Road for $300, and paid $750 dollars to have a one-room frame schoolhouse for black children built on the site. Though the school was located in an area that had been strongly pro-Southern during the Civil War, the president of the school board, Philadelphia-born lawyer Thomas Allen, believed in educating all children. But after a few months, the school's attendance dropped off and it closed. Students then traveled by train to Normandy to attend classes in the old Grace Lutheran Church building, located on Lucas and Hunt Road. Vernon came into use again, but the student body soon outgrew its building. In 1927, a new two-room brick building was constructed at 5764 Mable Avenue, and the Florissant Road school closed.

Mount Olive Missionary Baptist Church ⬭213

Middle of the north side of Eddy Avenue

Mount Olive Missionary Baptist Church was built around 1880 by black residents of Ferguson on land given by Thomas T. January to his former slaves after the Civil War. The church was located to the north of his estate; early baptisms were performed in January Pond. Mount Olive served the black residents of Ferguson and Kinloch before the opening of the First Baptist Church of Kinloch. It was demolished during the early 1980s.

Bridgeton Baptist Church ■ 214
327 Hall Street

The Bridgeton plantation of William Norris was on the Underground Railroad. Norris, an abolitionist, considered escaping slaves to be free men. He gave them some of his land and then a log cabin for a church. They organized the church, originally called First Baptist of Bridgeton, in 1853.

Elzy R. Smith Elementary School ○ 215
440 Hall Avenue at Fee Fee Road

This school was built in 1958 and named for Elzy R. Smith (1900-1974), a Lincoln University graduate who served as its first principal. Hired as a teacher in the predominantly black Scudder School District, Smith rose to become chief administrator of the district before it became part of the Berkeley School District. He was employed by the district from 1927 to 1967. Elzy R. Smith Elementary School closed at the end of the 1976-77 school year.

Fairmount School ○ 216
336 Summit Avenue

Until 1958, Fairmount Elementary School was the Scudder School District's only black school. It was desegregated under pressure from the St. Louis County superintendent of schools and after the election of a majority black school board.

St. Peter Claver Church ○ 217
Northside of Fairview Avenue, four blocks west of Bellair Avenue

St. Peter Claver was a Jesuit mission, opened in 1916. The church became part of the Archdiocese in 1949. It closed in 1956 and its parishioners were added to St. Mary's parish. It was named for St. Peter Claver (1581-1654), the son of a Spanish farmer, who went to Cartagena in Central America as a Jesuit priest in 1610. There he dedicated his life to the service of slaves taken from Africa. Claver was canonized in 1888, and in 1896 he was declared the patron saint of all the Catholic missions among black people.

See also: Shrine of St. Joseph

Bridgeton Baptist Church

Photo by David Schultz.

Robertson Firehouse ○ 218
355 Fairmount Avenue

The Robertson Fire Protection District was started by the black residents of Robertson as a volunteer bucket operation, and individual residents were taxed for service. It provided protection for much of the area around Robertson. In its early years, the firehouse also served as a movie theater.

Black Jack

In his *History of St. Louis County*, published in 1911, William L. Thomas established the existence of the village of Black Jack around 1840 at the intersection of Parker and Old Halls Ferry roads. Some say the name Black Jack derived from a cluster of three enormous black jack oak trees, which provided shelter and a resting place for farmers hauling their produce to market. Another legend claims that the community was named for Jack, a well-known slave who lived in the area. Once an agricultural area, Black Jack experienced urban growth after World War II; it was incorporated in 1970.

New Cold Water Burying Ground ■ 219

Old Halls Ferry Road

This African-American cemetery, adjacent to the Paddock Golf Course entrance, was created in 1886 by five trustees who purchased the one-half acre lot for fifty dollars. The deed specified that the land was to be used "as a graveyard or burying ground under the name of "New Cold Water Burying Ground."

The 1878 atlas shows that a black school and church were located across the street from the cemetery site. The 1909 atlas shows "African Church and School" still at this location, but they subsequently disappeared. A sign and a few remaining tombstones mark the site.

Parkview Heights ■ 220

Parker and Old Jamestown roads

In 1970, the Inter-Religious Center for Urban Affairs proposed building a federally subsidized, moderate-income, multiracial housing project on an 11.9-acre site in an unincorporated part of North County. Area residents protested that the project, Parkview Heights, would overcrowd schools and lower property values; at their request, the County Council incorporated the area as the city of Black Jack. After the city was formed, one of its first acts was to pass a zoning code that limited all development to single-family homes.

In 1971, the American Civil Liberties Union filed a two-million-dollar lawsuit on behalf of the Parkview Heights Corporation in United States District Court in St. Louis. The suit asked that the zoning law be declared invalid since it denied lower-income residents the chance for better housing. In an attempted out-of-court settlement, Black Jack agreed to pay $450,000 to the non-profit housing development for the land on which the complex was to be built. But in August 1979, the Eighth Circuit Court of Appeals ruled that Black Jack was in violation of the 1968 Fair Housing Act and that city officials must meet with federal officials and the United States district court judge to work out a plan for low-income housing. Since the United States Supreme Court refused to review the appellate court's ruling, Black Jack was forced to develop the housing units, now located on this site as the Kendelwood Apartments, for low- and moderate-income families.

Paddock Woods subdivision ■ 221

Parker Road and Sheffield Avenue

On September 2, 1965, Joseph Lee Jones filed a complaint in the United States District Court against Alfred H. Mayer Company, contending that the company refused to sell him a home in the Paddock Woods subdivision because he was black. The suit, *Jones v. Alfred H. Mayer Co.*, was dismissed both in district court and in appellate court. But on June 17, 1968, the United States Supreme Court ruled 7-2 in Jones' favor, basing its opinion on an 1866 federal law that prohibited all racial discrimination in the sale or rental of property. The court's opinion stated that "all citizens of the United States shall have the same right, in every State and Territory, as is enjoyed by white citizens thereof to inherit, purchase, lease, sell, hold, and convey real and personal property." Jones and his family, who had meanwhile bought a home in another part of St. Louis County, settled out of court with the Alfred H. Mayer Company, which agreed to pay the cost of all legal proceedings.

Elmwood Park, Overland, Creve Coeur, Maryland Heights, Breckenridge Hills

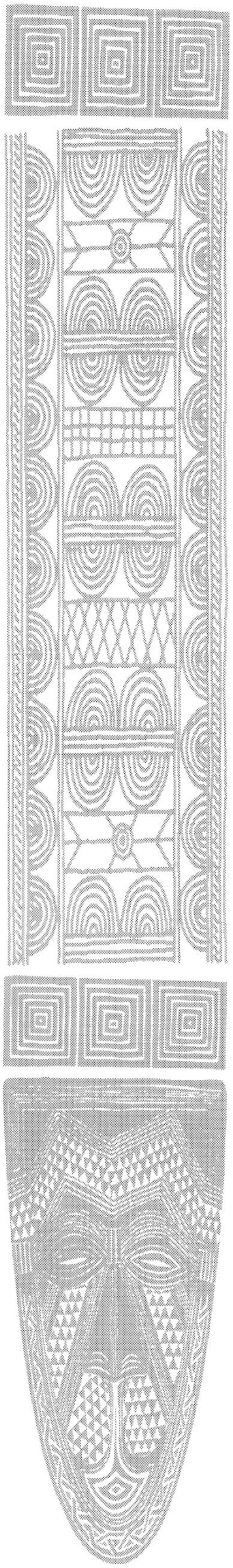

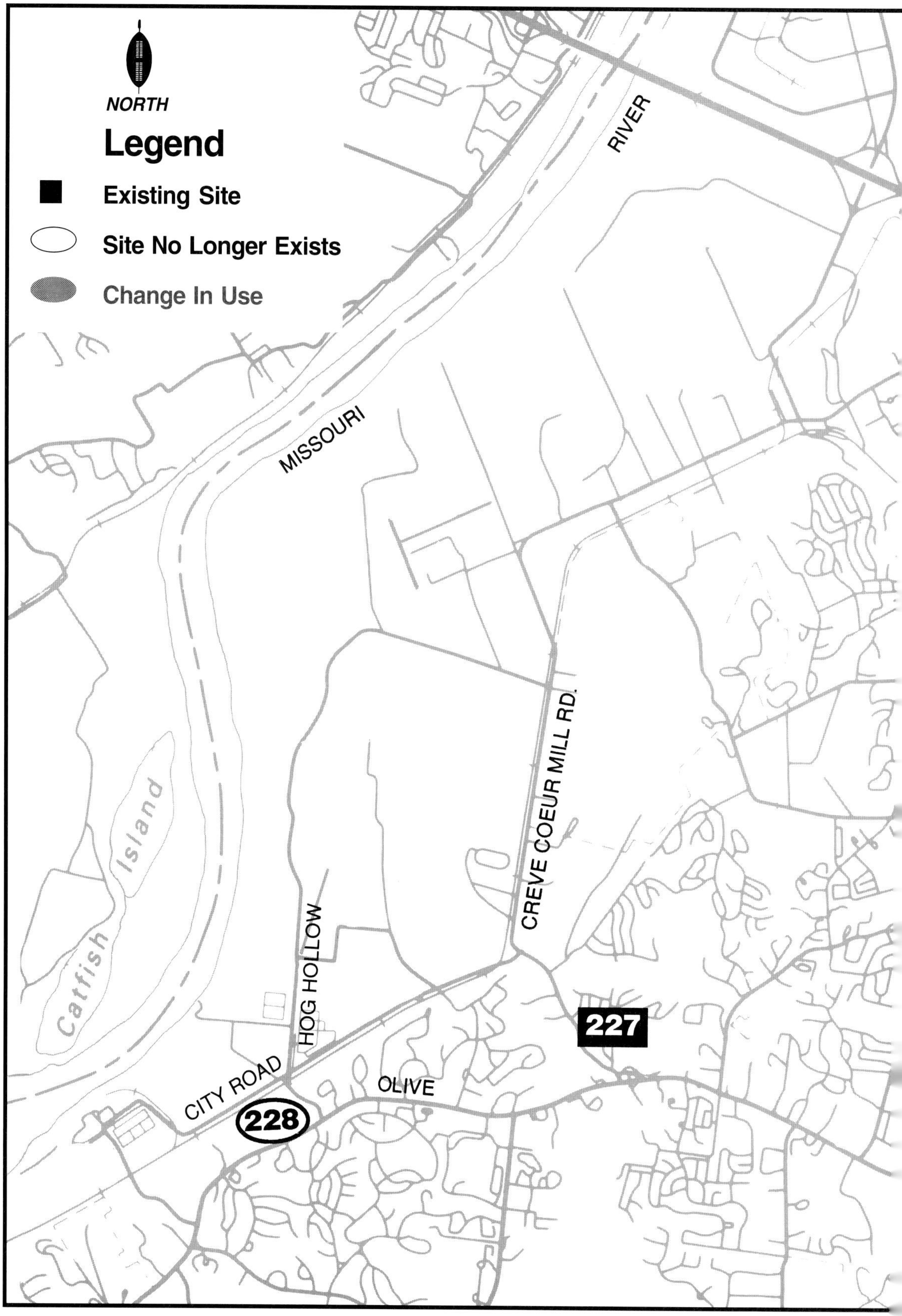

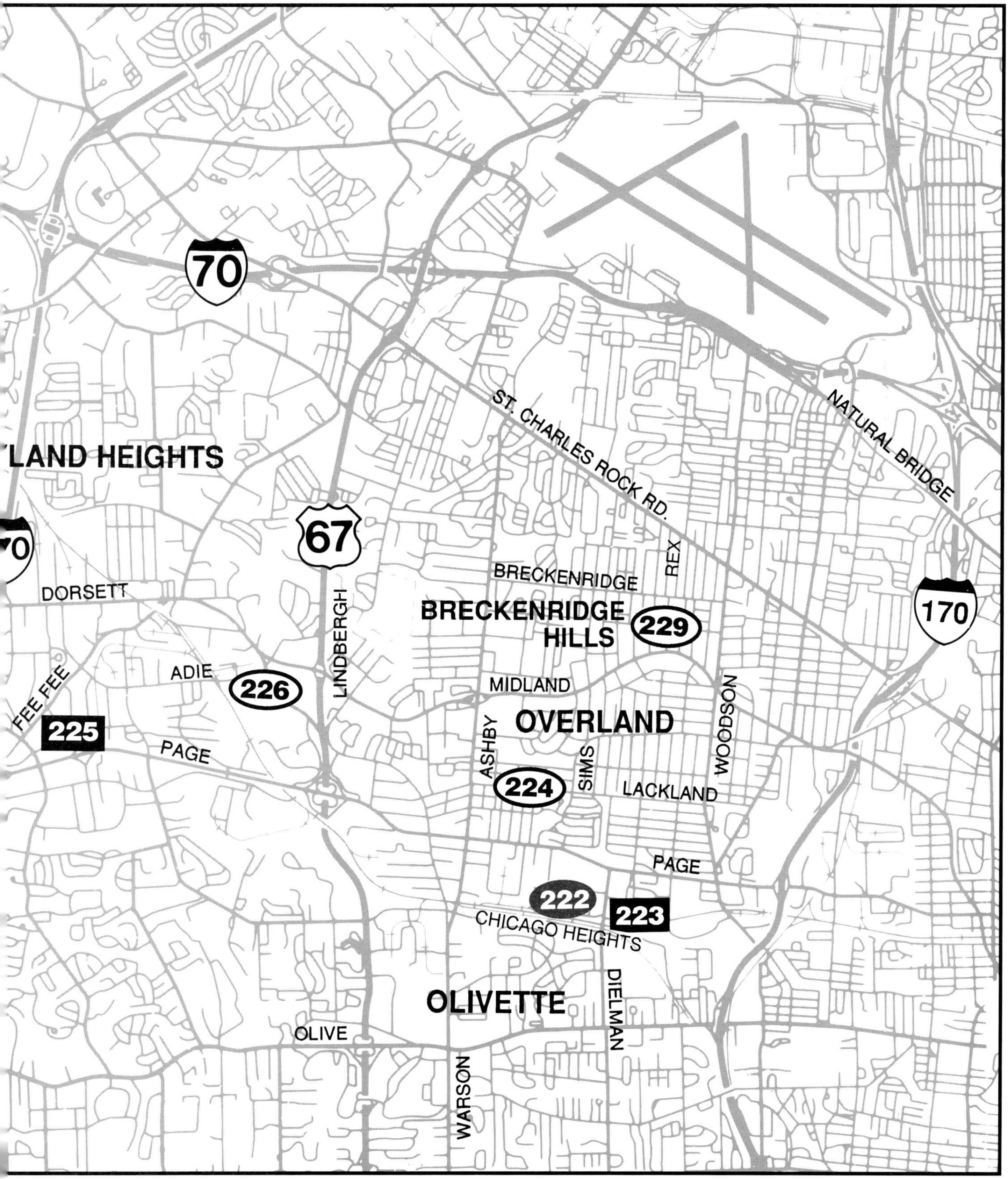
70
LAND HEIGHTS
67
ST. CHARLES ROCK RD.
NATURAL BRIDGE
REX
BRECKENRIDGE
170
DORSETT
BRECKENRIDGE
HILLS
229
LINDBERGH
ADIE
226
MIDLAND
WOODSON
FEE FEE
225
OVERLAND
ASHBY
PAGE
SIMS
224
LACKLAND
PAGE
222
223
CHICAGO HEIGHTS
DIELMAN
OLIVETTE
OLIVE
WARSON

Elmwood Park, Overland, Creve Coeur, Maryland Heights, Breckenridge Hills

Cemetery at Musick Baptist Church

Photo by Lee Harris.

Elmwood Park, Overland, Creve Coeur, Maryland Heights, Breckenridge Hills

Chapter 8

Elmwood Park

Elmwood Park is a small, predominantly black community located between Olivette and Overland. It was settled after the Civil War by families who worked on farms in the area. The area south of the railroad tracks was annexed by Olivette in the 1950s. From the mid-1960s to the early 1970s, the community, which had consisted of some seventy or seventy-five African Americans, underwent extensive urban renewal. After the land was cleared, new homes and housing units were constructed on the Overland side. Olivette tried to replace the blighted homes with light industry but was forced to build a development called Rothwell Heights for those who were displaced. Today, Elmwood Park has several sites with connections to black history, including a county park, located at Meeks and Dielman avenues, named for slain civil rights leader Martin Luther King, Jr.

Elmwood Elementary School ● 222

9707 Chicago Heights

Elmwood Elementary, a two-room brick building, was opened in 1915 for black students in the Ritenour School District. It closed in 1976 after a 1973 United States District Court decision, *Adams v. Richardson*, which required the Department of Health, Education and Welfare and the Office of Civil Rights to seek immediate desegregation of school districts. Of eleven Missouri districts cited by the court for possible discrimination, eight were in the St. Louis area. One of them was Ritenour, which had long operated Elmwood Elementary as a separate school for black students. The building was later used as a vocational preparatory school and now houses Christ Holiness Temple United Holy Church.

First Baptist Church of Elmwood Park ■ 223

1452 Dielman Road

First Baptist Church was established in 1900 after an inspirational prayer meeting at the home of Joe Davis, one of the first residents of Elmwood Park. Ministers from various local black churches, including Musick Baptist Church in Maryland Heights and Harrison Avenue Baptist Church in Kirkwood, helped to organize the new congregation. In 1901 the parishioners bought a lot at the west end of Meeks Avenue, where they built their first sanctuary. After the demolition of the old church building as part of the areawide urban renewal program, the congregation built a new sanctuary in the early 1970s, and an even larger one on the adjacent lot in 1985.

Overland

Lackland Avenue Colored School ⬭ 224

Lackland and Sims avenues

The Lackland Avenue Colored School, which opened in 1888, served not only students of the Ritenour School District in which it was located but also students from the Mount Pleasant and Wellston districts. In 1913, Ritenour became the first district in St. Louis County to offer high school courses to its black students when it added high school classes to Lackland. Washington Reed, one of the early black landowners in Breckenridge Hills, was a teacher.

In 1915, the school was closed and the elementary students were transferred to the Elmwood Elementary School, another school for blacks in the district. The high school program was dropped, but in April 1917 some black parents in the district asked the Board of Education to reinstate the high school classes. They were told to return a month later and present their request in writing. When black parents came back, the superintendent told them that the state had just adopted legislation that would establish a high school in Clayton for all black students in St. Louis County. That school, however, was never created. In 1922 the board agreed to pay tuition to send two black Elmwood Park students to high school in St. Louis. Six years later, the board voted to send black high school students from the district to Douglass High School in Webster Groves.

Maryland Heights

Musick Baptist Church ■ 225

790 Fee Fee Road

Musick Baptist Church was organized in 1811 after Eddy Musick, a white landowner, attended a prayer meeting held in his barn by his slaves. Musick was so moved by the prayers and the singing that he deeded his slaves a tract of land on which to build a church and set up a cemetery. The church was named "Musick" in honor of its benefactor. The current church building is of unknown date and has been remodeled many times. It is said to have a cornerstone dated 1924, but this is no longer visible. Over time, this church spawned offshoot congregations throughout the area: Creve Coeur Baptist Church, First Baptist of Elmwood Park, and Pilgrim Baptist in Richmond Heights.

Carver Elementary School ⬭ 226

2402 Adie Road

In 1951, the old Carver School for black students, located on Adie Road, was replaced by a new building on Magg Avenue. This new, two-room school, part of the Maryland Heights School District, served black students who had previously attended school in the Moore and Webster Groves districts. The school was named for George Washington Carver (1864?-1943), a prominent black botanist, agricultural chemist, and educator. Carver closed in 1962, and the students were transferred to the white Remington Elementary School in the Pattonville School District.

Creve Coeur

First Baptist Church of Creve Coeur ■ 227

1553 Creve Coeur Mill Road

First Baptist Church of Creve Coeur was organized in 1895 by the Reverend John Sibley. The original church building, located about one block north of the present church, was constructed on property donated to local black residents by landowner John Schacht, who also gave ten dollars toward the new building. The congregation purchased a new plot of land in 1941 and completed another building in 1946. In 1990, with a rapidly growing membership, the congregation dedicated a larger sanctuary on the same site.

Lake Colored School 228

Hog Hollow Road, between Olive Street Road and City Road

The one-room Lake Colored School served a small population of black students from around the turn of the century until 1955, when it was closed by the Parkway School District.

Breckenridge Hills

The Reed home and farm 229

Southeast corner of Rex and Breckenridge

Before the Civil War, a young black man named Washington Reed came to the area which is now Breckenridge Hills, where he rented and farmed land. After the war started, Reed enlisted in the Union Army on October 17, 1863, in Providence, Rhode Island. He served as a sergeant in "G" Company of the Eleventh Regiment, United States Colored Artillery, fought until the end of the war, and was honorably discharged in New Orleans in 1865.

Musick Baptist Church

Photo by David Schultz.

After the war, Reed returned to Missouri and married Belle Lackey. Seven children were born to them. During these years, the Reeds worked on rented farms and operated a dairy. Washington Reed also taught black children to read and write. By 1889, he had amassed enough money to pay $125 an acre for a forty-four-acre section of the Breckenridge Estate when it was auctioned off at the County Courthouse. This area is bounded by present-day Baltimore Avenue, West Milton, Breckenridge Avenue, and Quiet Lane.

Washington Reed died in 1915, leaving his property to his widow, Belle. Upon her death, the land passed to the Reed children, all of whom, except Carrie Reed Carter, subdivided and sold their holdings between 1948 and 1950. Some Reed descendants still live in Breckenridge Hills.

University City, Clayton, Richmond Heights, Frontenac

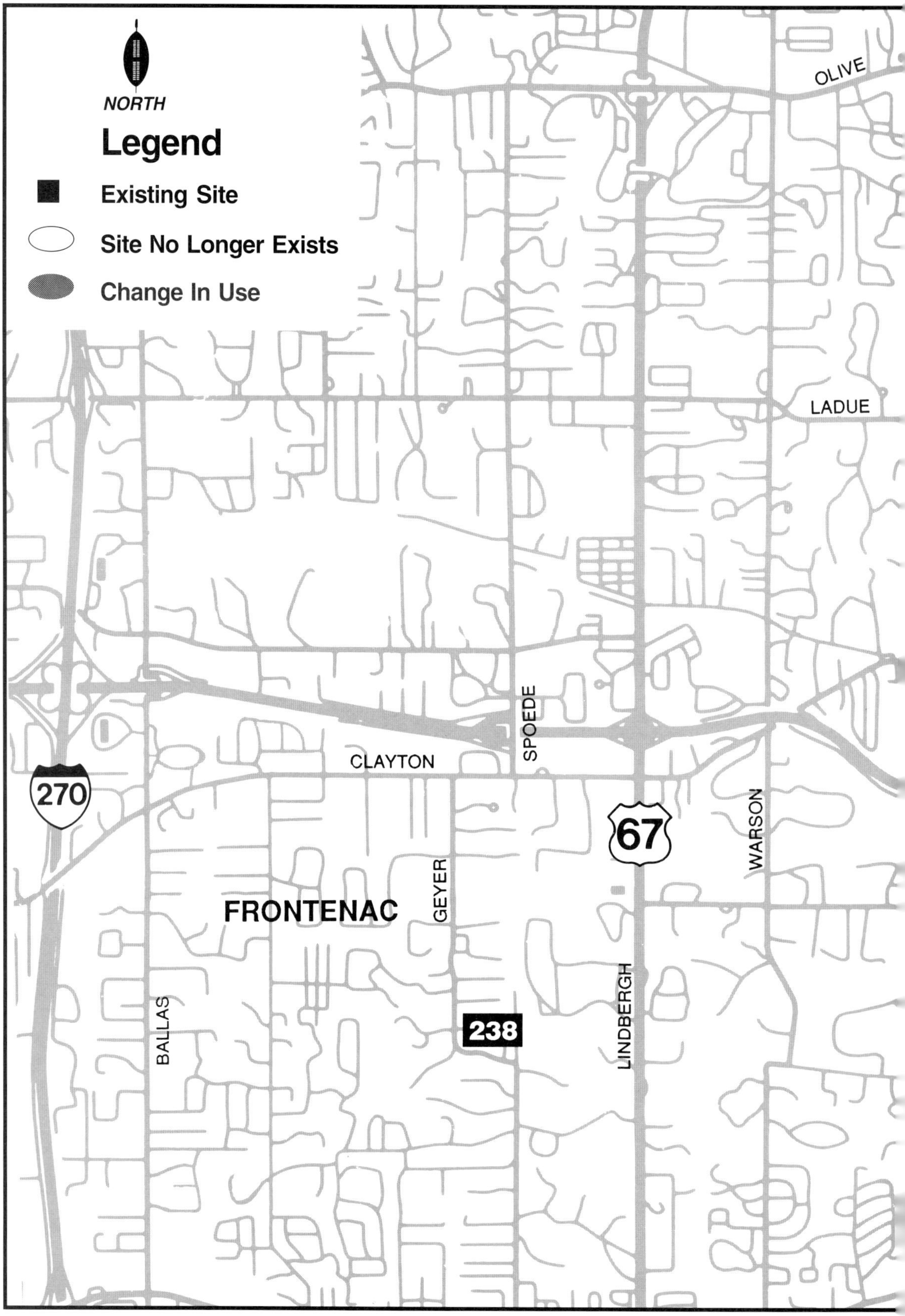

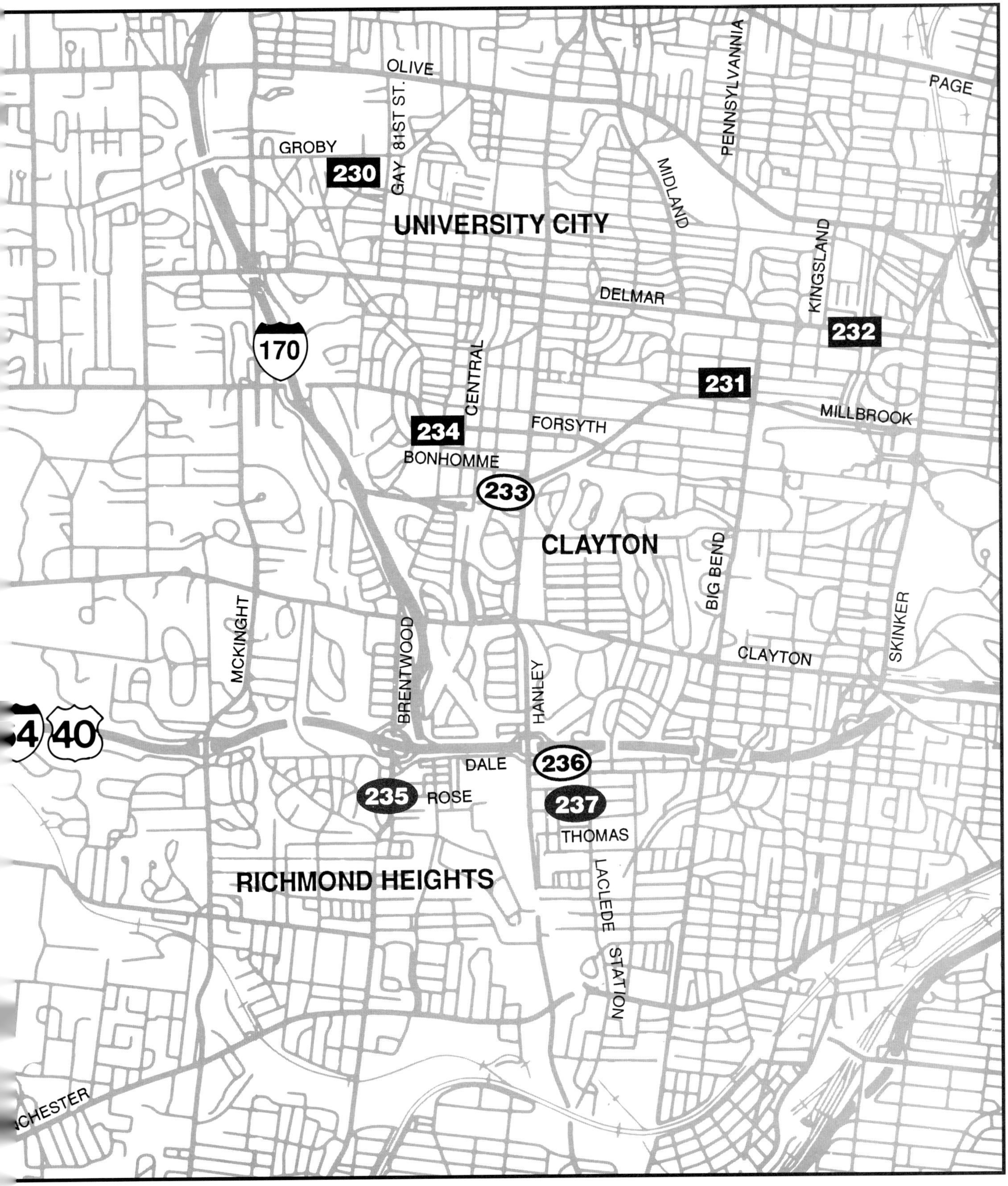
OLIVE
PAGE
GROBY
81ST ST.
GAY
230
PENNSYLVANNIA
MIDLAND
UNIVERSITY CITY
KINGSLAND
DELMAR
232
170
231
CENTRAL
MILLBROOK
234
FORSYTH
BONHOMME
233
CLAYTON
BIG BEND
MCKINGHT
BRENTWOOD
CLAYTON
SKINKER
HANLEY
40
DALE
236
235
ROSE
237
THOMAS
RICHMOND HEIGHTS
LACLEDE
STATION
CHESTER

University City, Clayton, Richmond Heights, Frontenac

Katherine Dunham's star

Photo by Lee Harris.

Josephine Baker's star

Photo by Lee Harris.

Miles Davis star and plaque on the St. Louis Walk of Fame

Photo courtesy of the St. Louis Walk of Fame.

University City, Clayton, Richmond Heights, Frontenac

Chapter 9

University City

McNair Sixth-Grade Center ■ 230

8125 Groby Road

During 1992-93, this school had 425 sixth-grade students; its curriculum emphasizes science. Previously known as Brittany Annex, it was renamed several years ago for Ronald McNair (1950-86), the African-American astronaut who lost his life when the space shuttle *Challenger* exploded. McNair, a South Carolina native, received a Ph.D. in physics from Massachusetts Institute of Technology in 1976. He was recognized nationally for his work in the field of laser physics. Selected from a pool of ten-thousand applicants for the astronaut program in 1978, he became the second black American to fly in space. He also received three honorary doctorates and a score of fellowships and commendations.

Santoro's Restaurant ■ 231

Corner of Big Bend and Millbrook Boulevards

This restaurant, now renamed Bernie Federko's, was the site of a 1959 sit-in by Washington University students, who were protesting its refusal to serve blacks. With the news that sit-in participants had been arrested on trespassing charges, a committee of concerned citizens formed to fight discrimination and push for passage of a public accommodation ordinance. In February 1960, the University City Council defeated the bill, but established a Human Relations Commission to promote racial and religious tolerance. University City finally approved a public accommodations bill in 1963, the first St. Louis County municipality to pass such legislation.

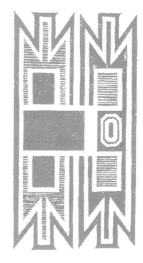

St. Louis Walk of Fame ■ 232

Delmar Boulevard, in the Loop area

This project, begun in 1988, commemorates famous St. Louisans with bronze stars and plaques set in the University City sidewalks. Each year, ten more names are chosen. Among the fifty selected so far are many prominent African Americans with local ties: writer Maya Angelou (1928-), singer Josephine Baker (1906-75), baseball great James "Cool Papa" Bell (1903–91), rock 'n' roll star Chuck Berry (1926-), opera star Grace Bumbry (1937-), dancer and choreographer Katherine Dunham (1910-), actor/comedian Redd Foxx (1922-91), ragtime musician Scott Joplin (1868-1917), musician Albert "Blues Boy" King (1923-92), gospel singer Willie Mae Ford Smith (1904-), and rock singer Tina Turner (1939-).

Chuck Berry with his Walk of Fame star

Photo by Wes Paz. Courtesy of the St. Louis Post-Dispatch.

Clayton

Attucks Elementary School ⬭ 233

Bonhomme Avenue and Hanley Boulevard

Attucks Elementary School, a one-room brick building with basement playrooms and manual training room, opened in 1923 to serve the black students in the Clayton School District. It took the place of a one-room frame building at Coleman Avenue, opened in 1893, which had been the first black school in the district. Attucks School had an average attendance of twenty-five students until it closed in 1954, when the Clayton schools were desegregated. The school was named for Crispus Attucks (1723?-1770), a black man, who died in the Boston Massacre of 1770.

St. Louis County Courthouse ■ 234

Central Avenue and Forsyth Boulevard

The old St. Louis County Courthouse, built in 1878, was connected to the adjoining jail by a second-floor corridor known as "the Bridge of Sighs," where condemned men were hanged. In July 1894, Harrison Duncan, an African American, was hanged from this bridge for killing James Brady, a police officer. While in jail, Duncan would often sing from his cell to crowds that gathered outside. On the afternoon before his death, he invited newspaper reporters into his cell, where he maintained his innocence. All he could hope for now, he said, was to meet death like a "true man." Before the reporters left, Duncan sang a final concert for them, including the songs "My Mother's Picture" and "Night to the Grave." A reporter later recalled that Duncan's voice sounded firm and could be heard beyond the courthouse itself.

At daybreak next morning, four hundred spectators gathered in the square outside to watch the hanging. R. Lee Mudd, the county's prosecuting attorney, was outspoken following Duncan's execution. "I say Duncan should never have been convicted of murder in the first degree. I say Duncan should never have been hanged." Duncan's hanging was memorialized in the folk song "Ballad of Brady and Duncan."

See also: Ballad of Brady and Duncan

Attucks Elementary School

Photo. Courtesy of Dr. John Wright.

Richmond Heights

L'Ouverture Elementary School ● 235

8616 Rose Avenue

L'Ouverture Elementary School, now closed, opened in 1925 to serve black students who had previously attended school in Webster Groves. The school was named for Pierre Dominique Toussaint L'Ouverture (1743-1803), a Haitian slave, who began an eleven-year slave rebellion in Saint Dominique that resulted in the establishment of Haiti as a black-governed French protectorate.

Old Lincoln Elementary School ⬭ 236

8023 Dale Avenue

This one-room school opened in 1909 for the black students in the Maplewood-Richmond Heights School District. The school's first teacher, Harvey J. Simms, named it for Lincoln Institute (now Lincoln University in Jefferson City). Before it became Lincoln Elementary, the school was known as the "Colored School on Dale." It was sold in 1955 and its students were transferred to New Lincoln Elementary School.

New Lincoln Elementary School

Photo by David Schultz.

New Lincoln Elementary School ● 237

7917 Thomas Place

New Lincoln was constructed in 1933 and used together with Old Lincoln for the education of black students in the Maplewood-Richmond Heights School District. Grades one, two, three, and four were housed in the Old Lincoln facility; kindergarten was added later. Grades five, six, and seven were housed in New Lincoln. New Lincoln was sold to the Special School District in 1964; the building has since changed hands and is currently vacant. The City of Richmond Heights hopes to convert it into a recreational facility.

Old Des Peres Meeting House and Cemetery

Photo by Lee Harris.

Old Des Peres Meeting House

Photo by David Schultz.

Frontenac

Old Des Peres Meeting House and Cemetery ■ 238

Geyer Road, south of Clayton Road

This Presbyterian church, built of stone in 1833, could hold one hundred worshipers. From 1833 to 1836, the Reverend Elijah Parish Lovejoy (1802–37) was its minister. The church, given the name "Old Stone Meeting House" by Yankee soldiers, was also used as a station on the Underground Railroad. Some slaves are buried in the adjoining cemetery, which was established at the same time as the church.

Webster Groves, Rock Hill, Crestwood, Kirkwood

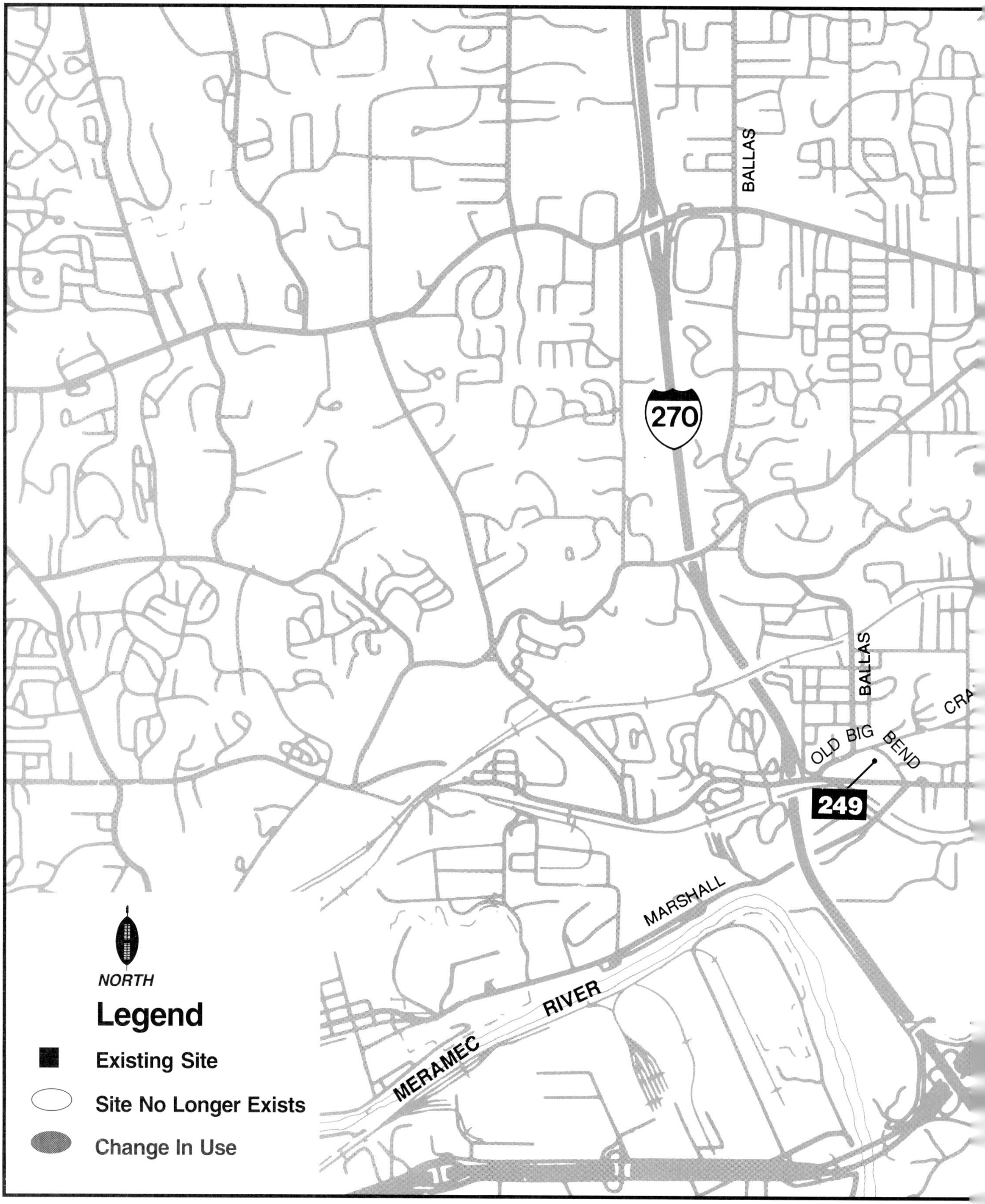

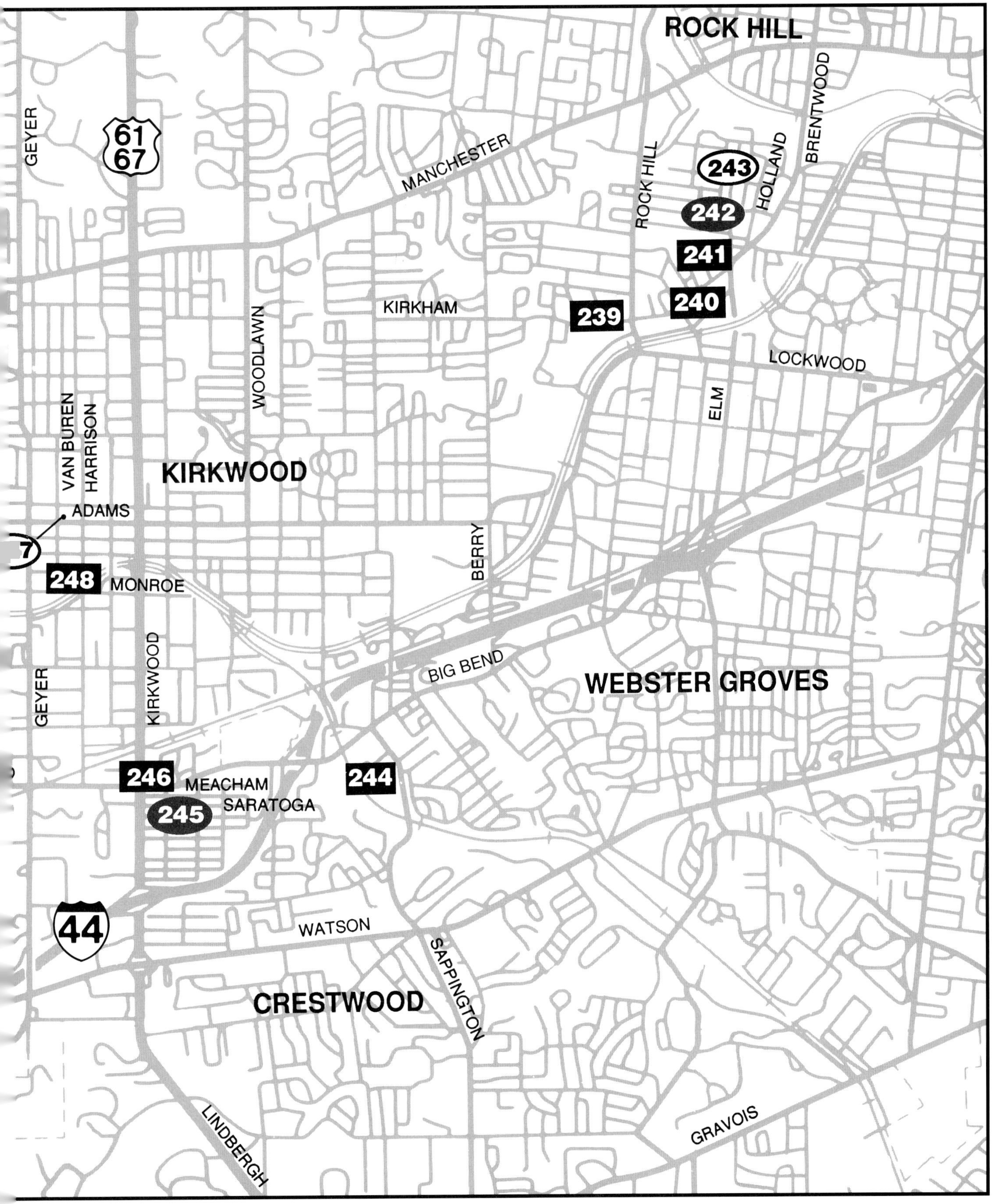
ROCK HILL
BRENTWOOD
HOLLAND
243
ROCK HILL
242
241
240
239
MANCHESTER
61
67
GEYER
KIRKHAM
LOCKWOOD
ELM
WOODLAWN
VAN BUREN
HARRISON
KIRKWOOD
ADAMS
248
MONROE
BERRY
BIG BEND
WEBSTER GROVES
GEYER
KIRKWOOD
246
MEACHAM
245
SARATOGA
244
44
WATSON
SAPPINGTON
CRESTWOOD
LINDBERGH
GRAVOIS

Webster Groves, Rock Hill, Crestwood, Kirkwood

Entrance to Olive Chapel African Methodist Episcopal Church

Photo by David Schultz.

Webster Groves, Rock Hill, Crestwood, Kirkwood

Chapter 10

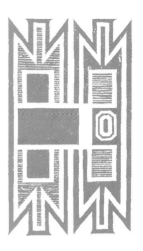

In 1804, Louis Bompart bought eleven hundred acres of timberland about eight miles west of the village of St. Louis and built a homestead near what is now 8700 Manchester Road. He was the first person in the area to own slaves. Other settlers in the area, John and James Marshall and John Marshall's parents-in-law, Thomas and Cynthia Berry, also owned slaves. Along with the Bompart slaves, they became the nucleus of Webster-Rock Hill's pre-Civil War black population. After the war, many freed blacks settled in what is today northern Webster Groves and southeastern Rock Hill. Some former slaves of the Berry and Marshall families were given tracts of land along Kirkham Road, then called Shady Avenue. Slave quarters once stood behind the Marshall house, a few lots from what is currently the southwest corner of Rock Hill and Manchester roads.

In 1845, the Marshall slaves helped build a nearby stone church (now the Rock Hill Presbyterian Church, Manchester and McKnight roads). They are said to have quarried the stone for the building and worked on Sundays to construct the roof as their special gift to the church. In 1858, four female slaves were part of the congregation.

As more blacks came to the area during the following decades, the area around Rock Hill Avenue and Kirkham became known as the "Old Community." African Americans continued to live all over Webster, but as more whites moved into the suburbs during the 1910s and 1920s, many blacks moved to north Webster Groves around their churches and the Douglass School.

Webster Groves

First Baptist Church of Webster Groves ■ 239

159 Kirkham Road

The First Baptist Church of Webster Groves, founded in 1866, was the first Baptist church, white or black, to be established in Webster Groves. The original church was on Kirkham Road near North Gore Avenue. Many members lived some distance from it, so in 1923 the congregation purchased property at 159 East Kirkham Road. When the new building was opened in 1929, part of the congregation chose to remain at the original location as the Old Community Baptist Church. A new sanctuary was completed in 1955, and in 1964 an addition was built over the Fellowship Hall.

See also: Old Community Baptist Church

First Baptist Church of Webster Groves

Photo. Courtesy of the Western Historical Manuscript Collection, University of Missouri–St. Louis.

Old Community Baptist Church

Photo. Courtesy of the Western Historical Manuscript Collection, University of Missouri–St. Louis.

Blackwell Chapel African Methodist Episcopal Zion Church

Photo by David Schultz.

Old Community Baptist Church ■ 240

238 West Kirkham Road

In 1929, a group of former members of the congregation retained the original building of the First Baptist Church and renamed it Old Community Baptist Church.

See also: First Baptist Church of Webster Groves

Blackwell Chapel African Methodist Episcopal Zion Church ■ 241

511 North Elm Avenue

The Blackwell Chapel traces its beginnings to 1889, when members worshiped in a little storefront church on Gore and Moody avenues. The church later moved to Kirkham Road and, in 1916, to its present location.

Douglas Manor Apartments, formerly Douglass Elementary School

Photo by David Schultz.

Douglass Elementary School • 242

546 North Elm Avenue

In 1866, Emma Babcock, a white woman, began classes for African-American children in the First Baptist Church on Kirkham Road. The Webster School Board, established in 1868, soon took over administration of the school and appointed its first black teacher, T. A. Bush, in 1871. With a growing number of students, the school moved in 1872 to a one-room cabin just west of the church. When this building burned down in 1890, a new school was erected in 1892 on Holland Avenue between Fox and Ravine. In 1895, it was renamed for Frederick Douglass (1817?-1895), the prominent black abolitionist. Born a slave in Talbot County, Maryland, Douglass secretly taught himself to read and later escaped from his owner. He became a leading orator, writer, and editor, fighting not only for black rights but for the rights of all the oppressed.

The new Douglass Elementary School on North Elm was dedicated in 1947; the old building remained as the Douglass High School. In 1967, Douglass became the first of two integrated demonstration schools in the Webster School District. In 1978, when enrollment in the district decreased, Douglass Elementary was closed. It was refurbished in 1983 as the Douglass Manor Apartments, a forty-one-unit subsidized housing complex for older adults and disabled families. The cafeteria area of the old school was renovated and named the Howard B. Goins Community Center; Goins was the principal of Douglass Elementary and High School for thirty-one years.

Douglass High School

Photo. Courtesy of Dr. John Wright.

Douglass High School and recreation field ○ 243

Holland Avenue

Before 1925, black Webster Groves students went on to Sumner High School for further studies; afterwards, rooms were added to Douglass Elementary for a new high school program. By 1928 a complete high school curriculum had been established there. A library was also added to the school, and it was used by residents and students alike.

Douglass was the only black high school in the county until 1938, when Kinloch High School opened for the black students of the Kinloch School District. Until 1954, when all schools were desegregated after the United States Supreme Court decision, Douglass remained the only accredited high school for blacks in St. Louis County. Students came from throughout the 497-square-mile area of the county and beyond.

By 1947, the building had become too crowded for all its programs, and a new elementary school was built on North Elm. The old building remained as the Douglass High School until it was demolished in 1956. Several single-family homes were constructed on the site in the 1980s.

Crestwood

Father Dickson Cemetery ■ 244

845 South Sappington Road

Father Dickson Cemetery was founded in 1903 and named for the Reverend Moses Dickson (1824-1901), the black abolitionist. As president of the Colored Refugee Relief Board in 1878, Dickson helped relocate thousands of former slaves, who were moving to the West from southern states. He was originally buried in St. Peter's Cemetery in Normandy, but in 1903 his body was moved to Father Dickson Cemetery. In 1915, a monument to Dickson was erected in the cemetery; it bears the names of all the states that took in the black refugees.

Among those buried in the cemetery is James Milton Turner (1839?-1915), who led the fight for free public education of Missouri blacks, helped organize the Missouri Equal Rights League in 1865, campaigned throughout the state for the rights of blacks to vote, and served as consul general to Liberia from 1871 to 1878.

Kirkwood

There are records of African-American residents, both free and slave, in the Kirkwood area from before the Civil War. Following the war, some blacks stayed on to form the nucleus of a community near the business district, particularly along East Argonne Avenue, a settlement known as "Kentucky Town." Others spread out within the town limits. Descendants of these early settlers are an integral part of the community today.

Three street names in Kirkwood bear witness to the importance of African Americans in the community: Bouyer Street, a short street off the 300 block of South Fillmore, named for the Bouyer family, who came to the area as slaves in 1830; Whitsun Street, running parallel to Fillmore from East Clinton, named for Arthur Whitsun, president of the first

Civic Club among Kirkwood blacks; and Del Reed, off Harrison, named for the owner of a drayage business in Kirkwood.

Black people moved into Meacham Park, then an unincorporated area of St. Louis County adjacent to Kirkwood, in the early 1900s. Although today the area is predominantly black, it was a racially mixed community after World War I. Though some people mistakenly assume that Meacham Park was named for John Berry Meachum, it was actually named for a white man who purchased the area in 1904. In November 1991, voters in both Kirkwood and Meacham Park approved annexation of Meacham Park by Kirkwood; the area was annexed in May 1992. Streets in this area are named for such prominent African Americans as Crispus Attucks and W. C. Handy.

James Milton Turner Elementary School ● 245

245 Saratoga Avenue

At the turn of the century, black children in Meacham Park went to the Booker T. Washington School in Kirkwood. In 1911, after several years of petitioning the Kirkwood School Board, the black residents of Meacham Park obtained a school for their children, which opened in a rented building. The school was closed in 1921, but a new building on Saratoga Avenue was opened in 1925 as the Meacham Park Elementary School. In 1932, the school's name was changed to honor James Milton Turner (1839?-1915), a black educator and civil rights leader, born in St. Louis County. Population shifts led to the closing of the Booker T. Washington School in 1950, and all black students were sent to the James Milton Turner Elementary School. The school building currently houses five private businesses.

First Baptist Church of Meacham Park ■ 246

304 Meacham Street

In 1900, a few Meacham Park families began holding Friday night prayer meetings and Sunday afternoon services in their homes. Five years later, the Reverend Hill, pastor of Compton Hill Baptist Church in St. Louis, came to the aid of the fledgling congregation. He preached at their services and urged them to build a rough, brushwood shelter at Saratoga and Shelby avenues for their services. After a few months, Hill left and the "brush harbor" came down, though the prayer meetings continued in members' homes.

In June 1907, the Reverend J. A. Jackson became pastor and the congregation officially incorporated as a church. During the same year they built their first sanctuary; in the 1960s it was replaced by a new sanctuary.

Booker T. Washington Elementary School ⬭ 247

Adams Avenue between Harrison and Van Buren avenues

In 1867, the Kirkwood School District rented space in a church for the education of local black children. A temporary building, in the area of Adams Avenue and Geyer Road, opened in 1869, and night school classes for adults were added in 1874-75. Richard Hudlin, who later became Clayton's first postmaster, was appointed the school's first black teacher in 1878 and principal in 1879. The school, which was renamed the Booker T. Washington Elementary School in 1908, was demolished in 1914, and portable buildings were erected to replace it.

The school closed in 1950 and its students were sent to James Milton Turner School. Some parents protested and tried to enroll their children at white schools; later in the year, they brought suit against the Kirkwood District because it had failed to provide equal facilities.

Olive Chapel African Methodist Episcopal Church

Photo by David Schultz.

Olive Chapel window

Photo by David Schultz.

Olive Chapel African Methodist Episcopal Church ■ 248

301 South Harrison Avenue at Monroe Avenue

Olive Chapel, the second church founded in Kirkwood, was organized and built in 1853 at 330 West Washington. For many years, a circuit rider served the congregation. In 1867, the church was the site of Kirkwood's first public school for blacks. In 1923, the congregation moved to the former Friedens Evangelical Lutheran Church, dating from 1896, at the corner of Monroe and Harrison.

Other early African-American churches in the area were the Rose Hill Baptist Church (First Baptist Church) organized in 1870; the Second Baptist Church at Taylor and Monroe (now the Unity Baptist Church at 328 South Taylor), organized in 1878; and the Harrison Avenue Baptist Church (now the Harrison Missionary Baptist Church), 355 Harrison, organized in 1880.

Quinette Cemetery ■ 249

Ballas Road and Old Big Bend Boulevard

The first recorded owner of this property was Luke Brockway, who allowed his slaves, and others in the area, to use this piece of land as a cemetery. He sold the property in 1866 to William Martin, Henry Nash, and George Sleet. In 1873, Olive Chapel African Methodist Episcopal Church in Kirkwood acquired title to the 2.7-acre property. There are no official records of burials, partly because many of those interred were indigents. The cemetery is believed to be the site of more than one hundred graves. The most recent burial was in 1973.

Quinette Cemetery

Photo by David Schultz.

Ballwin, Chesterfield

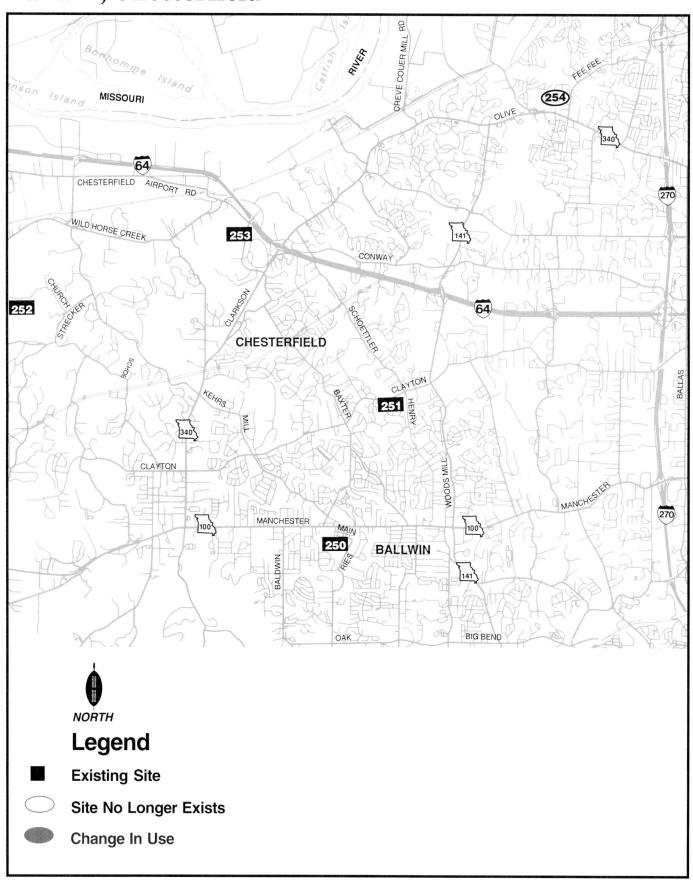

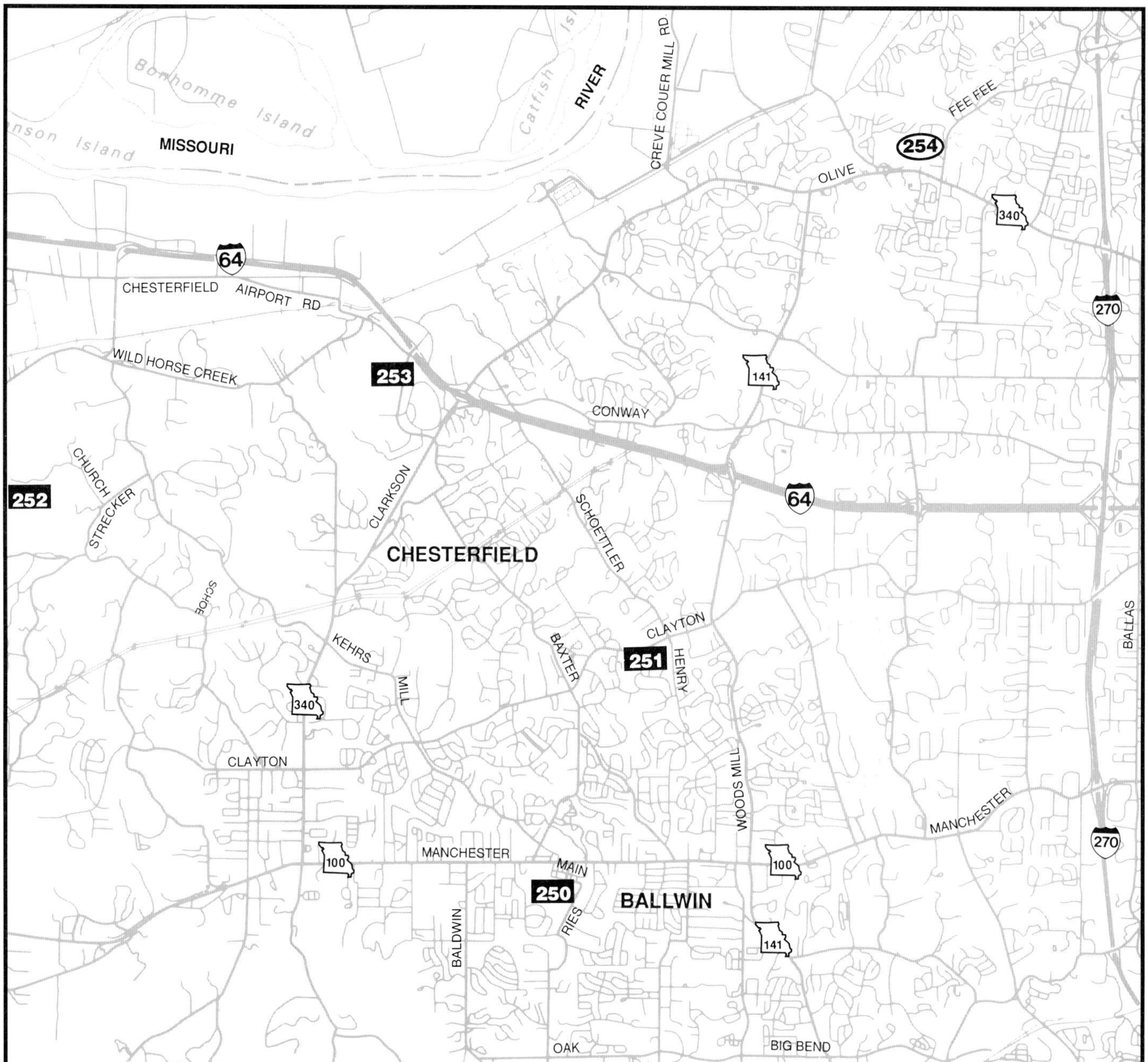

NORTH

Legend

■ Existing Site

Site No Longer Exists

Change In Use

Ballwin, Chesterfield

Chapter 11

First Baptist Church of Ballwin

Photo by David Schultz.

Ballwin

First Baptist Church of Ballwin ■ 250

302 Main Street at Ries Road

According to St. Louis County records, First Baptist is the oldest Baptist church west of the Mississippi River. The corner on which the church stands was once an agricultural center and slave-trading post. The church was organized early in the first decade of the 1800s, when the town of Ballwin was still a wilderness. In 1832, Judge Higgins of Ballwin issued an order to permit the congregation to build a house of worship.

Before that time, harassment from vigilantes had kept the black congregation from meeting openly for worship. Church members are said to have gathered in a grape arbor and hidden under iron pots to keep their voices from being overheard. They even strung ropes and wire fencing around the prayer area to deter horseback-riding vigilantes just long enough for the worshipers to slip safely away.

Chesterfield

Ballwin Colored Cemetery ■ 251

Off Clayton Road just west of Henry Road and Schoettler Road

The 2.55-acre Ballwin Colored Cemetery is shown in the 1909 county atlas as the "African Cemetery." In 1989, the title to the property was deeded to the First Baptist Church of Ballwin by the trustees of the Ballwin Cemetery Company.

Union Baptist Church in Westland Acres

Photo by David Schultz.

Westland Acres Colored School

Photo. Courtesy of Dr. John Wright.

Westland Acres ■ 252

17033 Church Road

The area known recently as Westland Acres and earlier as "the Hill," straddles Chesterfield and an unincorporated area of St. Louis County. It is named for former slave William West who, with his wife Pollie, purchased approximately 343 acres in 1868 from pioneer settler Norris Long, for whom Long Road is named. More than fifty West family members still live in Westland Acres, which currently consists of 141 acres. Area residents are working to bring county water and sewer lines into the community.

The Union Baptist Church in Westland Acres is a family church, built in 1984 to replace a 1921 church that was destroyed by fire. Near the church is the West-Gumbo Cemetery, now known as John W. West Cemetery, which contains about thirty graves from several generations of the West family.

Also located in the community is an old one-room schoolhouse once operated by the Rockwood School District for black students. A later school, built in 1952, stands near the entrance to the old schoolhouse. It is a two-room concrete-block building with two classrooms, a playroom, and a kitchen. When the United States Supreme Court handed down its desegregation decision in 1954, the board decided not to complete the school since it would eventually be closed. Thus, brick facing was never added as planned. Black elementary students continued to attend the school until 1963, when Westland Acres parents petitioned the Board to close the school and integrate the students into other schools in the system.

First Baptist Church of Chesterfield ■ 253

16396 Chesterfield Airport Road

First Baptist Church was organized on its present site in 1856. Slaveholder Mary Long gave the church property to the founding members of the congregation, but it did not officially become theirs until 1875. The church was originally built to serve as a school and a church. The present structure was completed in 1975.

Stafford Colored School ⬭ 254

Fee Fee Road north of Olive Street Road

The Stafford Colored School in the Moore School District (now a part of the Parkway School District) opened around the turn of the century, serving students both from the immediate vicinity and from neighboring communities. The school closed in 1946 and the building became a residence. Its students were sent to Webster Groves on a tuition basis.

First Baptist Church of Chesterfield

Photo by David Schultz.

Stafford Colored School

Photo. Courtesy of Dr. John Wright.

St. Charles

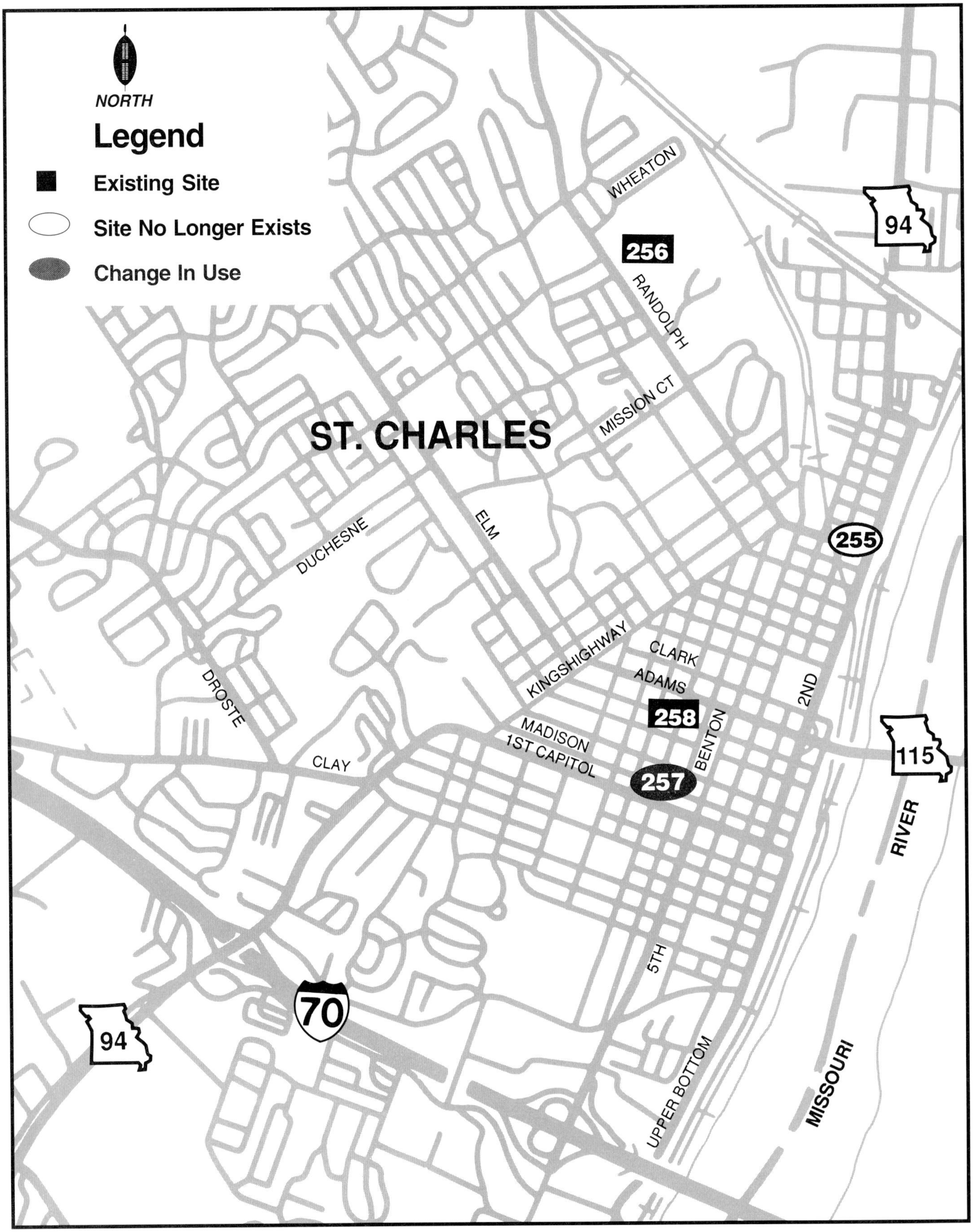
NORTH
Legend
Existing Site
Site No Longer Exists
Change In Use
ST. CHARLES
WHEATON
256
RANDOLPH
MISSION CT
94
ELM
DUCHESNE
255
KINGSHIGHWAY
CLARK
ADAMS
2ND
DROSTE
258
MADISON
1ST CAPITOL
BENTON
115
CLAY
257
RIVER
5TH
70
94
UPPER BOTTOM
MISSOURI

Les Petites Côtes (the Little Hills), or St. Charles, was settled by Louis Blanchette in 1769. French immigrants followed. By the early 1800s, the population of the village of St. Charles listed a number of slaves. Free blacks, such as Jean Baptiste Point Du Sable, also lived there.

Jean Baptiste Point Du Sable home

Photo. Courtesy of Dr. John Wright.

Jean Baptiste Point Du Sable home 255

701 North Second Street

A stone house, once on this site, was built in 1797 by Pierre Rodin, a free black. He subsequently sold it to Jean Baptiste Point Du Sable, who in 1806 deeded the property to Alexander McNair (1775-1826), elected Missouri's first governor in 1820. The house was torn down in 1929.

Du Sable (1745-1818) was a Haitian-born fur trader of French and African descent, who in the 1770s became the first non-Native American settler of the Chicago area. Du Sable returned to St. Charles in 1800. A prosperous man, he purchased farm lands and other property. All of his local holdings were transferred to a granddaughter upon her assurance that he would be buried in the St. Charles Borromeo Church cemetery. The Du Sable Museum of African-American History in Chicago's Washington Park area was named for Du Sable.

See also: St. Charles Borromeo Church Cemetery

African Methodist Episcopal Church

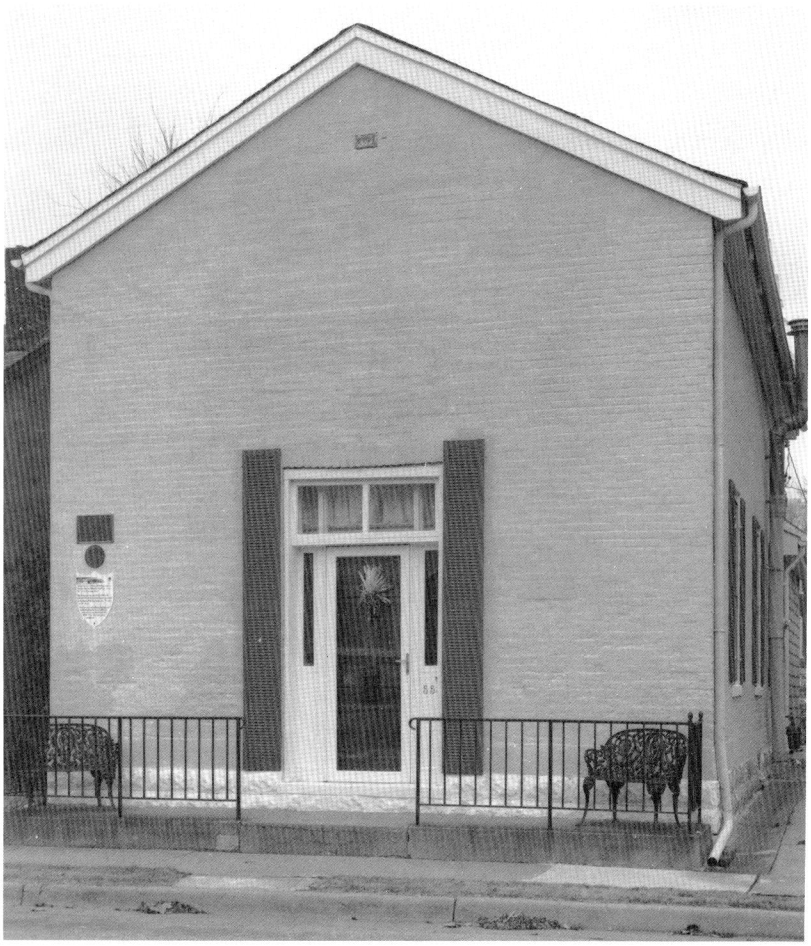

Photo by David Schultz.

St. Charles Borromeo Church Cemetery ■ 256

West Randolph Street between South Wheaton Drive and Mission Court

Jean Baptiste Point Du Sable died in August 1818 and was buried in the St. Charles Borromeo Church Cemetery, at that time located on South Main Street. His grave was moved to the cemetery on Randolph Street. On October 26, 1968, a contingent of more than one hundred people, many from Illinois, watched Chicago Auxiliary Bishop Michael Dempsey, St. Louis Auxiliary Bishop George Gottwald, and St. Charles Borromeo pastor Father Michael P. Owens dedicate a large marble stone commemorating Du Sable as founder of Chicago. The stone was then placed in the old section of the cemetery.

See also: Jean Baptiste Point Du Sable home

African Methodist Episcopal Church ● 257

554 Madison Street

In 1855, Jeremiah Fletcher Riggs purchased the land on which this building now sits and sold it to seven white trustees for one hundred dollars so that a church could be erected for blacks and mulattos. The parishioners were most likely the slaves of St. Charles mayor Ludwell Powell and other landowners in the area. After the Civil War, the seven original trustees signed over the land to five black trustees for one dollar. The congregation built the existing church by hand with bricks they had made. This building was used until 1868, when a larger building was constructed on Washington Street. In 1874, the old church was sold to the Union Benevolent Society, a black religious organization, and in 1947 it was converted into a private residence. It was designated a state landmark and placed on the National Register of Historic Places in 1982.

Mount Zion Baptist Church

Photo by David Schultz.

Church cornerstone

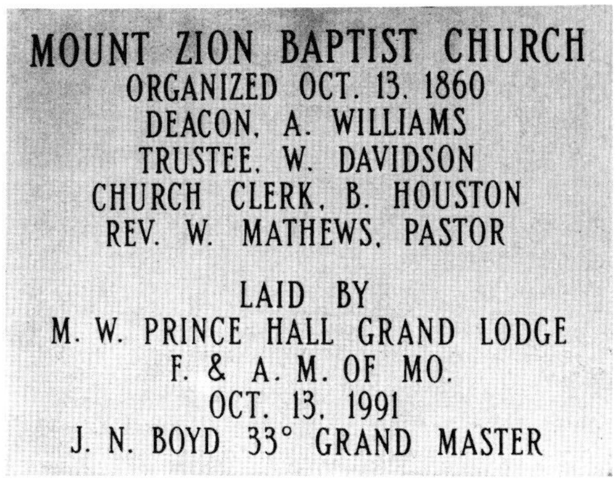

MOUNT ZION BAPTIST CHURCH
ORGANIZED OCT. 13. 1860
DEACON. A. WILLIAMS
TRUSTEE. W. DAVIDSON
CHURCH CLERK. B. HOUSTON
REV. W. MATHEWS. PASTOR
LAID BY
M. W. PRINCE HALL GRAND LODGE
F. & A. M. OF MO.
OCT. 13. 1991
J. N. BOYD 33° GRAND MASTER

Photo by Lee Harris.

Mount Zion Baptist Church ■ 258

520 North Benton

The Mount Zion Baptist Church was organized in 1860 after Lydia Lewis, brought from Virginia as a slave and later freed by her owners, gathered other blacks together for home prayer meetings. This congregation formed a church under the direction of its first pastor, Father Wills, and secured a building at Fifth and Pike. In 1896, the church moved to 427 Clay (now First Capitol Drive). Later, the church moved to its present location and the building on Clay was demolished.

East St. Louis, Illinois

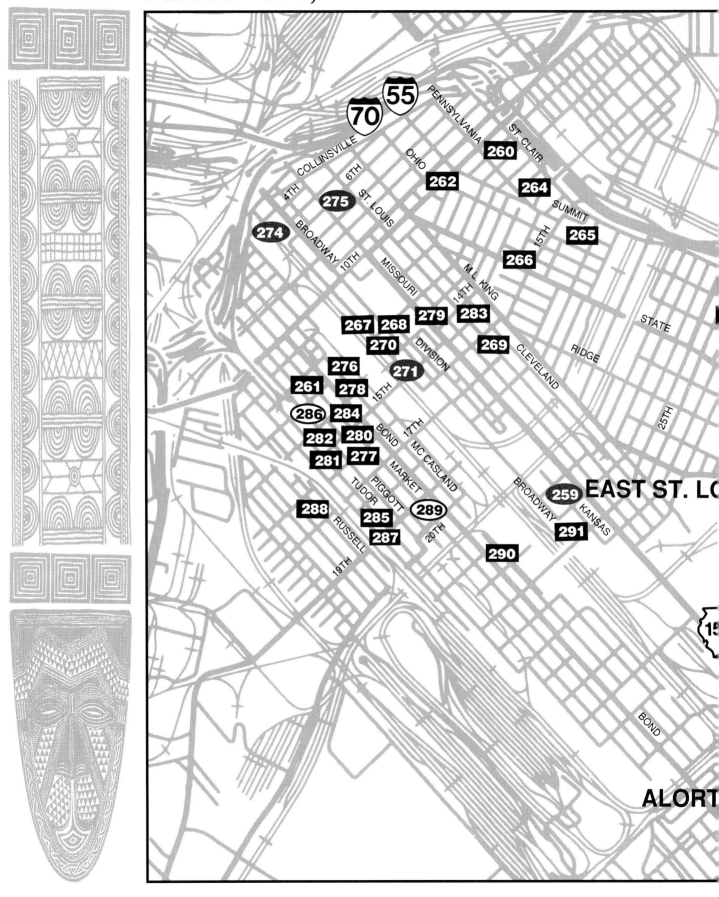

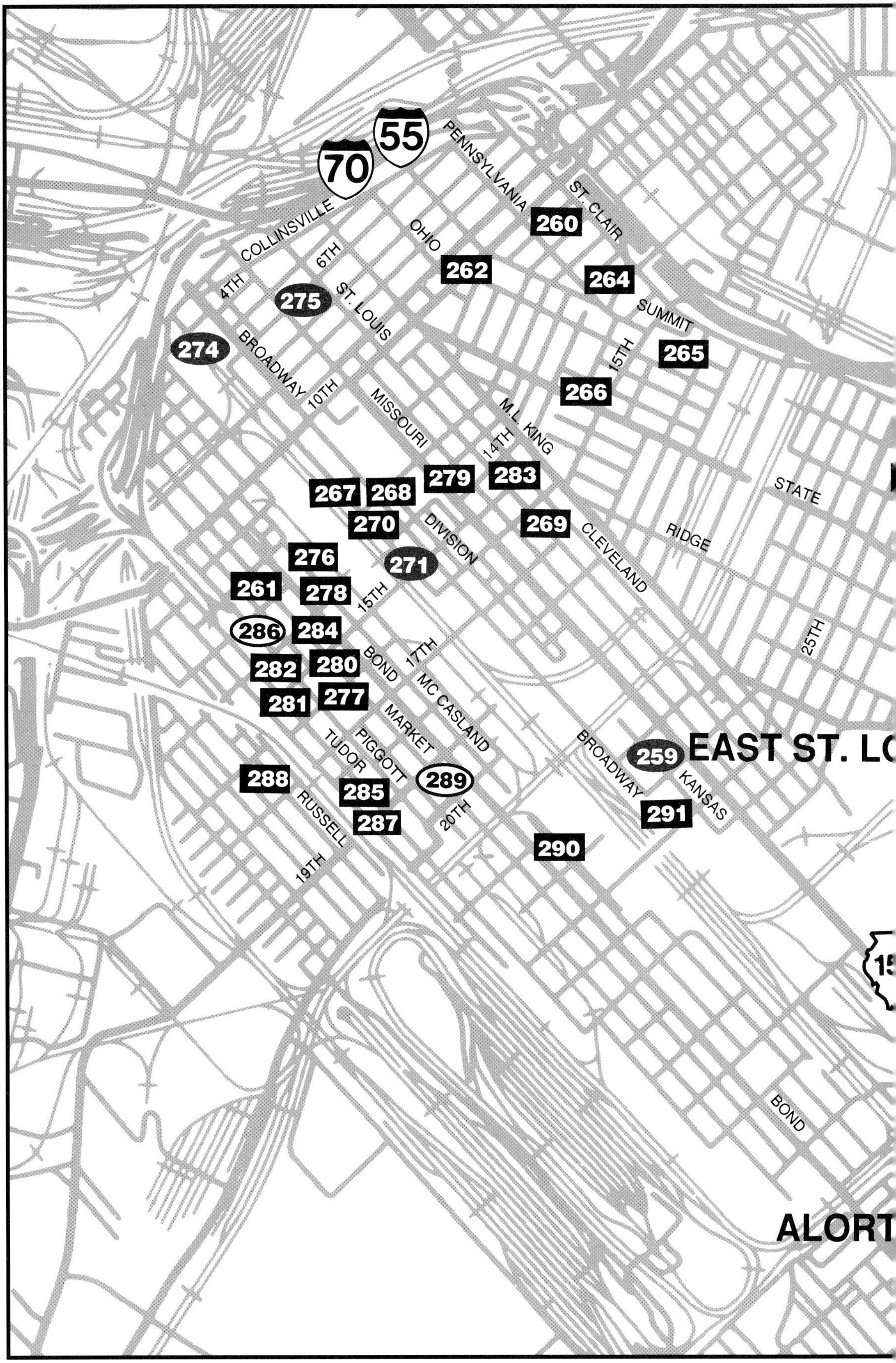

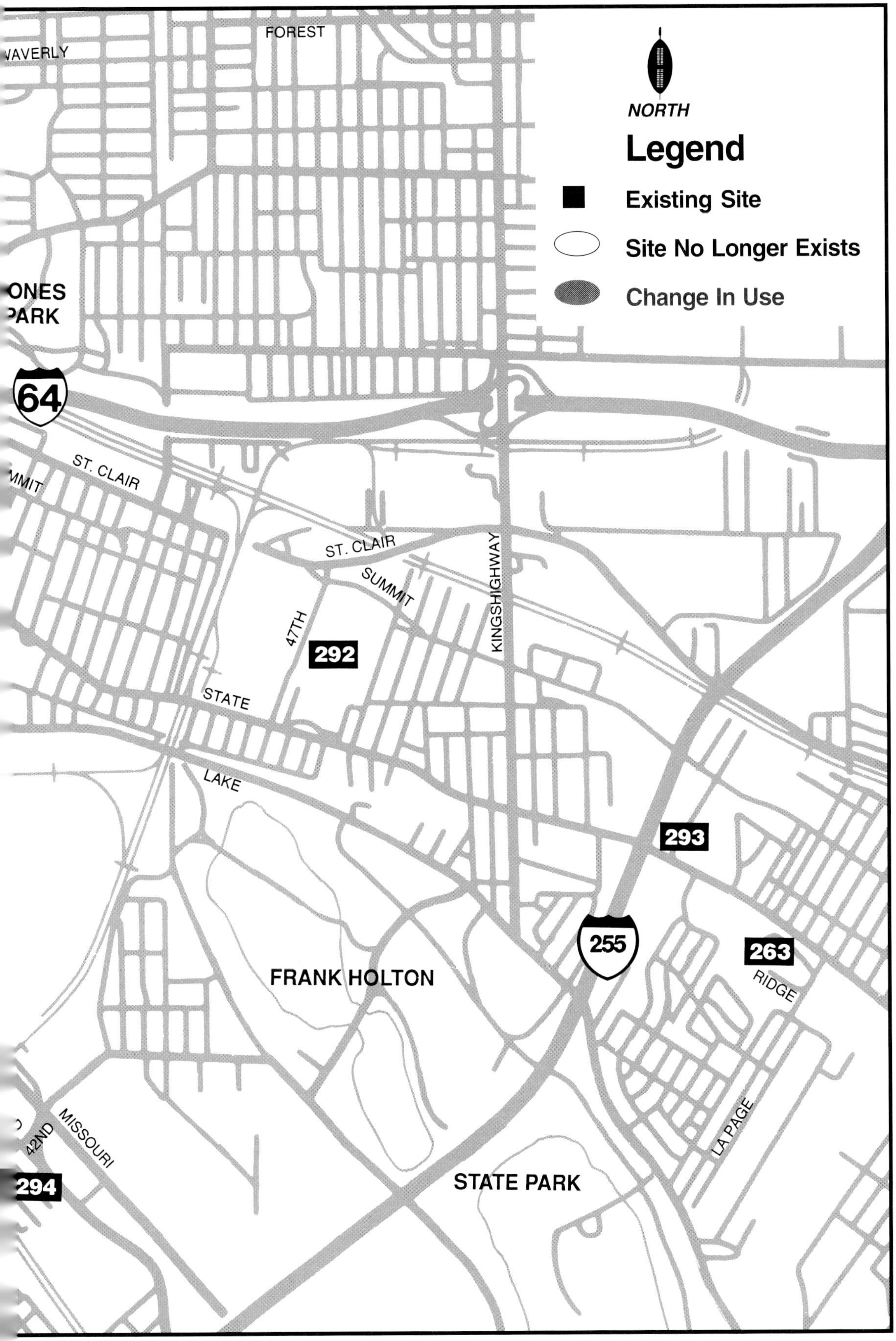
FOREST
WAVERLY
NORTH
Legend
Existing Site
Site No Longer Exists
Change In Use
JONES PARK
64
ST. CLAIR
SUMMIT
ST. CLAIR
SUMMIT
KINGSHIGHWAY
47TH
292
STATE
LAKE
293
255
263
RIDGE
FRANK HOLTON
STATE PARK
LA PAGE
42ND
MISSOURI
294

East St. Louis, Illinois

Katherine Dunham Museum entrance

Photo by Lee Harris.

East St. Louis, Illinois

Chapter 13

The area that later became East St. Louis was still forest and prairie land when Richard McCarthy, the first white settler, arrived in 1765. In 1808, Illinoistown was established on the site; East St. Louis was chartered in 1865. The first African Americans are thought to have arrived on the east side of the river after 1720. For decades, free Illinois was a land of hope for blacks escaping from slavery in Missouri.

Until World War I, blacks lived for the most part undisturbed in East St. Louis, though they were relegated to the lowest rung of the occupational ladder. They were also expected to conform to a rigorous system of racial segregation. In the large factories they had separate washrooms and dressing rooms, they often worked in segregated labor gangs, and they ate meals in "the colored section" of the lunchrooms. Black children went to "black schools," even though an 1874 Illinois law prohibited a racially segregated school system. Though the Illinois legislature passed one of the country's first public accommodations acts in 1885, public places in East St. Louis—theaters, restaurants, and hotels—ignored it.

By 1910, six thousand blacks lived in East St. Louis. Seven years later, the black population had grown to more than ten thousand, as blacks from the South poured into the city, seeking jobs that they could not find at home. With this influx, the white population felt increasingly nervous and resentful. In July 1917, the tenuous peace that had existed between the races suddenly ended as East St. Louis erupted in a tragic race riot. For decades afterwards, a legacy of death, guilt, and fear haunted the city.

Yet East St. Louis has survived and produced many outstanding individuals: Donald McHenry (1936-), United States representative to the United Nations under President Jimmy Carter (1924-); Jackie Joyner-Kersee (1962-), Olympic Gold Medal winner; Miles Davis (1926-91), internationally known musician. Lincoln high school's jazz band and East St. Louis High School's football team are nationally recognized.

Today, African Americans comprise 98 percent of the East St. Louis population and hold key offices in education and government. Schools and other institutions bear the names of such black leaders as Nelson Mandela (1918-), Martin Luther King, Jr. (1929-68), Crispus Attucks (1750?-70), Paul Laurence Dunbar (1872-1906), and Clyde C. Jordan, Sr. (1930-87). Many churches that served as a refuge for local blacks when they were excluded from area facilities still play a major role in the community today.

East St. Louis *Crusader* newspaper

A humanitarian

A Great Day In St. Louis

The second Annual Dr. Martin Luther King, Jr. Memorial Benefit Program will be held at Powell Symphony Hall on January 15, 1973 at 6:00 p.m. The program, a spectacular musical, will feature outstanding choirs, instrumental groups and recording artists. Among some of these will be the O'Neal Twins, Martha Bass, Interfaith Choir, Austin Layne, Rev. Cleophus Robinson, Lee Scott Singers, The Alvin Major Messenger Singers and many more.

Recipients of presentations will be Herman Davis, the young high school athlete who was paralyzed from injuries suffered during a football game. Herman is to be transported by ambulance to the program from Jewish Hospital. Also to receive a presentation will be Mrs. Helen Warnecke, the widow of the slain Police Officer, Harold Warnecke along with Wilma Chestnut.

Among recipients of the Dr. Martin Luther King Award plaques will be Mayor A.J. Cervantes, the late Austin Wright (posthumously) Mrs. David P. Wohl and Norman Seay.

A special segment of the program will be presented by the HDC Ensemble in honor of the late Austin Wright.

Also bronze recording awards will be presented to radio stations and artist who helped popularize the Dr. King Funds theme song, "I HAVE A DREAM". A limited number of tickets are available for this event at several local churches and record shops in the city. You may also call 531-8919 for additional ticket information.

All companies, organizations or persons wishing to contribute to this non profit effort may send checks or money orders to: Dr. Martin Luther King, Jr. Memorial Fund of St. Louis, 2850 N. Grand Blvd., St. Louis, Mo. 63107.

Some of the projects supported by the King Memorial Fund are the Dr. King Student Aid Fund (Junior College District), Feed the Hungry Program (Progressive Baptist), Sickle Cell Anemia Foundation (St. Louis Chapter), Youth Job Placement and Counseling Service, and the Distribution of Christmas Boxes to the needy.

Tickets are available on a first come first serve basis. Anyone having items to exhibit or sell which pertain to the memory of Dr. King, should send the information to the Memorial Fund Office, 2850 N. Grand Blvd., or call 531-8919.

All churches and organizations which help us in this effort will be recognized in the newspaper the following week.

Lorraine Harris, Public Relations; Rev. Willie E. Harris, Executive Director

"I have a dream"

Only 15¢ The CRUSADER

Vol. 31 — East St. Louis, Ill., Thursday, January 11, 1973 — No. 41

Announced candidates for township supervisor

Will McGaughey

Charles Merritts, Sr.

Francis Foley

Three persons have announced their candidacy for the East St. Louis township supervisor's office in the April elections. They are Will McGaughy, dir-

189 Board of Education; and Francis "Red" Foley, incumbent supervisor and chairman of the St. Clair County Board.

their candidacy in January, 1973. No formal petition has

actually been filed by any of the announced candidates. The fil-

Council discusses Phase II

Mayor Williams has announced that the City's Fourth Action Year Planned Variations Program has been approved. The program grant of 5.833 million dollars provides for a combination of the Fourth Action Year of the Model Cities Program and Second Action Year of the Planned Variations Program.

The Planned Variations modification of the Model Cities Program has permitted the City to expand Model Cities services to the whole City through an additional 3.8 million dollar anual grant to its normal 2.083 million dollar grant under Model Cities. Planned Variation was instituted under the Nixon Administration to test the concept of Federal revenue sharing.

In addition to more funding and City wide programming, Planned Variations has imple-

matching the funding of both programs, the City sought to maximize employment, training and public services.

(4) Industrial Development: The plan provides for continuation of the Industrial development Dept. of the City and Ascending Citizens Development Corporation. These units are respectively now involved in administering the City's Industrial Park project (this project was funded in the first year of Planned Variations and has not yet been completed) and assisting in development of small businesses through loans and technical assistance.

(5) Education: A high priority component of the plan will be to assist School District 189 in expanding its vocational education program. The plan, as well, seeks to improve school

Katherine Dunham Museum

Photo by Lee Harris.

The *East St. Louis Crusader* newspaper ● 259

2206 Missouri Avenue

In February 1941, John M. Kirkpatrick started a newspaper, the *East St. Louis Crusader*, in the basement of his home. Several years later, the paper moved to new quarters at Fourth and Missouri, then in the mid-1950s to its Missouri Avenue location. As the newspaper grew, Joe Weathers Lewis, Sr. (1939-), became the editor. It was one of the largest weekly black newspapers in southern Illinois during the 1970s. In 1980, because of declining advertising revenue, the paper ceased publication. The Crusader Publishing Company still operates at Tenth and State; it is the second largest black printing company in the country.

Katherine Dunham Museum ■ 260

1005 Pennsylvania Avenue

Katherine Dunham (1910-), world-renowned performer, choreographer, and teacher, attended the University of Chicago, where she studied anthropology. With the help of a Rosenwald Fellowship, she did further research in the Caribbean and in Brazil. In 1931, she founded her first school for the study of black Caribbean dance in Chicago, then began her own professional dance career three years later. She came to East St. Louis in 1967 as a faculty member at Southern Illinois University, where she founded a performing arts training center and created a curriculum in dance anthropology. Among her many awards and honorary degrees, she was named a Haitian Legion of Honor and Merit Chevalier in 1950.

In the late 1970s, a group of supporters formed a "friends" organization and acquired a Victorian mansion on Pennsylvania Avenue to serve as the Katherine Dunham Museum. She added the term "dynamic" to the title, to indicate the museum's vitality. In her autobiography, she wrote:

> A museum is one of the concrete expressions of a city's interest in art. I think it's terribly important for both the young and the old people of East St. Louis to be able to come out of their poverty environment and identify with their heritage and see what black cultures in other parts of the world have achieved.

Today, the museum exhibits African and Caribbean folk and contemporary art, performance costumes from the Dunham Company, original paintings by Dunham, and musical instruments. It is open by appointment and admission is free.

John Robinson Homes ■ 261

1200 Market Street

Built in 1943, this development was renovated in the late 1980s and in 1993 included 132 units. It is named for Captain John Robinson (1829-1919), a turn-of-the-century East St. Louis civil rights leader who recruited blacks for the army and was president of the Afro-American Protective Emancipation League.

See also: John Robinson Elementary School

Hughes Quinn-Rock Junior High School ■ 262

Tenth and Ohio streets

Hughes Quinn-Rock Junior High School, which had 811 pupils in 1992-93, represents the blending of the old Hughes-Quinn and Rock Junior High schools at the start of the 1990-91 school year. It was named for John Wesley Hughes (1867-1937), a black principal in East St. Louis for twenty-three years. Hughes, a graduate of Berea College in Kentucky, served as principal of a Wheeling, West Virginia, high school before coming to East St. Louis in 1914. At the time of his death, he was principal of Lincoln High School. A member of St. Paul Baptist Church, he was a leader of the Negro Baptist organization in Illinois and lectured frequently on Middle Eastern countries.

The school was also named for Governor V. Quinn (1895-1949), a Mississippi native who worked as a coach and principal in southern Illinois schools before moving to East St. Louis in 1937. He served as principal of old Lincoln High School from 1937 until 1949.

Martin Luther King Junior High School

Photo by Lee Harris.

Martin Luther King Junior High School ■ 263

7000 Ridge Avenue

In 1971, this school was founded and named for Martin Luther King, Jr. (1929-68), the prominent minister and civil rights leader. It is located at Seventieth Street and Ridge Avenue, in the same complex as Kennedy Elementary School. In 1992-93, it had 678 students.

Miles Davis Elementary School ■ 264

Fifteenth Street and St. Clair

In 1982, this school, formerly known as Longfellow School, was rebuilt and reopened. It was renamed for legendary jazz musician and composer Miles Davis (1926-91), a graduate of Lincoln High School. In 1983, Davis came back to East St. Louis to attend ceremonies that established it as the Miles Davis Elementary School. In 1992-93, it had 639 students from kindergarten through sixth grade.

See also: Miles Davis home

East St. Louis Monitor

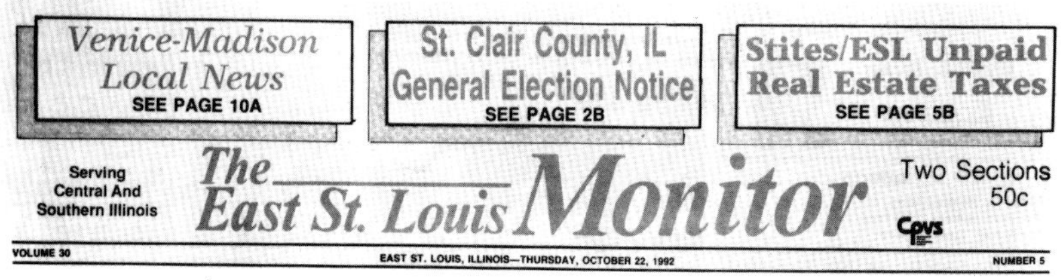
Venice-Madison Local News SEE PAGE 10A

St. Clair County, IL General Election Notice SEE PAGE 2B

Stites/ESL Unpaid Real Estate Taxes SEE PAGE 5B

Serving Central And Southern Illinois

The East St. Louis Monitor

Two Sections 50c

VOLUME 30 EAST ST. LOUIS, ILLINOIS—THURSDAY, OCTOBER 22, 1992 NUMBER 5

A. M. Jackson School ■ 265

1798 Summit Avenue

This school, which had 278 students from kindergarten through eighth grade in 1992-93, has a math and science emphasis. It is named for Arthur Mells Jackson (1883-1945), prominent black citizen and educator, who was the district's second black board member.

Jackson, a Georgia native and 1907 graduate of Morehouse College, began his long career in education as a coach at Roger Williams University in Tennessee. In 1915, he was hired by the East St. Louis Board of Education to teach at Lincoln High School. For the next thirty years, he remained at Lincoln, teaching Latin and coaching basketball and baseball. The district's first football coach, he won 70 percent of his games.

The *East St. Louis Monitor* newspaper ■ 266

1501 State Street

This newspaper, which has a circulation today of seventeen thousand, was started by Clyde C. Jordan, Sr., in 1963. It carries local news and important national stories to a readership in East St. Louis and across the nation.

See also: Clyde C. Jordan Senior Citizen Building
Clyde C. Jordan Stadium

Lilly-Freeman Elementary School ■ 267

1236 Broadway Street

Lilly-Freeman School was established in 1969 for students from kindergarten through sixth grade. Formerly a Model City Demonstration and Experimental School, it had 425 students in 1992-93. The first school in East St. Louis named for black women, it honors two local teachers: Minnie Scott Lilly and Maggie Freeman.

Minnie Scott Lilly (1868-?), born in Murphrysboro, Illinois, moved to East St. Louis as a child. One of the first three graduates of old Lincoln High School, she did undergraduate work at Wilberforce University and the University of Montana and graduate work at the University of Illinois. An inspiring teacher who urged many black East St. Louis students to attend college, she became known for this slogan: "Keep on keeping on, climb the ladder to success, and never stop keeping on." A long-time English teacher and chairman of the English Department at old Lincoln High School, she directed memorable dramatic performances at the school. She was also quietly insistent on her civil rights. At monthly teachers' meetings, blacks were assigned to sit in a certain section of the hall. One day, she took a seat among the white teachers, and the other black teachers followed—thus breaking down that racial barrier. Minnie Scott Lilly lived at 1833 Bond Avenue. She retired from teaching in 1933.

Maggie Freeman (1884-1966), a native of St. Clair County, graduated from Belleville High School and the University of Illinois at Carbondale. After a forty-nine-year career teaching social studies at Denverside (later Dunbar) and old Lincoln High School, she retired in 1951. She lived at 1720 Market Street. When neighborhood children came to her home, she willingly gave them treats, but she insisted that they each learn a little black history, too. She was a member of Wilkerson AME Chapel in Belleville, which was established by her grandfather.

Norman E. Owens Plaza ■ 268

1161 Division Avenue

This plaza, which consists of seventy-two rental units, was built in 1974 and named for the Reverend Norman E. Owens, Sr. (1934-), pastor of Macedonia Baptist Church since 1967, who served as president of the East St. Louis Housing Authority from 1970 to 1981. During the first months of his tenure on the board, he was faced with a two-year-old rent strike by residents of East St. Louis public housing projects, who were protesting the authority's failure to maintain and repair its property. Under Owens' leadership, the board settled the strike, improved conditions in the projects, and initiated tenant advisory boards to give residents a voice in the administration of their housing.

Judge Billy Jones Elementary School ■ 269

1601 Cleveland Street

The school had 416 students in kindergarten through sixth grade in the 1992-93 school year. Formerly Monroe Elementary, it was renamed in 1987 for Judge Billy Jones (1912-87), the first black associate circuit judge in the Twentieth Judicial Circuit Court of Illinois.

Jones, a 1945 graduate of Howard University School of Law, became an attorney in East St. Louis. In 1949 he gained national publicity when he took black children into nine all-white public schools at the beginning of the fall semester. On behalf of the NAACP, he later filed a successful suit to integrate the public schools, first in East St. Louis, then in Sparta and Cairo, Illinois. In 1952, he served as a consultant in the various school desegregation cases which were then before the United States Supreme Court; they culminated on May 17, 1954, in the *Brown v. Board of Education, Topeka, Kansas* decision which struck down segregation in public schools. Jones served as president of the Illinois NAACP and in 1967 as president of the National Bar Association; in 1992 he was inducted posthumously into the National Bar Association Hall of Fame. By mayoral proclamation, the third Monday in September each year is officially Judge Billy Jones Day in East St. Louis.

Macedonia Baptist Church ■ 270

1335 East Broadway Avenue

According to church records, Macedonia, originally known as First Colored Baptist Church, was founded in 1863 on Kerr Island, near East St. Louis. Later it moved to 506 Grady and in 1892 built its first frame building, which was used as a school during the week. In 1929, it moved to Fourteenth Street and Broadway Avenue. The name first changed to Macedonia Colored Baptist, then to Macedonia Baptist of East St. Louis, Inc. Its new building was constructed in 1905.

Walk of Fame star

Photo by Lee Harris.

Miles Davis home ● 271

3 North Fifteenth Street, near Broadway

Miles Dewey Davis III (1926-91), the internationally known jazz musician, was born in Alton, Illinois. Around 1927, his family moved to East St. Louis, where his father, Miles Dewey Davis, Jr., a prosperous dentist, had a practice over Daut's Drugstore on North Fifteenth Street. In 1989, Davis recalled the neighborhood in *Miles: The Autobiography*, which he wrote with Quincy Troupe. His family lived upstairs, behind the dental office, in an integrated area "with Jews and Germans and Armenians and Greeks living all around us." His family moved to a house at Seventeenth Street and Kansas Avenue in the mid-1930s.

Davis' parents encouraged him to become a musician; on his thirteenth birthday, his father gave him a trumpet. He took private lessons from Harold "Shorty" Baker (1914-66), Duke Ellington's lead trumpet player, and by the time he was fifteen he and a group of musicians were playing gigs at clubs and churches in East St. Louis. At age seventeen, Davis began playing with Eddie Randle and his Blue Devils, which he called "one of the most important steps in my career. It was with Eddie Randle's band that I really started opening up with my playing, really got into writing and arranging music. . . . We traveled some and played all over the St. Louis and East St. Louis areas."

After graduating from Lincoln High School, Davis enrolled in the Juilliard School of Music in New York, then left to play with such jazz greats as Charlie Parker (1920-55). He later emerged as one of the most influential modern jazz trumpeters, both in nightclubs and on records. He was well known for his soft, rich, lyrical tone and his unconventional styling.

Donald McHenry Elementary School

Photo by Lee Harris.

Donald McHenry Elementary School ■ 272

2700 Summit Avenue

This school reopened in 1980, five years after a fire had destroyed its building; it had originally been the Slade School, established in 1909. In 1992-93 the school had 533 students in kindergarten through sixth grade.

The school was renamed for Donald F. McHenry (1936-), a native of East St. Louis who graduated from Lincoln High School. He went on to Illinois State University, earning his bachelor's degree in 1957 and his master's degree in 1959. After a teaching stint at Howard University in Washington, D.C., he joined the Department of State in 1963 and rose through the ranks. In 1971 he was guest scholar at the Brookings Institution, then became a project director at the Carnegie Endowment for International Peace. President Jimmy Carter named McHenry to the post of Deputy Representative to the United Nations Security Council in 1977.

On September 23, 1979, McHenry was sworn in as the fourteenth and youngest-ever United States Permanent Representative to the United Nations. He served until January 20, 1981. As chief United States representative to the United Nations, he was also a member of President Carter's Cabinet. He is currently University Research Professor of Diplomacy and

International Relations at Georgetown University and president of the IRC Group, Inc., an international consulting firm. In 1980, an East St. Louis street on which McHenry had lived as a child was renamed to honor him.

Nelson Mandela Elementary School ■ 273

1800 North 25th Street, at Waverly

Founded in 1904, this school was originally named for Thomas Jefferson (1743-1826), third president of the United States. In 1992-93, it served 392 students from kindergarten through sixth grade.

In 1990, the school was renamed for Nelson Mandela (1918-), president of South Africa's African National Congress (ANC), which seeks political rights for South African blacks. A political prisoner for more than twenty-seven years because of his opposition to South Africa's white minority government and its apartheid system of racial separation, Mandela has become a symbol of the struggle for equality. Since his release from prison on February 11, 1990, Mandela has reclaimed his position in the once-banned ANC and is engaged in talks with government leaders about South Africa's future. Mandela, winner of the 1993 Nobel Peace Prize, has also received other awards from various governments and honorary degrees from universities around the world.

East St. Louis race riots of 1917 ● 274

Scattered sites, primarily in "Black Valley," between Fourth and Sixth streets and Broadway to Railroad Avenue

In July 1917, East St. Louis was the scene of one of the bloodiest race riots in American history. Racial tension in the community had been increasing throughout the spring of 1917. The city's black population had increased rapidly between 1910 and 1917, and white workers at local stockyards, packing plants, and factories resented the influx of cheap new labor. In April, Aluminum Ore Corporation, one of the city's largest plants, went on strike—and some of the strikebreakers were black. After management crushed the strike, white workers blamed the blacks for their defeat. Late in May, rioting broke out briefly after a meeting in which white labor leaders appeared before the city council to protest the black migration.

On the evening of July 1, some whites in a speeding car shot randomly into homes in a black neighborhood. When detectives arrived to investigate, a crowd of black residents—apparently mistaking the detectives for more drive-by murderers—fired on their car, killing one detective and fatally injuring the other.

On July 2, 1917, rioting erupted in East St. Louis. White mobs pulled innocent black citizens off streetcars and clubbed or stoned them; later, mob leaders murdered black victims who lay wounded in the streets. Whites set fire to homes owned by blacks, then shot black residents as they tried to escape the flames. By evening most remaining blacks had fled the city or been escorted to safety by arriving state militiamen. At least thirty-nine blacks and nine whites died in the rioting, and 312 buildings were destroyed. As a result of the riot, a large portion of the black population left East St. Louis, many never to return.

A congressional subcommittee investigated the incident and filed a scathing report condemning corrupt East St. Louis politicians, as well as local industrialists who used black workers to undermine unions. In court trials that followed the riot, eleven blacks were convicted of murdering the detectives, but only four whites went to prison for murder.

Lincoln High School (present location)

Photo by Lee Harris.

Lincoln High School (old) ● 275

Sixth Street and St. Louis Avenue

When it was founded in 1886, Lincoln School was a combined elementary and high school for black students, located at Sixth Street and St. Louis Avenue. A 1902 school census shows that 287 students were enrolled that year, and the school had an 89 percent attendance rate. Minnie C. Scott, Mary E. Scott, and Fannie Edwards made up the first class of high school graduates in 1894. As Principal B. F. Bowles wrote in a 1901 letter to the East St. Louis superintendent, "the greater number of the graduates of this department become teachers."

In 1909, the Lincoln building became the headquarters for the East St. Louis Board of Education, and Lincoln moved to 1100 East Broadway. The school's many prominent alumni include jazz musician Miles Davis (1926-91), who graduated in 1944. Today, the original building is used as a halfway house.

The school was named for Abraham Lincoln (1809-65), sixteenth president of the United States, who led the nation during the Civil War. Though personally opposed to slavery, he declared at the beginning of the war that he would not interfere with slavery, since he did not want to lose important border states to the Confederacy. But on January 1, 1863, under pressure from the Radical wing of his Republican party, he issued the Emancipation Proclamation, which freed all slaves living in the states that were in rebellion against the Union. Three-quarters of all slaves fell under the provisions of the proclamation, which could only be enforced as southern states yielded to military force. The remaining slaves received their freedom in December 1865 when the Thirteenth Amendment to the Constitution was adopted.

See also: Lincoln High School (new)

Lincoln High School (new) ■ 276

1211 Bond Avenue

In 1950, Lincoln High School moved from its Broadway location to this building, where it currently serves 1,155 senior high students. Among its well-known graduates is Olympic gold medalist Jackie Joyner-Kersee (1962-), who was a member of Lincoln track teams, coached by Nino Fennoy, that won consecutive Illinois high school Class AA championships in 1978, 1979, and 1980. In 1988, Joyner-Kersee attended ceremonies at Lincoln High in which she was inducted into the school's Hall of Fame.

See also: Lincoln High School (old)
Jackie Joyner-Kersee and Al Joyner home

Lincoln Park ■ 277

Fifteenth to Seventh Street

Fourteen-acre Lincoln Park, established in 1907, has a baseball diamond, four tennis courts, a playground, and picnic area with shelter. In 1958 a large swimming pool was added. Also located in the park is the Mary E. Brown Community Center, named for a local leader who had a special interest in young people. The center, which closed in 1980, is known as the place where a number of well-known professional football stars got their start: Kellen Winslow, Johnnie Poe, Victor Scott, Eric Wright, and Jerome Heavens. Olympic gold medalist Jackie Joyner-Kersee (1962-) began her athletic career at the center when she was nine years old.

John DeShields Homes ■ 278

1235 McCasland Avenue

This housing development was built in 1954 and named for the Reverend John DeShields (1860-1950), minister at St. Paul Baptist Church for more than fifty years. It includes three hundred two-floor rowhouses.

DeShields was born in Collinsville, Illinois, the third of eleven children. Self-educated in his early years, he first became a licensed minister in the Methodist Church, then changed to the Baptist faith. In 1896 he came to St. Paul Baptist Church in East St. Louis and saw the church through its growth from North Seventh Street to its present site at Fifteenth and Bond. For twenty years, DeShields was the moderator of the Wood River Baptist Association. A well-known community leader, he also served on the East St. Louis Housing Authority.

See also: St. Paul Baptist Church

Lincoln Park

Photo by Lee Harris.

Orr-Weathers Apartments ■ 279

1300 Missouri Avenue

This development, built in 1961, consists of two high-rise buildings and 156 rowhouses—a total of 588 units in all. Two other buildings were closed during the mid-1980s after funds earmarked for their renovation were misappropriated. The unit is named for two prominent black East St. Louisans, who were members of the housing board: Louis Orr (1907-61), an attorney, and Dr. Henry H. Weathers, Jr. (1903-50), a heart surgeon.

Dr. Weathers was a well-known physician in East St. Louis. After his death, the city purchased his office site as a location for a public housing development. Louis Orr urged authorities to have the new development named for Dr. Weathers, but Orr died before achieving his goal. The city then decided to honor both men; the dedication ceremony was held in 1963 at the Orr-Weathers Apartments.

St. Paul sign

Photo by Lee Harris.

St. Paul Baptist Church

Photo by Lee Harris.

St. Paul Baptist Church ■ 280

1500 Bond Avenue

In 1895, a small group of black East St. Louisans founded St. Paul's in the old Garfield School at Fourth and Winstanley. The church grew quickly, and members soon bought a lot on Seventh Street and built their first sanctuary at a cost of twelve hundred dollars. By 1903, the congregation was large enough to construct a second building on Baugh Avenue. Though the exodus from East St. Louis after the 1917 race riots decimated its membership, the church managed to build its third sanctuary at 1500 Bond Avenue in 1922. This building was completely renovated in 1957, then six years later it was destroyed by fire. For more than three years services were held in Lincoln High School, but the congregation dedicated a new building in 1967. The Willie Shaw Educational Building was added in 1991.

Friendship Baptist Church ■ 281

1648 Tudor Avenue

Established in 1908 at Sixteenth Street and Russell Avenue, the church moved to its present location on July 4, 1911. On April 14, 1940, it became the first black church in the nation to broadcast over the radio on a program sponsored by Morton Salt Company and Shaw Clothing Company. The present structure was built in 1956.

Truelight Baptist Church ■ 282

1535 Tudor Avenue

This congregation was organized in April 1910 by the Reverend James A. Lampley. First located at Fourteenth and Baker streets, the church later moved to 1510 Tudor Avenue; in the 1920s it moved down the street to its present site. Reverend Lampley remained the pastor until his death in February 1956. The church has had only two ministers in its history.

St. Luke's African Methodist Episcopal Church ■ 283

414 North Fourteenth Street

Founded in 1880, this congregation first met in members' homes. It was formally organized seven years later. In 1960, the church moved to its present location, but in 1989 a fire destroyed the building, which the membership soon rebuilt. St. Luke's served as a community center before public facilities were open to blacks and as a school when regular classrooms were overcrowded. Church members have been active in civil rights and in public housing issues.

John Robinson Elementary School ■ 284

1435 Market Avenue

John Robinson Elementary School was founded in 1931. Miles Davis (1926-91), the famous jazz trumpeter, was a student at the school. In 1992-93, it had 306 students from kindergarten through sixth grade.

The school was named for Captain John Robinson (1829-1919), an early East St. Louis civil rights leader and community activist. He came to East St. Louis in 1878 from Harper's Ferry, Virginia, where he had reportedly witnessed the 1859 execution of abolitionist John Brown (1800-59). In the late 1870s, when the black population of the city reached four hundred, Robinson went to the East St. Louis School Board and asked that a school be established for blacks. Finally, the board agreed to provide some space over a blacksmith shop on Collinsville Avenue. Robinson also recruited blacks to serve in the army and in 1882 founded the Afro-American Protective Emancipation League.

See also: John Robinson Homes

Dunbar Elementary School ■ 285

1900 Tudor Avenue

In 1992-93, Dunbar had 596 pupils from kindergarten through sixth grade. It opened in 1917 and was named for Paul Laurence Dunbar (1872-1906), the famous black poet, novelist, and short-story writer.

John Robinson Elementary School

Photo by Lee Harris.

Dunbar Elementary School

Photo by Lee Harris.

Shiloh African Methodist Episcopal Church

Photo by Lee Harris.

Jackie Joyner-Kersee and Al Joyner home ⬭ 286

1433 Piggott Avenue

Olympic star Jackie Joyner-Kersee (1962-), often called "the world's greatest athlete," grew up in a small Piggott Avenue home, which burned in 1986. In 1977, 1978, and 1979, she won the Amateur Athletic Union national Junior Olympic pentathlon championship. She graduated from Lincoln High School in 1980 and went on to the University of California at Los Angeles, graduating in 1986 with a bachelor's degree in history. In 1984, she and her brother, Al Joyner (1960-), both competed in the Olympic Games. He became the first American in eighty years to win the triple jump gold medal, while Jackie, who was injured, won a silver medal in the heptathlon, an event that consists of 100-meter hurdles, the high jump, shot put, 200-meter run, long jump, javelin throw, and 800-meter run. At the 1988 Olympics she won her first gold medal for the heptathlon, and in 1992 she became Olympic champion in the heptathlon for the second time. She is the first person ever to win medals in a multievent in three consecutive Olympics.

Shiloh African Methodist Episcopal Church ■ 287

815 South Nineteenth Street

Shiloh was organized in 1884; its first building was located a mile and a half south of Cahokia on Camp Jackson Road (now Route 157). The congregation moved to East St. Louis in 1908 and merged with the older but smaller St. Mark's Methodist Church. For fifty years, Shiloh was located at 1904 Tudor Avenue.

Martin Van Lucas Elementary School ■ 288

1620 Russell Avenue

Lucas School was established in 1956. In 1992-93, it had 259 students from kindergarten through sixth grade. The school is named for Martin Van Lucas (1870-1943), prominent black educator and school principal. A native of Wabash Country, Illinois, and graduate of Southern Illinois Teacher's College, he came to East St. Louis in 1900 and began his teaching career at the Rush City School, which he later served as principal. In a forty-two-year teaching and administrative career, he also served as principal at six other elementary schools, including Dunbar, Attucks, and Robinson.

Mary Martin Center ⬭ 289

Twentieth Street and Market Street

During the 1920s, East St. Louis resident Mary L. Martin (1869-1950) began caring for disabled and elderly people in her home at 1860 Baker Avenue. Soon she expanded her work to feeding the hungry, giving clothes to the needy, and finding medical help for the sick. When her programs outgrew her home, she moved them to the basement of Friendship Baptist Church. In 1937, she opened the Mary Martin Center, a refuge for homeless and orphaned children at

Attucks Elementary School

Photo by Lee Harris.

1945 Market Street. At first, the center was funded solely through private donations; later, it received support from the United Way. Over time the center became the site of senior citizen activities, Scout meetings, and sorority/fraternity events.

In 1980, the Mary Martin Center became a component of the Urban League of St. Louis. Members continue to meet twice weekly at the Urban League office, 3500 State Street in East St. Louis, to participate in arts and crafts, sewing, and field trips.

Mount Zion Baptist Church ■ 290

2235 Bond Avenue

Mount Zion was organized in 1901 in the home of Jennie Thomas in Rush City, Illinois. Its first building was constructed at Tenth Street and Cook Avenue in East St. Louis; the church later moved to Thirteenth Street and Tudor Avenue and from there to its current site. During the 1940s and early 1950s, the congregation grew to be one of the largest in the city. For nearly two decades, it has been involved in the redevelopment and construction of area housing, along with other kinds of community outreach. The church has built three homes in the Denverside area, established a mission church in East St. Louis, run a daily meals program, and provided thousands of food baskets to needy residents.

Attucks Elementary School ■ 291

2600 Kansas Avenue

Founded in 1929, Attucks School was named for Crispus Attucks (1723?-70), a black hero, who was killed in the Boston Massacre. In 1992-93, the school had 207 students ranging from kindergarten through sixth grade.

Clyde C. Jordan Stadium ■ 292

North Forty-seventh Street

The Clyde C. Jordan Stadium was built in 1991 as an athletic facility for Lincoln High School and for East St. Louis Senior High School. One of the teams using the field is the East St. Louis Flyers, the football team of East St. Louis Senior High School. Bob Shannon has served on the Flyers' coaching staff since 1970; he took over as the team's head coach in 1978. Through fifteen seasons, his team has won 152 of 173 games and the state championship six times. Shannon has also sent dozens of his players to college on football scholarships. He has five times been named High School Coach of the Year by the *Sporting News*. On January 18, 1993, Shannon and his wife, Jeanette, were invited to the pre-inaugural "Faces of Hope" luncheon by President Bill Clinton (1946-). They were among the fifty-four guests from thirty states who had left a lasting impression on Clinton and Vice President Albert Gore, Jr. (1948-).

See also: Clyde C. Jordan Senior Citizen Building
East St. Louis Monitor *newspaper*

Clyde C. Jordan Senior Citizen Building ■ 293

6715 State Street

Originally called the East St. Louis Senior Citizen Building, it was renamed after the death of Clyde C. Jordan, Sr. (1930-87), a newpaper publisher and philanthropist. Jordan, a community leader who served as East St. Louis township supervisor and president of District 189 of the East St. Louis School Board, received awards from more than one hundred local organizations. This center offers programs and activities to senior citizens.

See also: East St. Louis Monitor *newspaper*
Clyde C. Jordan Stadium

Vernice Neely Elementary School for Exceptional Children ■ 294

4400 Grand Street

In 1978, Neely School was established and named for Vernice Garner Neely (1923-1972), an educator and community leader. In 1993, it was a primary-intermediate school in special education.

Vernice Neely, a native of East St. Louis, graduated from Lincoln High School and from Illinois State University at Normal. She received a master's degree from the University of Illinois in 1958 and was one of the first blacks admitted to the school's honor society. In 1945, she began her teaching career in the Business Education department at Lincoln High School and was later appointed chairman of the department, a position she held until her death. She was an active member of the NAACP and of Truelight Baptist Church.

Entrance to Clyde C. Jordan Stadium

Photo by Lee Harris.

Alton, Illinois

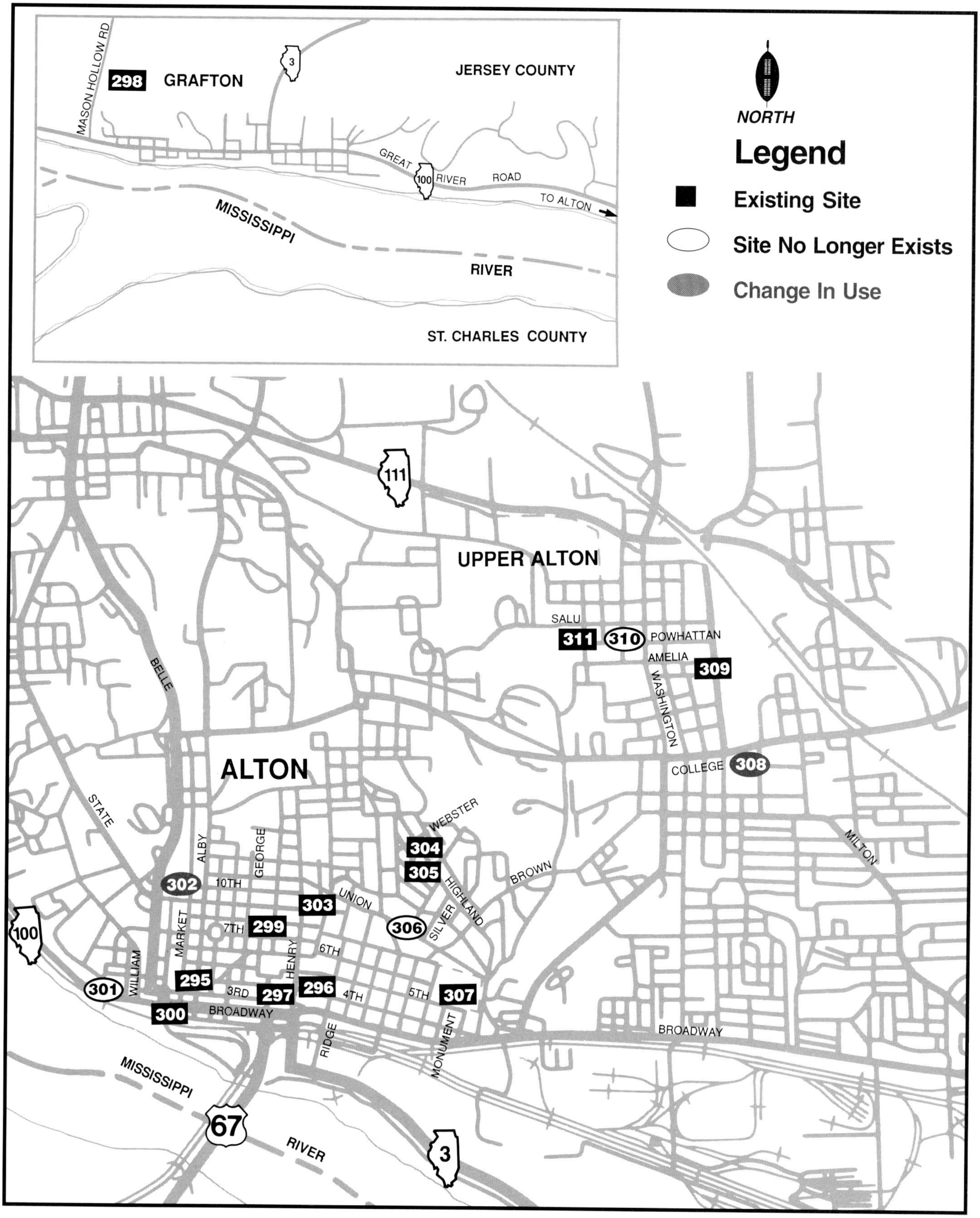

Alton, Illinois

Chapter 14

In 1817, Colonel Rufus Easton, a St. Louis resident, acquired land on the east side of the river and laid out a town which he named for his son, Alton R. Easton. Before the Civil War, many blacks escaped from Missouri through the free state of Illinois by way of Alton. For years, the old Rock House on College Avenue served as a station on the Underground Railroad.

Yet pro-slavery sentiment was also present in the divided community. In 1837, the Reverend Elijah Parish Lovejoy, editor of the Alton *Observer*, an abolitionist newspaper, was murdered by a mob while he tried to protect his press. And six years after Lovejoy's death, a black woman seeking freedom in the Alton courts was seized and taken across the river to Missouri and slavery. During his famous 1858 debate with Stephen A. Douglas in Alton, Abraham Lincoln argued that the enslaving of one race by another was a "tyrannical principle."

In 1895, despite an 1874 Illinois law prohibiting a racially segregated school system, Alton built the Douglass and Lovejoy schools for its black students. The father of Minnie and Ambrose Bibb, who wanted his children to attend the school closest to their home, filed proceedings on their behalf against the school board. The case remained in the courts for eleven years until it was finally decided by the Illinois Supreme Court. The ruling was in their favor, but it was a hollow victory for the Bibb children, who had already completed high school. Other black families were afraid to press the issue, and Alton elementary schools remained segregated for many years.

Today, blacks live scattered throughout Alton and their children attend neighborhood schools. Historic churches such as Campbell Chapel African Methodist Episcopal, Allen Chapel, Tabernacle Baptist, Union Baptist, and Webster Temple Church of God in Christ continue to serve the community and contribute to its improvement.

Each year on November 7, the anniversary of Elijah Parish Lovejoy's death, black and white citizens come together at his grave to honor his memory and pledge themselves to continue working for a better community and world.

Riot at Elijah Parish Lovejoy's Press

Wood engraving. Courtesy of the Missouri Historical Society Photograph and Print Collection.

Memorial Silhouette of Elijah Parish Lovejoy

Printed silhouette, ca. 1837. Courtesy of the Missouri Historical Society Photograph and Print Collection.

Elijah Parish Lovejoy press

Photo by Jill Sherman.

Elijah Parish Lovejoy press ■ 295

In the lobby of the Telegraph
111 East Broadway

After the death of the Reverend Elijah Parish Lovejoy, his fourth printing press was destroyed by an Alton mob and thrown into the Mississippi River. This section was recovered from the river in 1915 by the Sparks Milling Company during excavation for a mill building in downtown Alton. The company presented it to the *Telegraph,* which still displays it in the lobby.

See also: St. Louis Observer *office*
Lovejoy monument and grave site
Lovejoy assassination site

Campbell Chapel African Methodist Episcopal Church ■ 296

626 East Fourth Street, between Henry and Ridge streets

The church was organized around 1840 by William Paul Quinn, a bishop of the African Methodist Episcopal Church who came to the area to establish new congregations. The first church, built in 1844 on Third Street between Oak and what is now Central Avenue, was frame; later it was faced in stone. After a fire destroyed the old sanctuary, the congregation built a new brick church in 1973.

Enos Apartments ■ 297

325 East Third Street

This building, constructed in a pre-Civil War Italianate style, was the residence of Nathaniel Hanson in the early 1860s. It has hooded windows, elaborate cornices, and a glassed-in cupola. After 1910, a Dr. Enos used the building as a sanitorium, and enlarged the building by raising the eaves, roof, and cupola to add a floor.

A tunnel in the basement, now closed to the public, was once a station on the Underground Railroad. From the 1830s through the Civil War, Alton was an important starting point for a line of the Underground Railroad which crossed the state and continued on to Jacksonville, then to the Illinois River and by that route to Ottawa, Illinois. Escaped slaves traveled the line along trails through the forest to secret rooms in homes and barns and well-concealed spaces in wood piles or haystacks. A series of hand signals helped them recognize white friends along the route who were willing to hide them.

Boone-Kelly cabin ■ 298

304 East Sixth Street (now on Mason Hollow Road, Grafton, Illinois)

This 1830s-era, hand-hewn log cabin is one of the oldest structures built in the city of Alton. It was constructed by Samuel Boone, who had come to Alton from Pennsylvania with his wife, Sarah. Originally the cabin had a dirt floor; around 1838 sawed timber joists were added and later a plank floor was placed over the joists.

When Boone sold the cabin in 1855, Isaac Kelly, a freed slave from Georgia, moved in. For several generations the Kelly-Blodgett family occupied the cabin. Hidden for years under a house which was built around it, the cabin was rediscovered in 1974 by Alton preservationist Robert St. Peters, who rescued it from demolition. In 1991, it was reconstructed in Grafton, Illinois, on the Wildflower Farm, Mason Hollow Road, where it is now open to the public.

Union Baptist Church ■ 299

Seventh and George streets

Probably the oldest black church in Alton, the Union Baptist Church dates from 1836. It was organized by the Reverend E. Rogers at the home of Charles Edwards in Upper Alton. After meeting in members' homes for several years, the congregation built this church at the corner of George and Seventh streets.

Boone-Kelly cabin

Photo. Courtesy of Robert St. Peters.

Union Baptist Church

Photo by Lee Harris.

Site of the last Lincoln-Douglas debate

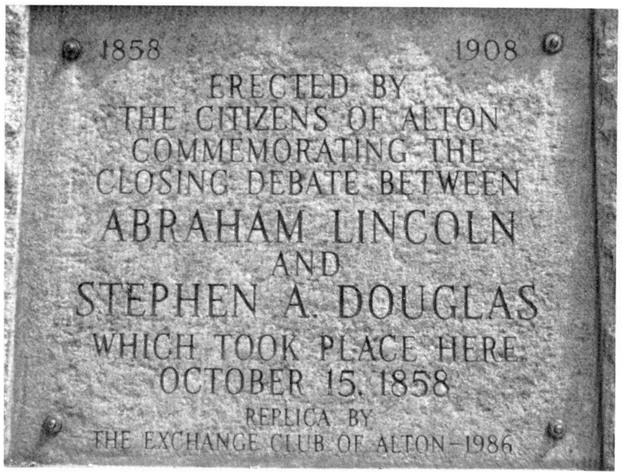

Photo by Lee Harris.

Site of the last Lincoln-Douglas debate ■ 300

At Broadway and Market

In 1858, two candidates—Abraham Lincoln and Stephen A. Douglas—were vying to become United States senator from Illinois. They spent four months on the campaign trail making dozens of speeches and staging a series of seven debates around the state. Their final platform debate occurred in Alton on the morning of October 15, 1858. It was one of the biggest political events ever held in the city. Steamboat and railroad excursion cars brought crowds of St. Louis passengers for the contest, which took place on the northeast side of what was then city hall.

As they had in their previous debates, the two candidates discussed their positions on the slavery issue. Senator Douglas insisted that "in my opinion this government can endure forever . . . divided into free and slave States as our fathers made it,—each State having the right to prohibit, abolish or sustain slavery just as it pleases." Lincoln argued that the fundamental issue was one of right versus wrong, and that the enslaving of one race by another was a "tyrannical principle." The marker is now only a few feet from where the platform was erected.

Lovejoy assassination site ⬭ 301

William Street, at Broadway

Along the river, near the foot of William Street, was the four-story Godfrey-Gilman warehouse, where the Reverend Elijah Parish Lovejoy was shot and killed on November 7, 1837. Lovejoy and nineteen companions were defending his newly arrived press, on which he printed the Alton *Observer*, against attack by an Alton mob. One member of the mob, Lyman Bishop, was also shot to death in the street by the warehouse defenders.

See also: St. Louis Observer *office*
Lovejoy monument and grave site
Elijah Parish Lovejoy press

Douglass Elementary School ⬬ 302

Market and Tenth streets

In 1895, a school for black children was constructed on the corner of Market and Tenth streets at a cost of five thousand dollars. In 1974, it became the first black school in the city to be closed. The school was named for Frederick A. Douglass (1817?-95), prominent black writer, orator, and abolitionist, who was born a slave in Maryland in 1817. At twenty-one he escaped to Massachusetts, where he joined the anti-slavery movement. Later, he became a prominent publisher in New York with his well-known newspaper, *North Star*.

Senator Lyman Trumbull house ■ 303

1105 Henry Street

This Greek Revival house was built in 1820 by Benjamin Ives Gilman, then purchased and renovated in 1849 by Lyman Trumbull (1813-96), United States senator from 1855 to 1873. He was the author of the Thirteenth Amendment to the Constitution, which abolished slavery, and he also wrote much of the Reconstruction legislation after the Civil War. Senator Trumbull was present at the 1858 Lincoln-Douglas debate in Alton.

The home has a native limestone foundation, with hand-made brick walls on the main and upper floors. It features supporting interior beams of black walnut, white pine floors, and several fireplaces on the first and second levels. In 1975, the house was recognized for its architectural and historic significance when it was named to the National Register of Historic Places.

Webster Street ■ 304

In October 1978, a one-block portion of Fletcher Street in Alton was renamed for Bishop Henry H. Webster (?-1989) of Webster Temple Church of God in Christ, who was celebrating the fiftieth anniversary of his pastorate. Webster Street runs between Hampton Street and Highland Avenue.

Webster Temple Church of God in Christ ■ 305

1100 Highland Avenue at Webster Street

This congregation formed around 1915 after members began meeting in private homes. They built a frame sanctuary at Highland Avenue and Fletcher Street and called the new church the Highland Avenue Church of God in Christ. In 1928, Bishop Henry H. Webster began a pastorate that lasted more than sixty years, until his death in 1989. The church was renamed in his honor in the mid-1970s.

Senator Lyman Trumbull house

Photo by Lee Harris.

Lovejoy Elementary and Junior High ○ 306

Union and Silver streets

In 1895, this school for black children was completed at Union and Silver. In 1949, Lovejoy was consolidated with Central Junior High, located at 1043 Tremont Street. The combined school closed as a junior high in 1980 and reopened as Lovejoy Elementary School. The original school building was sold in 1979 and subsequently demolished. The school was named for the Reverend Elijah Parish Lovejoy (1802-37), the abolitionist editor who was killed by an Alton mob while defending his press.

Trumbull house detail

Photo by Lee Harris.

Lovejoy monument and grave site

Photo by Lee Harris.

Monument detail

Photo by Lee Harris.

Lovejoy monument and grave site ■ 307

Fifth and Monument streets

The Reverend Elijah Parish Lovejoy was buried in Alton Cemetery, under a simple pine board that soon rotted away. His grave was forgotten. In 1888, Illinois Lieutenant-Governor Thomas Dimmock (1830-?) spoke to a St. Louis congregation about the importance of a memorial to Lovejoy; his speech was printed and circulated by the Lovejoy Monument Association. As a result, the Illinois Assembly voted to appropriate twenty-five thousand dollars, if the association could raise another ten thousand dollars.

The finished monument, created by St. Louis designer Louis Mullgardt and sculptor Robert P. Bringhurst, was dedicated on November 7, 1897, near the entrance to Alton Cemetery. It consists of a ninety-foot granite column with a winged figure of Victory, trumpet in hand, on top. The column is mounted on a pedestal with four bronze panels representing different phases of Lovejoy's career. His grave and a marker in memory of his wife, Celia Ann French Lovejoy (1813-70), are close by. Lovejoy's marker was donated by Burton Bernard, a Granite City attorney.

See also: Lovejoy assassination site
Elijah Parish Lovejoy press
St. Louis Observer *office*

Old Rock House ● 308

2705 College Avenue

This stone house was built in 1834-35 for the Reverend T. B. Hurlbut, pastor of the Upper Alton Presbyterian Church and friend of the Reverend Elijah Parish Lovejoy. In October 1837, it was the site of a meeting at which the State Anti-Slavery Society of Illinois was organized, with sixty members. Lovejoy was present at this meeting; he was killed less than two weeks later. The house served as a station on the Underground Railroad. Reportedly, it was also a recruiting center used by the Union Army during the Civil War. An upper story with six dormer windows was later replaced with the present concrete-block addition. This building is now the Lovejoy Apartments.

Old Rock House

Photo by Lee Harris.

Tabernacle Missionary Baptist Church ■ 309

2621 Amelia Street

This historically black church, originally called Second Baptist Church, was founded in March 1869. Its first sanctuary, a small frame building, was located at 2620 Amelia Street. In 1918, its name changed to Holy Temple, and it also spun off another congregation, St. John's Baptist Church. Its name changed once again in 1930 to Tabernacle Missionary Baptist Church. In 1989, the congregation tore down its original building and built a new brick sanctuary across the street.

Tabernacle Missionary Baptist Church

Photo by Lee Harris.

Dunbar Elementary School ○ 310

Washington Avenue and Powhattan, Upper Alton

Dunbar, an elementary school for black children, was founded in 1895 in a building that had first been used as the church and school for Allen Chapel African Methodist Episcopal Church. After it closed in 1974, the school was sold and subsequently torn down.

It was named for Paul Laurence Dunbar (1872-1906), the famous black poet, novelist, and short-story writer. An early book of poetry, *Lyrics of Lowly Life*, won him national recognition in 1896. He was the first black poet to express the lyrical qualities of black life, using black dialect. His *Collected Poems* appeared posthumously in 1913.

Church cornerstone

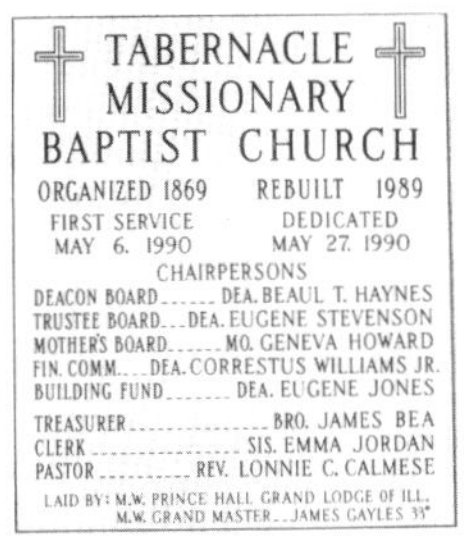

TABERNACLE
MISSIONARY
BAPTIST CHURCH
ORGANIZED 1869 REBUILT 1989
FIRST SERVICE MAY 6. 1990
DEDICATED MAY 27. 1990
CHAIRPERSONS
DEACON BOARD...... DEA. BEAUL T. HAYNES
TRUSTEE BOARD...DEA. EUGENE STEVENSON
MOTHER'S BOARD......MO. GENEVA HOWARD
FIN. COMM....DEA. CORRESTUS WILLIAMS JR.
BUILDING FUND....... DEA. EUGENE JONES
TREASURER..............BRO. JAMES BEA
CLERK.................SIS. EMMA JORDAN
PASTOR..........REV. LONNIE C. CALMESE
LAID BY: M.W. PRINCE HALL GRAND LODGE OF ILL.
M.W. GRAND MASTER...JAMES GAYLES 33°

Photo by Lee Harris.

Allen Chapel African Methodist Episcopal Church

Photo by Lee Harris.

Stained glass window

Photo by Lee Harris.

Allen Chapel African Methodist Episcopal Church ■ 311

2213 Salu Avenue

Allen Chapel and an affiliated school were established in 1876 by the Reverend William B. Hammond in a building that would later become the Dunbar School. In 1879, Hammond sold a piece of property in the Salu addition of Upper Alton to his congregation; the present church building was completed in 1880. In the early 1940s, this structure was remodeled and covered with brick siding.

A Guide for Further Research

Missouri Historical Society
Library and Collections Center
225 South Skinker Boulevard
Mailing Address: P.O. Box 11940
St. Louis, MO 63112-0040
(314) 746-4599; FAX (314) 746-4548

The Missouri Historical Society operates the History Museum, located in the Jefferson Memorial Building in Forest Park, and the Library and Collections Center at the South Skinker address. The library and archival collections include more than 70,000 non-circulating volumes, pamphlets, and periodicals; approximately 1,600 distinct manuscript collections; a significant sheet music collection; large newspaper and map collections; and more than 430,000 prints and photographs. Collections preserve the history and culture of the St. Louis area, the state of Missouri, the Louisiana Purchase Territory, and the opening of the American West. Regional African-American history is documented throughout the collections, especially in government records, private and family papers, scrapbooks, St. Louis imprints, and photographs. Collections include materials on the institution of slavery; the status and circumstances of free blacks in both antebellum and post–Civil War St. Louis; civil rights and desegregation; and African-American culture, organizations, institutions, and demographics.

The St. Louis Mercantile Library
Association
510 Locust Street, sixth floor
St. Louis, MO 63101
(314) 621-0670; FAX (314) 621-1782

The St. Louis Mercantile Library has more than 300,000 titles, 250,000 historical photographs, 10 million news clipping files, 1 million manuscripts, extensive collections of early regional newspapers, and historical map and print collections. Special collections focus on the history and culture of the St. Louis region and the American West, and on the history of railroad and river transportation. Of particular interest to African-American research are the H. R. Helper Collection, comprising anti-slavery pamphlets and books; the John Mason Peck Collection, including early regional religious pamphlets; and extensive holdings on the local civil rights movement and on African-American history. The library also has the complete photo and clipping file of the *St. Louis Globe-Democrat*, a local newspaper for 135 years.

St. Louis Public Library
Central Library
1301 Olive Street
St. Louis, MO 63103
(314) 241-2288; FAX (314) 539-0393;
TDD (314) 539-0364

The library system includes Central Library, twelve branches, the Charing Cross Location, an audiovisual library, and Community Services. Altogether, it holds more than 4.5 million items, including 100,000 maps; 500,000 graphics; current and retrospective periodicals and newspapers; federal, state, and local government documents; clippings, pamphlets, and other ephemera. At Central Library, the St. Louis Information Center provides current economic, demographic, and government information on the St. Louis metropolitan area. The St. Louis Area Studies Center serves as a focal point for information on the area's history and culture. A strong genealogy collection contains resources for family history research. Regional African-American authors and history are represented in the holdings of the Rare Books and Special Collections. Information on area African-American artists can be found in the Fine Arts department collections. Of special interest is the Julia Davis Research Collection on subjects dealing with African Americans, their achievements, and their contributions to society. This collection is housed at the Julia Davis Branch, 4415 Natural Bridge Avenue.

Southern Illinois University at
Edwardsville
Lovejoy Library
Edwardsville, IL 62026-1063
(618) 692-2603; FAX (618) 692-2381

In its collection, the Lovejoy Library has 800,000 volumes, 34,000 sound recordings, and 150,000 maps and aerial photos. Special collections include regional history materials, especially pertaining to the Mississippi River valley, and the Jazz Archives and Music Research collections. The library has collections of East St. Louis mayors Alvin Fields, William E. Mason, and James E. Williams, and the clipping file of the *East St. Louis Journal* (later *Metro East Journal*), 1930s-79.

University of Missouri–St. Louis libraries
Thomas Jefferson Library
8001 Natural Bridge Road
St. Louis, MO 63121
(314) 553-5060; FAX (314) 553-5853

The University of Missouri–St. Louis, one of four campuses in the University of Missouri system, has more than 570,000 volumes in its collection. The Western Historical Manuscript Collection (553-5143), located in the Thomas Jefferson Library, contains manuscripts related to St. Louis and Missouri history, with a particular strength in African-American history. It includes extensive photograph and oral history collections. Of special interest are the University of Missouri–St. Louis Black History Project Collection, 1911-83, and the oral history collections of approximately one thousand taped interviews with St. Louis immigrants, black leaders, jazz and rock musicians, union members, and labor and political leaders.

Washington University libraries
Olin Library
1 Brookings Drive, Campus Box 1061
St. Louis, Mo 63130-4899
(314) 935-5444; FAX (314) 935-4045

Washington University libraries, consisting of the central Olin Library and department and school libraries, hold more than two million books and bound volumes. Of special interest are its Missouriana and St. Louis collections. It has the papers of the Urban League of St. Louis, the American Civil Liberties Union of Eastern Missouri, and other St. Louis history collections relating to twentieth-century St. Louis.

Selected Bibliography

Adams, Patricia. "Fighting for Democracy in St. Louis: Civil Rights During World War II." *Missouri Historical Review* 80, no. 1 (October 1985): 58-75.

Ashe, Arthur. *A Hard Road to Glory: A History of the African-American Athlete*. 3 vols. New York: Warner Books, 1988.

Athearn, Robert G. "The Spirit of St. Louis." In *In Search of Canaan: Black Migration to Kansas, 1879-80*. Lawrence, Kans.: The Regents Press of Kansas, 1978.

Bellamy, Donnie. "Free Blacks in Antebellum Missouri, 1820-1860." *Missouri Historical Review* 67, no. 2 (January 1973): 198-226.

Betts, Robert B. *In Search of York: The Slave Who Went to the Pacific with Lewis and Clark*. Boulder, Col.: Colorado Associated University Press, 1985.

Blassingame, John W. "The Recruitment of Negro Troops in Missouri During the Civil War." *Missouri Historical Review* 58, no. 3 (April 1964): 326-38.

Board of Education of the City of St. Louis. *Facts Concerning One Hundred Years of Progress in the Public Schools of St. Louis, 1838-1938*. St. Louis: Department of Instruction, St. Louis Public Schools, 1938. [*Public School Messenger* 35, no. 5 (3 January, 1938)].

Chomeau, Mary B. "Some Early Negro Families of Kirkwood." *Kirkwood Historical Review* 4, no. 3 (September 1965): 3-5.

Christensen, Lawrence O. "Cyprian Clamorgan, The Colored Aristocracy of St. Louis (1858)." *Missouri Historical Society Bulletin* 31, no. 1 (October 1974): 3-31.

—— "Race Relations in St. Louis, 1865-1916," *Missouri Historical Review* 78, no. 2 (January 1984): 123-36.

—— "The Racial Views of J. W. Wheeler," *Missouri Historical Review* 67, no. 4 (July 1973): 535-47.

Clayton, Sheryl H. *Black Men Role Models of Greater St. Louis*. East St. Louis, Ill: Essai Seay Publications, 1984.

Commemorative History of the St. Louis Public Schools 1838-1988. Saint Louis: St. Louis Public Schools, 1988?

Corbett, Katharine T. "Missouri's Black History: From Colonial Times to 1970." *Gateway Heritage* 4, no. 1 (Summer 1983): 16-25.

Corbett, Katharine T., and Mary E. Seematter. "Black St. Louis at the Turn of the Century." *Gateway Heritage* 7, no. 1 (Summer 1986): 41-48.

—— "No Crystal Stair: Black St. Louis, 1920-40." *Gateway Heritage* 8, no. 2 (Fall 1987): 8-15.

Crossland, William A. *Industrial Conditions Among Negroes in St. Louis*. St. Louis: [Press of Mendle Printing Company], 1914.

Cunningham, Lyn Driggs, and Jimmy Jones. *Sweet, Hot and Blue: St. Louis' Musical Heritage*. Jefferson, N.C.: McFarland & Co., 1989.

Davis, Julia. *St. Louis Public Schools Named for Negroes; Biographical Sketches*. [St. Louis]: The author, 1968.

Day, Judy and M. James Kedro. "Free Blacks in St. Louis: Antebellum Conditions, Emancipation and the Postwar Era." *Missouri Historical Society Bulletin* 30, no. 2 (January 1974): 117-35.

Dreer, Herman. "Negro Leadership in Saint Louis: A Study in Race Relations." Ph.D. diss., University of Chicago, 1955.

Ehrlich, Walter. *They Have No Rights: Dred Scott's Struggle for Freedom*. Westport, Conn.: Greenwood Press, 1979.

Employee's Loan Company (St. Louis). *Negroes, Their Gift to St. Louis*. [Text and Research Committee, John D. Buckner, Julia Davis, John H. Purnell, James A. Scott, and others]. St. Louis: Employee's Loan Company, 1964.

Evans, J. W. "A Brief Sketch of the Development of Negro Education in St. Louis, Missouri." *Journal of Negro History* 7, no. 4 (October 1938): 548-52.

Faherty, William Barnaby, and Madeline Barni Oliver. *The Religious Roots of Black Catholics of Saint Louis*. St. Louis: St. Louis University, 1977.

Greene, Lorenzo J., Gary R. Kremer, and Anthony F. Holland. *Missouri's Black Heritage*. St. Louis: Forum Press, 1980.

Hermann, Janet S. "The McIntosh Affair." *Missouri Historical Society Bulletin* 26, no. 2 (January 1970): 122-43.

Hodges, Carl G., and Helene H. Levene, comps. *Illinois Negro Historymakers*. Chicago: Emancipation Centennial Commission, 1964.

James, Ivan C. *History of Black Catholicism in St. Louis*. [St. Louis]: [The author], 1989.

James, Lloyd. "Blacks in St. Louis History." *St. Louis Globe-Democrat*, 20 February, 1979.

Kelleher, Daniel T. "St. Louis' 1916 Residential Segregation Ordinance." *Missouri Historical Society Bulletin* 26, no. 3 (April 1970): 239-48.

Kinloch History Committee, comp. *Kinloch: Yesterday, Today and Tomorrow*. Kinloch, Mo.: Kinloch History Committee, 1983.

Kremer, Gary R. *James Milton Turner and the Promise of America: The Public Life of a Post-Civil War Black Leader*. Columbia, Mo.: University of Missouri Press, 1991.

Lange, Dena Floren. *Century of Achievement in the St. Louis Public High Schools, 1853-1953*. St. Louis: St. Louis Public Schools, 1953.

LeFlore, Shirley, ed. *And We Rise: An Anthology of St. Louis Afro-American Poets*. St. Louis: Community Press, 1979.

Levy, Scott Jarman. "Tricky Ball: 'Cool Papa' Bell and Life in the Negro Leagues." *Gateway Heritage* 9, no. 4 (Spring 1989): 26-33.

Lipsitz, George. *A Life in the Struggle: Ivory Perry and the Culture of Opposition*. Philadelphia: Temple University Press, 1988.

—— *The Sidewalks of St. Louis: Places, People and Politics in an American City*. Columbia, Mo.: University of Missouri Press, 1991.

McKoy, Kathy. "Afro-American Cemeteries in St. Louis." *Gateway Heritage* 6, no. 3 (Winter 1985-86): 30-37.

Moore, N. Webster. "The Black YMCA of St. Louis." *Missouri Historical Society Bulletin* 36, no. 1 (October 1979): 35-40.

—— "James Milton Turner, Diplomat, Educator, and Defender of Rights (1840–1915)." *Missouri Historical Society Bulletin* 27, no. 3 (April 1971): 194-201.

—— "John Berry Meachum (1789–1854): St. Louis Pioneer, Black Abolitionist, Educator, and Preacher." *Missouri Historical Society Bulletin* 29, no. 2 (January 1973): 96-103.

Painter, Nell Irwin. *Exodusters: Black Migration to Kansas after Reconstruction*. New York: Knopf, 1977.

Parrish, William E. *Missouri Under Radical Rule, 1865-1870*. Columbia, Mo.: University of Missouri Press, 1965.

A Policy Framework for Racial Justice: An Agenda for the 1980s, St. Louis. [Sponsored by Harris-Stowe State College, Sigma Pi Phi Fraternity, and the Danforth Foundation]. N.p. 1986.

Primm, James Neal. *Lion of the Valley: Saint Louis, Missouri*. 2d ed. Boulder, Colo.: Pruett Publishing Co., 1990.

Proud: A History of Black People in the State of Missouri. St. Louis: Proud, Inc., 1976-77.

Richard, Maximilian. "Black and White on the Urban Frontier: The St. Louis Community in Transition, 1800-1830." *Missouri Historical Society Bulletin* 33, no. 1 (October 1976): 3-17.

Richards, Frank O. "The St. Louis Story: The Training of Black Surgeons in St. Louis, Missouri." In *A Century of Black Surgeons: The U.S.A. Experience*. Edited by Claude H. Organ, Jr., and Margaret M. Kosiba. 2 vols. Norman, Okla.: Transcript Press, 1987.

Rodabough, John. *Frenchtown*. St. Louis: Sunrise Publishing, 1980.

Rudwick, Elliott M. *Race Riot at East St. Louis, July 2, 1917*. Carbondale, Ill.: Southern Illinois University Press, 1964. Reprint. Urbana, Ill.: University of Illinois Press, 1982.

Schwendemen, Glen. "St. Louis and the 'Exodusters' of 1879." *Journal of Negro History* 46, no. 1 (January 1961): 32-46.

Slavens, George E. "The Missouri Negro Press, 1875-1920." *Missouri Historical Review* 64, no. 4 (July 1970): 413-31.

Smith, JoAnn Adams. *Selected Neighbors and Neighborhoods of North St. Louis, and Selected Related Events*. St. Louis: Friends of the Vaughn Cultural Center, 1988.

Strickland, Arvarh E. "Aspects of Slavery in Missouri, 1821." *Missouri Historical Review* 65, no. 4 (July 1971): 505-26.

Tabscott, Robert W. "Elijah Parish Lovejoy, Portrait of a Radical: The St. Louis Years, 1827-1835." *Gateway Heritage* 8, no. 3 (Winter 1987-88): 32-39.

Thomas, James P. *From Tennessee Slave to St. Louis Entrepreneur: The Autobiography of James Thomas*. Edited by Loren Schweninger. Columbia, Mo.: University of Missouri Press, 1984.

Toft, Carolyn Hewes, ed. *Carondelet. The Ethnic Heritage of an Urban Neighborhood*. St. Louis: Social Science Institute, Washington University, 1975.

—— *St. Louis: Landmarks & Historic Districts*. St. Louis: Landmarks Association of St. Louis, 1988.

—— *The Ville: The Ethnic Heritage of an Urban Neighborhood*. St. Louis: Social Science Institute, Washington University, 1975.

Trexler, Harrison A. *Slavery in Missouri, 1804-1865*. Baltimore: The Johns Hopkins Press, 1914.

Troen, Selwyn K. *The Public and the Schools: Shaping the St. Louis System, 1838-1920*. Columbia, Mo.: University of Missouri Press, 1975.

Troen, Selwyn K., and Glen E. Holt, eds. *St. Louis*. New York: New Viewpoints, 1977.

Van Ravenswaay, Charles. *Saint Louis: An Informal History of the City and Its People, 1764-1865*. Edited by Candace O'Connor. St. Louis: Missouri Historical Society, 1991.

Woods, Mrs. Romeo D., Ora Fairchild, and Julia Davis. *Contributions of Blacks to St. Louis from A to Z*. St. Louis: St. Louis Public Library, 1976.

Wright, John A. *No Crystal Stair: The Story of Thirteen Afro-Americans Who Once Called St. Louis Home*. St. Louis: Ferguson-Florissant School District's Interracial Advisory Action Committee, 1988.

Young, Nathan B. *Your St. Louis and Mine*. St. Louis: N. B. Young, 1937.

Index

References to illustrations are printed in boldface type.

–T–